To Le Clan,
With Best
Wishes,

Uncommon
Heart

Uncommon Heart

Anne Audain

and

John L. Parker, Jr.

Cedarwinds Publishing

C_W

Uncommon Heart
©2000 by Anne Audain
and John L. Parker, Jr.

Published by Cedarwinds Publishing Company
P.O. Box 13618
Tallahassee, Florida 32317
850-224-9261
850-561-0747 (fax)
runnersbooks@aol.com   www.runnersbooks.com

Orders:
P.O. Box 351
Medway, Ohio 45341
800-548-2388
937-849-1624 (fax)

Front cover photo courtesy *New Zealand Herald*
Cover Design by Oliver W. Bitman
Manufactured in the United States

Library of Congress Cataloging in Publication Data
Anne Audain, 1955-
Parker, Jr., John L., 1947-
Uncommon Heart
1. Audain, Anne, 1955- . 2. Runners (Sports)—United States—Biography. 3.
Runners (Sports)—New Zealand—Biography
I. Parker, John L., Jr., 1947- . II. Title.

796.4´26 [B]

ISBN 0-915297-28-0

V 10 9 8 7 6 5 4 3 2 1

This book is dedicated to Valerie and the late Ivan Garrett, my mum and dad, with as much love and appreciation as a daughter can express.

—Anne Audain

For Jim, Jerry and Jeff, my three brothers, who rounded out our house full of J's, and who are no doubt thinking: well, it's about time.

—John L. Parker, Jr.

1 ~ *The Power of Words*

The thing I remember mostly was how big and rough his hands were. And how stained they were from the ink, particularly at the fingertips, from tracing along miles of words flowing in mirror image in the lead galleys.

He was a big strong man, as many printers were in the days when words found their way to paper through streams of molten metal, and when he lifted me into his lap so easily I was always surprised that the ink didn't come off on me. But his hands were clean. The ink was a part of him.

And the words, too, were part of him. Being a master printer for the country's largest newspaper, he understood well the power of words. Looking upon this incredibly fragile creature in his lap, this adopted stick figure of a daughter, he must have known how much she would need the strength of his words.

So he made up a story.

"You're a very special girl, you know," he would say. "Most parents don't get to pick their babies, but we did. Your mum and I went to a place where all the babies were, and we walked down the row looking at this one and that one. And when we got to the end there you were! And you looked up and smiled at me. You were the only one who smiled, so we knew you were the right one."

As Joan Didion says, we tell ourselves stories in order to sleep, and that was a very pretty story. I found out later of course that it wasn't entirely true, but I never felt the least bit of anxiety about being an adopted child. Just the opposite, in fact. I knew that not only was I loved and wanted, I was chosen especially from row upon row of babies.

I smiled at the big man with the rough, ink stained hands and he picked me to be his little girl...

2 ~ The Island

It seems so exotic these days to think that much of my childhood was spent as a barefoot waif with the run of an enchanted island in the South Seas, but at the time it was just everyday life. I was born in New Zealand, a wild and beautiful country of primal forests, active volcanoes and animal species isolated from their cousins for thousands of years. Spend any time there at all and you'll get the distinct feeling God has only just finished up His work.

I was three years old when my father called me in from my room, where I was drawing pictures in my notebook, and hoisted me up to his lap.

"Your mum's going to hospital," he said. "She's all right, but the doctors want to be very careful with the baby. So you're going to go live with Nana and Granddad Garrett on the island for a while, all right?"

If this was supposed to be upsetting news, I'm sure I took it all too well. My mother had problem pregnancies from the start, and had lost three babies before they adopted me. Now she was pregnant again and the doctors wanted to keep close watch over her.

Nana, my father's mother, lived with my ailing grandfather on Waiheke, a rugged island of about 1000 souls in the Hauraki Gulf, an hour-and-a-half ferry ride from Auckland, the largest city in New

Zealand.

To everyone on the island, Nana was Mrs. Garrett, the justice of the peace (which is like a notary public in America) as well as the secretary of the local Labor Party (Democrats!). She was a well-known figure, riding about the island on "The Red Terror," her aptly named, bright red rattletrap of a bicycle.

I remember very little of my grandfather. He was quite a bit older than Nana, a war veteran, and his health wasn't good. He had worked in a kapok factory where they made insulation, and he had emphysema from breathing the fibers. I mostly remember him sitting, rocking in a big rocking chair with a wooden parrot attached to the back while Nana bustled around the place.

There was electricity but no indoor plumbing and we had to collect rain for water. To take a bath we had to pour cold water into the tub and heat it with heating irons. And though beautiful, the terrain was unforgiving. Strong and healthy as she was, Nana had to push the Red Terror up many a hill. Some were hard to even walk up. The ancient local buses often could not make it up the infamous Palm Beach Hill if too many people were on board, so the driver would occasionally ask us to get off and walk.

There was quite a self-sufficient little barter economy on Waiheke and Nana was very much a part of it. She grew fruits and vegetables, and at a very young age I was enlisted as her agent. Either on foot or pedaling the Red Terror, I would go from cottage to cottage, trading beans, cabbage, tomatoes and fruit for eggs and other vegetables and fruit.

On Mondays we would ride and walk three miles into the little community of Surfdale, where many of the other seniors on the island would gather to play cards. We'd stop at a little store called Rosie's where we would get a meat pie—the New Zealand counterpart to the ubiquitous American hamburger—and then go on to the little community center.

I was expected to be seen but not heard while they played their card games and I sat beside her, watching the hands and listening to the grownup chatter. At afternoon teatime my job was to serve the cakes and biscuits—New Zealand for cookies—and when I got older, though I was still tiny, I was entrusted to cart around the big tray with the tea service, a duty I was inordinately proud to perform. Nana constantly reminded me to watch my manners.

Nana would often give me cooking lessons but her kitchen was so small it became more of an exercise in mental telepathy. She would lose patience with me if I didn't read her mind and move in the right direction, especially when she was carrying something hot. If I made a mistake, created a mess, or dropped something, she was ready with a well-worn homily. When she said something like, "There's no use crying over spilt milk," she often meant it literally.

Shy as I was in school, I must have been quite the conversationalist with Nana. I would sit on the back steps and chatter away while she worked. One day she just stopped what she was doing, turned to me with unambiguous exasperation on her face, and said, "Annie, will you please just shut up for a while?"

I was shocked because she was usually so "proper," a matron of the old school. To this day my mother laughingly recalls the telephone conversation during which I excitedly reported Nana's break in composure.

But most of the time Nana was exceptionally patient and quite the willing teacher. She had a mirror in the kitchen that had ceramic pigs around the frame. I loved it but one day I was touching it when I had been told not to, and it fell and broke. I was so afraid of her reaction that I hid in her closet until she found me. Her lesson: A broken mirror is nothing compared to being able to own up to the truth.

We would play card games in the evening, some difficult at that, and she made absolutely no allowances for my age. She would challenge me to think, and if I got upset with a mistake or a loss she would say, "You only get better by making mistakes; you have got to keep learning."

Thus, pleasant though it was, life on the island wasn't all frolicking in the surf and napping under palm trees. I learned a great deal about discipline and self-reliance there, about how to shape your own life if you find yourself in a place without a lot of structure.

What I learned there as a child would stand me in good stead later as an athlete: You must have a routine. Nana certainly had hers.

Her house was tiny, her kitchen big enough for only one cook to stand in, with no washing machines or other conveniences, and she had to catch the rain for drinking water. But she would get up every morning, wash up, get breakfast, and then go about the everyday tasks of living: cooking, baking, cleaning, tending her garden, and visiting her neighbors. And, of course, reading.

Like my father, she was an avid reader and she had her routine of lying down to read after lunch every day. Of course I quickly fell into this pattern as well. This reading session often flowed quite naturally into a nap session, and thus I learned another skill that would stand me in good stead later as an athlete doing serious training.

In so many ways, my foundation as an athlete and a person was built on that beautiful, rugged little island. Later, after my sister Katie was born, in the summers she and I would spend 10 hours a day at the beach, unsupervised, playing in the surf, searching for shells and crabs, climbing about the rocks. In this day and age, it sounds like some kind of fantasy world, this place where children can be left to ramble so freely in safety, but we knew nothing else. Nana would bring lunch down to us so we wouldn't miss even a few minutes, and then around eight o'clock she would come to literally drag us away for supper and bed.

As a family we spent our summer holidays at Palm Beach as well, renting any cottage that was available (Nana's was too small for all of us). Dad taught me to fish and we would climb around the rocky seashore to our favorite spots, often getting caught by the tide and having to scramble up the hills to get home in the evening.

Such was life as a child on my primitive little South Sea island. Sometimes I miss it still.

3 ~ *Growing up in a Garden*

K athryn, or Katie as we called her, was born in 1959 somewhat prematurely, and as expected both she and my mother struggled to survive. But survive they did, and I came home from my island to our house outside Otahuhu, a little town in the suburbs of Auckland. Life there wasn't as primitive as at Nana's, but there were similarities.

For one thing, it was two miles by dirt road just to get to Otahuhu, which was no metropolis itself. It was another 10 miles to Auckland, where my father worked at the *New Zealand Herald*.

My parents had built the house themselves on an acre divided in the middle, with a hedge between the house and my dad's fruit farm. He always took great pride in having "52 different varieties of fruit," though many were just different kinds of peaches. He also had a large vegetable garden. My mother kept the other half blooming with flowers.

Katie was such a beautiful baby, with a head full of blond curls and a sweet disposition, and we were all very proud of her. The bond between her and my mother was very strong right from the start and I can now see that my parents, whether consciously or unconsciously, seemed to divide the emotional labor of the household in that way.

Though my mum lavished care and attention on both Katie and

me, my father instinctively knew how much an adopted child would need continuous and unconditional acceptance and love, and he set out from the start to provide that. There was no question that I was "his little girl."

Only as I look back now do I realize how much of my mother is in me. Not only did she teach me to cook, sew and knit at a young age, she always looked on the bright side of things. Nothing got her down and to this day she is a bundle of energy.

But I understood even then that Mum and Katie were bound by blood and their birth ordeal and that it was a special relationship. As Katie grew older and we began to realize that she had developmental problems stemming from her difficult entry into the world, it only seemed to draw them closer.

The two of us inhabited our own little worlds together, Katie and I. Out behind the fruit trees we had a playhouse and a tree house and we would spend entire days together out there, each going about our separate projects. Because of my father and grandmother's influence, I spent a lot of time writing in journals, copying pictures and drawings, studying encyclopedias, dictionaries, books of all kinds. Today I'm much more of a talker and less a writer, but that was how I spent much of my childhood.

"A book can take you farther and faster than a boat or an airplane," my dad would say. When he would work overtime on weekends at the *Herald*, sometimes I would go with him. He would challenge me to read the news items even though they were far beyond my comprehension. He would make me read out loud and get me to tell him what I thought it was about. If I got frustrated he would say: "Annie, this is how you learn. People who read and understand things know more about the world. Having knowledge is a powerful thing in life. Okay, now start again. Read it to me." He would never let me give up. He even taught me how to read type backwards, as the typesetters had to do it in the composing room of the newspaper.

My father had been a good student, particularly in English, but like so many of his generation, he had to halt his education to earn a living, so he was determined that he would pass on his love of books and language to his children. As a result, by the time I was old enough to start school, I was way ahead of most of the other children.

But in New Zealand, because of the accident of my birthday, I started school younger than most of the other children at St. Joseph's, my Catholic grade school. (Mum was a staunch Catholic,

Dad a low-key Protestant.) I was still the frailest little slip of a thing; the school uniforms would billow around my pipestem arms and legs.

All of this must have made me a very appealing target right from the start, because other kids began picking on me almost immediately.

During my first day at school, they brought in several crates of milk bottles and we were supposed to file by and take a pint. By bad luck, I was first in line and had no idea what was going on. One little girl behind me took it upon herself to be my tormentor.

"She doesn't know what to do!" she laughed, and the others joined in.

It wasn't an auspicious start. I didn't know who John Paul Sartre was then, but even at that tender age I would have agreed with him that "hell is other people." I was too smart, too young, and too skinny and I didn't know the milk routine. Though I liked learning and being around books, I could have done without the rest of it. The nuns were very strict and I couldn't understand why my classmates were so mean.

Once, when I was in the third grade, I was sitting outside on a bench having lunch. At the end of the bench was a drinking fountain, one of those large, concrete fountains that look like a birdbath. I was at the end of the bench and the kids on the other end started this shoving game, trying to push everyone along so the end person—me—would get pushed off. So here I was, trying to eat my lunch, and all of a sudden I was struggling to keep my balance and stay on the bench. The next thing I knew I was flying off the end into the drinking fountain. My face struck the fountain and, as generally happens in those kinds of situations, I didn't really feel any pain. I knew I had hurt myself but didn't know how badly. It turned out that I had cut my eye severely. They rushed me to a doctor and I later found out that the cut was so close to my eye I almost lost it. I was lucky. To prevent scarring, they closed the cut with staples instead of stitches. Looking back on it, what was really curious was the school authorities didn't even notify my mother about what had happened. She didn't find out about it until she came to pick me up that afternoon.

Little wonder I preferred being with Katie back in the blossoming wonderland of our yard, or out on my enchanted island with Nana.

At an early age, I was developing into that cliché of distance running literature: a real loner. I simply preferred my own company to that of my classmates. As many friends as I have now all over the world, it's a strange thing to say that all through school I didn't develop a single lasting friendship among my classmates. Taunted as a "goody good" and "teacher's pet" in those very early years, I was so shy, such an outcast and object of scorn that I clearly wasn't a very good candidate for anyone looking for a pal. Later, as my world revolved more and more around athletics, I had more in common with those friends than my classmates.

At the time, though, had someone taken a good hard look at my class at school and tried to pick possible future athletic champions, I would surely have gone unnoticed.

Adding to the other problems my classmates had so quickly and ruthlessly identified, there was something terribly wrong with my feet. Wearing normal shoes was painful and even when barefoot I walked with a strange, pigeon-toed gait.

All in all, I was the quintessential ugly duckling, even down to the walk. My classmates never let me forget it.

4 ~ Feet of Clay

Mostly I remember the pain. I found myself walking on the outside edges of my feet to avoid the worst of it. My parents and grandparents were always trying to get me to "walk correctly," as if it were a matter of practice or will power. It was just no use.

I was born with bony protrusions on the inside forefoot of each foot, like giant bunions, and the doctors were perplexed by them. They finally decided that I needed surgery, but wanted to wait until I was older and my bones strong enough to handle the trauma.

I don't remember my feet ever keeping me from doing anything I wanted to do, but I do remember a constant backdrop of pain.

I suppose I must have suffered, but children really don't have anything to compare their experiences with, so I didn't feel particularly beset upon. I just kicked off my shoes and went barefoot as much as I could, and as New Zealand is a temperate country, I was able to do that a great deal. But when the weather did turn colder, I was in for it. Not only were the bony protrusions painful, but I had very poor circulation in my lower legs and that made the problem much worse in cold weather.

At school I wore soft house slippers, which were all right unless the weather got bad. I had all sorts of makeshift sandals and hard shoes with sections cut out, all to accommodate my poor little lumpy feet. Mostly I just endured.

I think I must have just put a lot of it out of my mind, but it was a very difficult thing for a young child. The pain was so unrelenting that I began to get migraine headaches regularly. I would wake up in the morning with double vision, which was always a sign that a migraine headache was coming on. I wouldn't tell my mother because I knew she'd keep me home from school, but by 10 in the morning, I'd be at the nurse's, nauseous, with my head exploding. I would black out and sleep it off, but at times the pain was so acute and lasted so long that I would have to stay at home in bed for a week at a time, with mum putting cold compresses on my head. I'm all but certain that those migraines were caused by the pain from my feet because after the surgery, I never had a single recurrence.

Despite these physical problems, because of my dad's early influence and my love of books and learning, I was always at or near the top in my classes. And despite the shabby treatment by my classmates, I never really felt like an outcast.

But we must have been quite the pair, Katie and I, once she started to school. It turned out that she was partially deaf and, as we later discovered, a slow learner. As she grew older and she fell further behind, we began to realize how serious her problems were. One day at school we were walking together and Katie said something to another girl about me being her sister.

"Oh, she's not your real sister," the other girl shot back, "She's adopted."

Because of all my father's careful nurturing, this didn't bother me in the least, but it upset Katie greatly, and just seeing her distressed was enough to get me upset. When our mum came to get us, Katie rushed out to her crying, "They said Annie's not my real sister!"

Our parents' way of handling this from the start was simple. Mum just said, "Annie's your real sister and don't let anyone tell you any different." I don't know to this day if Katie understands what adoption means or how it applies to us, but at the time she seemed satisfied with the reassurances.

And I, of course, knew there was nothing to be concerned about. Hadn't the man with the big, rough hands told me that I was special because he picked me out from all the other babies? To me, that was what being adopted meant: that I was special.

5 ~ *The Operation*

J ust after I turned 13, in January of 1969, the doctors decided I was old enough to tolerate the surgical procedure on my feet. Dr. Owen Nicholson, with whom I still keep in touch, performed the operation at Middlemore Hospital in Otahuhu, assisted by Drs. Lamb and Wilson.

"It wasn't a 'standard procedure' by any stretch of the imagination," Dr. Nicholson said. "Neither I nor my colleagues had ever really seen anything quite like it. Still haven't. It was a problem of excess bony growth out laterally from the first metatarsal. We could remove it but we couldn't guarantee that it wouldn't grow back..."

At one point in the preparation for surgery, they were doing all sorts of blood and cardiac tests, and they became a little alarmed at some of the results. Dr. Nicholson took my parents aside.

"We're concerned about her heart," he said. "Her pulse rate is very low, and her heart is larger than normal. She has an uncommon heart. We don't know exactly what it means, but it bears watching."

They had discovered something quite common in endurance athletes, but didn't know what it meant. In a short time it would become all too obvious that an uncommonly large heart was not an indication of more health problems. Far from it.

All I remember of the surgery, other than the pain, was a nurse coming into my room regularly to make a mark on my plaster casts to indicate how far up the casts the blood had seeped. If it rose too quickly, they would have to take the casts off to stop the bleeding.

They had to change the casts anyway after a while because there had been so much bleeding. The casts were so heavy that the first time I attempted to get out of bed, I swung them over the side and promptly threw myself onto the floor!

The doctors wanted me to immediately start learning how to walk all over again, even with the casts still on. They strapped these horrible rounded, rocking chair platform things to the bottom of my casts, then had me hobble up and down the hospital corridors with them. They were meant to get me in the habit of walking correctly, that is, straight ahead rather than my usual pigeon toed gait using the outer edges of my feet.

I must have been quite a sight, ambling noisily along the hallways. I looked and felt quite ridiculous. In fact, Mum nicknamed me "Mr. Plod" from a children's cartoon character of the time. Mr. Plod was a roly-poly, bumbling policeman, and I have to admit, my heavy-footed, get-out-of-the-way gait was not unlike that of the poor fellow.

&

"Well, where do you want to go on holiday?" Dad asked with a big grin when they came to fetch me home from hospital at long last.

I couldn't imagine. I was just so happy to be going home, I hadn't even thought about January holiday, which in New Zealand is the middle of summer, a time many New Zealanders go on vacation.

But there really wasn't any question about it. I wanted to go to the beach and I wanted to go fishing with my father, the happiest activity I knew. So that's what we did. We loaded up the car with all the fishing poles and whatnot and took off to nearby Laingholm Beach.

It was very nearly my last fishing trip. The first time I sat down on the wharf with my dad, I did the same thing I had done in the hospital, throwing my heavily casted legs over the side and practically going over with them. Fortunately my dad was watching me closely and snatched me up before I could go sailing over the side and straight to the bottom of Manukau Harbor.

The New Zealand school year begins in February so I started McAuley High School, a new private Catholic school for girls. I was attending with some of the girls I had gone to elementary school with, as well as with girls from all over the Auckland area and beyond.

There were three academic divisions for the first year of high school (what we called "the third form"): commercial, academic, and general. Strange as it seems in this day and age, at the time I felt that even though I had won an academic scholarship to the school, I would be better served by taking the commercial course and learning secretarial skills.

Opportunities for women in those days in New Zealand were so limited that we simply assumed that upon graduation we were either going to be nurses, teachers, or secretaries. I had not the foggiest notion about what I wanted to do in life, and it just seemed to be common sense to me to learn how to type and take dictation.

The school principals had other ideas, however, and I was put into the academic course, which was mathematics and languages. Far sighted though that may have been at the time, it was triple misery for me. I didn't want to be in the academic section; I was dealing with how ridiculous I looked with my funny feet, dressed in a school uniform so billowy I could practically turn around inside it, and I was still an object of much derision.

It's just miserable being different when you're a teenager, and I seemed to have been destined to be a sore thumb despite my best efforts to blend in. The girls in my own class more or less tolerated me, but the rest of the girls in the school singled me out for regular teasing.

There were times when we were sitting at lunch hour and girls would come up and take my lunch from me and run off, laughing, secure in the knowledge that I was in no condition to chase after them. The same thing happened in home economics class. I'd be working on a project at lunchtime and girls would come along and grab it and run away with it. It made for a pretty unhappy time. I can't say that my high school years were very pleasant because of all that teasing, but on the other hand my tormentors certainly gave me plenty of incentive to become quicker on my feet.

I managed to do well academically, probably because that's where I could put all my energy, but I didn't really enjoy classes at all. I was just surviving.

One glorious thing happened the summer after my operation: My migraine headaches totally disappeared! To this day I can remember the last one I ever had. I was sitting in Latin class, looking out the window at the playground as the teacher was talking about Latin numbers.

"Annie," she said, "Why don't you try counting the sea gulls on the playground, in Latin?"

I looked out the window and counted exactly twice the number of birds than were there. The teacher rapidly became frustrated with me, not realizing that my problem was neither Latin nor arithmetic, but double vision. I was soon back in the sick room with one of my crushing headaches. Remarkably, it was the last one I ever had.

Through February and March—summer in New Zealand, remember—I walked around in my casts with the rocker bottoms, and my feet were still somewhat painful even though the surgery had obviously fixed some things. Now, though, the pain came from the casts cutting into my swollen feet. Also, I was sweating inside the casts, which caused all sorts of problems with my skin. Bathing was a problem. The house I grew up in didn't have a shower, so I had to try to take baths with my legs outside the tub.

When the casts finally came off after about six weeks, I discovered my lower legs were covered in sores and blisters, just a terrible mess. And it was unsettling to walk around with no protection on my feet whatever. Talk about feeling vulnerable.

But I looked down at my feet and they looked perfect! The scars were still there and the stitches hadn't been taken out, but just to look at them and to see that they were so normally shaped was an exhilarating experience. On the other hand, to actually put them on the ground and to try to start using them was a frightening prospect. Even though I had been getting around fairly well on the rocker shoes it was still difficult to come out of those casts and try to walk normally.

My mother and father would take me to the beach or to the river to get my feet into the water and to allow me to run along the beach, and to make my legs strong by running in the salt water. It's kind of a New Zealand thing, this belief that the salt water and the coldness of the water are good for you. I had always liked such romps when I was younger, but after the surgery I had poor circulation in my feet and they became very sensitive to cold. To this day I cannot stand to have my feet in cold water, the pain is so great. And in the winter if my feet get cold it literally has me in tears.

So I'd go to the beach and walk in the water as much as I could stand, and it wasn't all that bad because the water in New Zealand is fairly warm in the summer. I'm sure that all that walking barefoot on the beach helped me recover quickly from the surgery.

I was back and forth to the doctors quite a lot, and they were wonderfully supportive and helpful, but still at that point there was no indication that I was going to run—or do anything else very strenuous for that matter. Their focus was on getting my feet strong, period.

I was fortunate indeed to have been born in New Zealand because at the time we had universal health care. I often wonder if I'd grown up in America whether my parents would have been able to afford all that was done to correct my feet.

But in New Zealand I got great care. Dr. Nicholson went on to lecture internationally and he even kept scrapbooks with clippings of my races, along with the records of my surgery, which he carried around when he lectured in Europe. He's retired now, and I still stop by to see him now and again when I'm in New Zealand. He always makes me take off my shoes so he can take a look at my feet and see how his handiwork is holding up after all the abuse I've put them through.

Clearly his skill radically changed my life for the better, but he has always maintained a modest demeanor, saying that my condition was so unusual that at the time he and his colleagues couldn't be sure if their course of treatment was the right one, and that he has always been delighted it turned out as well as it did.

6 ~ *Running Free*

Sports are important in New Zealand and some of my earliest memories are of watching rugby, tennis, horse racing, track and field and especially cricket with my father. I asked endless questions and he patiently explained the finer points to me. The Australian tennis champions Rod Laver and John Newcombe, big heroes of ours, were in their heyday then. And everyone in New Zealand, it seemed, kept up with the "All Blacks," our national rugby team. My father also belonged to the Auckland racing club, and he often took me to the horse races, where my proclivity for keeping scrapbooks necessitated my assembling everything l could find on my favorite thoroughbreds.

The Otahuhu Athletic Club also figured prominently in my early years, even before my surgery. Like a lot of children in the community, Katie and I took part in a variety of track and field events, including throwing the shot, high jumping and the like. We also participated in "scratch" races, a wonderful competition common in Australia and New Zealand, in which the slower runners are given a head start, thus allowing athletes of differing abilities to compete directly against each other in the same race. I have pictures of us, two little skinny kids, proudly holding up trophies we'd been given for something like trying the hardest, or good sportsmanship. It's obvious from looking at us that we were pretty hopeless at most of the events.

But after my feet were more or less "normal," the Otahuhu Athletic Club changed my life forever. Located in Sturges Park, the club is actually built into an old volcanic crater, with a grass track in the middle, grass embankments all around, old stone steps going up to the rim, and trees all around the top. Nowadays it looks to me like something out of the Middle Ages, some kind of athletic Stonehenge, but back then it was the only running track I knew.

And it was a wonderful one at that, with a well-maintained grass running surface and a little club room where we held a gathering every Wednesday night. Our neighbors, Rita and Jack Bates, were heavily involved with the club and they were both crazy about track and field. Their enthusiasm was contagious and though my parents were still concerned about my feet, they encouraged me to go out and try everything.

After my surgery I renewed my interest in the club, but because I was afraid of landing on my feet after a jump or dropping a shot put on them, this time I was more interested in running.

I started off doing the shorter distances and there was something about racing that I liked right away. On Saturdays we often had inter-club competition, traveling to Papatoetoe or some other club for competitions. Points were given for performances at all age levels and the winning team was determined by the total, so it was a true team effort.

These were long days of track and field, but they were lots of fun. The kids and adults supported each other in their different events, and the parents and relatives helped with the carpooling, officiating, and cheering. There was always a picnic atmosphere, with multicolored beach umbrellas cluttering the sidelines and the flags and pennants of each of the clubs proudly flying.

Later that summer Rita took me to a club meet where they were having an unusually long race for women, a mile run. For some reason, Rita entered me in that event. I had just turned 14 and I was going to be running against all these senior athletes, who were 20 and over.

I think I amazed both of us by finishing third in that race!

People started to talk right away because I had beaten a lot of senior women who were at the top of Auckland athletics at the time. This was a time when track and field (which we call "athletics") was just about the number one spectator sport in the country, so many of the women I beat were fairly well known. For this little slip of a 14-year-old to come out on the track barefooted and beat all but two of them certainly had people paying attention right away.

After that event, Rita entered me in the Auckland championship half-mile. At that time Mt. Smart Stadium was a cinder track, and I was going to need a pair of shoes to participate. We went to a Woolworth store and got a pair of white canvas sneakers, and that's what I wore in my first big track competition. I look back now and realize that Mum and Dad were probably apprehensive about all this, but they were much reassured that it was Rita who had entered me and would be taking me.

In this half-mile race I finished second to Anne Smith, one of the finest runners in the country at the time. Anne was being coached by an Englishman living in New Zealand, Gordon Pirie, who had been an Olympic silver medalist in Melbourne and had held several world records for the three and six miles in the 1950's.

At the time, I knew none of this. I was vaguely aware that I had done well in my races and that some people were talking about my running. I might have been aware that there was someone named Gordon around who was coaching some good runners, but that would have been the extent of it. I was mostly a wide-eyed kid who was enjoying the fact that her feet didn't hurt all time. At that time, everything else was icing on the cake. We were all very happy that I had finished second in the Auckland half-mile championships, but neither my parents, friends nor myself had any inkling what was to happen next.

That's when Gordon Pirie showed up at our front door.

7 ~ *Gordon*

Some people seem to change the lives of everyone they come into contact with. Gurus, seers, saints and madmen, they go about their business with supreme confidence. They are out to change the world or perhaps just the neighborhood, and whether or not they succeed, whether they end up in a jail, a palace or an asylum, they most assuredly change lives.

Gordon Pirie was such a person. I have never had any doubt that meeting him changed my life immeasurably and irrevocably.

I was 14 years old.

&

Gordon didn't so much immigrate to New Zealand as annex it. An Englishman, he had been a force on the world distance running scene for nearly 10 years. It was an era in which his countryman, Roger Bannister, had run the first four-minute mile, and his famous friend and mentor, the Czech Emil Zatopek, had challenged all existing training dogma.

Gordon was cocky, opinionated and thin-skinned, a problematic combination, particularly given the British sports media's penchant for faultfinding and second-guessing. He also didn't deal with authority well and often clashed with sports officials over one thing or another.

In his defense, Gordon's personality was almost the polar opposite of that of the British ideal of a champion sportsman—a mythical, glib, witty and well-rounded fellow who didn't take his training too seriously, won his meetings with easy grace, and (conveniently blessed with an independent income) earned only admiration, not money, from his talent. And—most importantly—he made it all look easy.

Gordon knew that distance running was becoming far too competitive for this laissez-faire gentleman's creed to succeed any longer. Instead, he took his cue from the bold, charismatic Zatopek, who joyously trained himself into a hungry whippet, and then ran opponents off their feet on the track. No stiff upper lip for Zatopek! On the contrary, he invited spectators to see what he was enduring as he snorted by the stands with a stunning lead, his head lolling about in pain, an awful grimace on his face. He was paying the price, his expression said, but he was leaving the world's best in his wake.

Gordon loved the awful *joie de vivre* of Zatopek's philosophy and sought to emulate it. But whereas Zatopek was the hero of a socialist state, an army officer and an Olympic champion with all his daily needs provided by a grateful nation, Gordon was a poor, striving athlete in a class-conscious society that still clung to the archaic code of the "gentleman athlete."

It irked Gordon that he was not only criticized for "training too hard," but that he was also expected to starve for the privilege of maintaining his amateur standing. Then, after his training methods had been ratified by his victories and records, he was criticized for merely being human. He pointed out that if he won a race but didn't set a record, the headline read: Pirie Fails!

When he finally retired from competitive athletics in 1961, he wrote a book entitled *Running Wild*. Where most successful athletes might have started such a work with a kind word for supportive parents, coaches or friends, Gordon felt so beset upon by detractors real and imaginary that he entitled his first chapter "My Critics." In a resounding remonstrance, he wrote:

> "... I ask myself why it is that I seem to have been so often involved in controversy when all I wanted was to get on with my job of giving all I had to athletics. At this rather solemn moment for me of saying goodbye to the

competitive field, I have had a long and earnest look at
myself, summoning up all the honesty and impartiality I
could muster. I have come to the conclusion that my
clashes with authority, with the self-appointed critics of
athletics, and sometimes with the public, were due to the
fact that my ideals, my aims, my training methods and
even my physical equipment, differed from those of
most of my British contemporaries. I have often trodden
a lone path and so have been called conceited, awkward,
self-opinionated, rebellious—even a bad sport. This
book may put the record straight by telling just what I
have tried to do, and how and why."

And so he does, for 224 pages. After his book came out he spent
much of the next several years burning many of his remaining
bridges in England before finally departing in the late 1960s for the
mild climate and sports-mad culture of New Zealand, a country he
had fallen in love with during his competitive days.

The feeling was pretty much mutual during his early years in the
country. His sometimes charming, sometimes prickly personality set
him apart from the great mass of easy-going, soft-spoken populace,
and he had curried a number of connections in his earlier travels in
the country. He had little trouble securing a teaching job at a high
school near Auckland, as well as a small part-time coaching stipend
from my own Otahuhu Athletic Club.

Anne Smith, an excellent English runner, was his pride and joy.
She had followed him from England and stayed with Gordon, his
wife Shirley and their two little girls, a living arrangement that raised
an eyebrow or two in our staid little country. But Gordon, as an
Englishman and a former world record holder, was initially accorded
a certain license for eccentricity.

He lived in an upscale area of Auckland called Remuera, and was
obviously doing fairly well at that time. He drove a Mercedes,
coached the Otahuhu Athletic Club and clearly enjoyed the status he
found in his newly adopted country.

☙

Of all this I, a shy and self-absorbed 14-year-old, knew next to
nothing. I was reveling in my newly straightened feet and the fact
that I seemed to have a knack for running. And so I had no idea
what in the world two older men were doing standing at our front

door, hats in hand, wanting to talk to my parents about me.

One was a man named Ferguson, the president of our club at the time, and it was with barely contained enthusiasm that he introduced the other man to us as if we should have known him already.

"This is Mr. Gordon Pirie!" he beamed.

My parents smiled politely. If Gordon was disappointed at the reception he received, he didn't show it.

"Mr. and Mrs. Garrett," he said, "I watched your Anne run second in the half-mile at Mt. Smart Stadium last weekend, and I think she has great potential. But she needs real training if she's to make the most of her gifts. I'd like to coach her."

He must have been at least a little taken aback when my parents didn't swoon with gratitude at the opportunity he was offering. But they were still more than a little worried about the stress and strain of athletics on my poor extremities, and I suspect that they weren't immediately won over by this highly excitable and exotic import, world records notwithstanding.

But he and Mr. Ferguson were quite persuasive, and after they left we discussed their proposal at some length. It was all quite heady stuff, the idea that I might actually become some kind of champion, travel with a national team to some big international events, perhaps even the Olympic Games! Nothing in our family's limited experience gave us anything to judge such notions by, so we finally by default just arrived at this timid but hopeful query: Why not give it a try and just see what happens?

I would like to be able to write that I went to bed that night with visions of gold medals dancing in my head, but as I say, I was mostly underwhelmed. The fact is that I had little idea that I was on a cusp of a new life. So I was now going to be coached by this Mr. Pirie, this energetic, hawk-faced man everyone seemed to respect and possibly to fear. Fine. A more immediate concern was no doubt some snippy remark a girl at school had made that day, or some project due for class.

&

I turned up for my first day for training and Gordon took one look at me and said, "Hello, Anne, nice to have you here. If you're going to train with me the first thing you're going to have to do is learn to dress correctly."

I suppose I should have been horrified, but of course he was right. It was extremely difficult to find women's athletic apparel in those days and I wasn't about to wear my huge balloon-like gym uniform. So I had cut off a pair of blue jeans at the knees, making sort of Bermuda shorts out of them, and I had found a sleeveless floral-patterned dress shirt. I wore no running shoes. That was it. That was how I showed up for my first training session with the great Mr. Pirie and the 30 aspiring world-beaters he was coaching at the time.

But that was my introduction to Gordon's personality. He certainly wasn't hesitant about saying exactly what was on his mind. It was, "Hi, nice to have you, don't come back until you dress the part."

In those days he coached us two nights a week, and we had club night on Wednesday and a competition on Saturday. On Sundays we would often drive somewhere to do a long run.

There were mostly teenagers in the group, with a sprinkling of adults, but we all trained together, starting at five o'clock in the afternoon. Some were sprinters, but most were middle-distance runners. There was no such thing as long distance for girls at the time; the longest race we ran was a mile or half-mile. The boys competed up to 5000 meters, which is a little over three miles.

Anne Smith was Gordon's star pupil. His wife, Shirley, who was a runner herself, and his two girls Joanne, 5, and Sarah, 4, would all come out to the track. There were lots of rumors at the time that Anne was more than a boarder with the family, and later that proved to be true. There was some obvious tension when they all turned up at the track together, but as a 14-year-old, I didn't really know what was going on and didn't care.

A lot of the parents used to turn up to watch the training sessions. My mother mostly would drop me off and come back later to pick me up. Sometimes the other parents would sit up in their cars and watch the workout sessions. When I joined, there were three sisters, Pauline, Margaret and Beverly Vercoe, and another girl, Sharon Thompson, who were all about my age. Among the teenagers, Beverly was the star.

Gordon's coaching method is not easy to describe. He was extremely loud, rude, dogmatic and abusive, but at the same time he was enthusiastic and motivating. He liked to play people off against each other, and as I began to improve, I found myself being used as a pawn in his little psychological games. He would even use me against the boys, saying things like: "If you don't do this series fast enough,

I'll throw Annie in with you and she'll likely beat the lot of you. How'd you like that, to be beaten by a girl, eh?"

With the other girls, he's say: "If you can't keep up with Anne, you're never going to be any good!" At the time it was flattering to always be the one held up as the ideal or the threat to the others. As I matured I saw this ruthless cruelty for what it was.

He even tried to spread this interpersonal rivalry to the parents, and it was an unpleasant thing to see that it often worked. He'd say to one parent, "Well, your kid just didn't do any good today; she couldn't keep up with Sally." And to another, "Sally is doing great and it's a shame Sue can't keep up with her."

He was an extremely manipulative person. It was sad that it was the way he chose to deal with everything. He had a vast amount of knowledge of the sport, but was extremely obsessive about it. He *had* to be right about everything. He wouldn't tolerate anyone else's point of view and anyone who tried to stand up to him ended up in a shouting match from which they'd eventually have to walk away. When crossed, Gordon could turn maniacal.

The club, though, was such a big, robust group that it could tolerate one Gordon Pirie. Most of the members who observed Gordon's antics said something like, "Well, that's just the way he is. We can handle it."

The overall club atmosphere was wonderful and the parents and the officials were very supportive. We had a great many people with a real passion for track and field, and a lot of enthusiasm. The club encompassed all levels and all ages, so you had a lot of parents competing, and they were great role models for the kids. So even Gordon couldn't entirely dampen the enthusiasm and friendship of the club. He was doing good things for many athletes, so everyone just tolerated the other side of him.

For me it was always, "Yes, Mr. Pirie" and "No, Mr. Pirie." He had just turned 40 and I had been brought up to respect my elders. That's the way I spoke to adults.

I just wanted to run, and I loved the rhythm of good, hard running. It so happened that was what Gordon wanted us to do most of the time anyway, so we usually got along fine. I really loved to turn up for training each night. Nothing was too tough for me and the passion I had for running hard and fast stayed with me through my entire career. It wasn't that I felt particularly competitive towards the other runners, I just wanted to run as hard and as fast as I could myself. I wanted to beat the clock. I never liked to run slowly.

That worked against me at times. My training diary is full of notations about problems with sore feet such that I'd had to take time off to let them recover.

I'd keep going back to the doctors and they'd say, "You're just going to have to be patient, your feet are getting stronger and you're trying to do something your feet aren't strong enough to do yet." But they were encouraging and taught me many ways to strengthen my feet. They never told me to stop, but they did warn me at times that I was pushing them too hard. My diaries show that I'd have to take two, three, four days off, sometimes even a week or two.

My dad was great about my newfound passion. He didn't know much about distance running in the beginning, so he bought a stopwatch and started to pay attention to lap times. I would come home from training and he would bathe my feet in a bucket of Epson salts and massage my legs. He felt that was his way to contribute to my effort.

I began to think of the club as my real life and school as something to be tolerated. I still disliked my classes and I still wasn't making any friends in school. My whole life was outside of school. Fortunately, I still had the discipline to do my homework and my grades were fine. Math was my best subject, but I was also taking Latin, French and biology. Though they were of no interest to me whatever, I managed to survive academically. In fact, I was in the top class and I tried to consistently be in the top 10 in my class, generally succeeding.

In New Zealand in those days, high school was as far as most people went in school. Most kids left high school for work at 16 or 17 with what we called a school certificate. Even if they failed, they could choose to stay until they earned it, or simply leave without it and start working. Apprenticeships were the way one learned a job. It was completely different from the United States. There wasn't much academic pressure for most people.

But it became a struggle for me to stay interested in academics, particularly as I began to be successful in sports. There was never any question, however, that I would stay in school and learn a profession. At the time, had anyone suggested that one day I would make a living—and a rather comfortable one at that—from athletics, I'm sure I would have considered them quite mad.

8 ~ Racing

The academic and athletic calendar in New Zealand goes all year around. Unlike athletes in other sports, distance runners just shift venues and distances and keep going. From November to March we have track and field season, April through July is cross country and August through October is road-racing season.

Competition was divided by age. At that time sub-junior was 13-15, junior was 16-20 and senior was over 20. The prevalent feeling then was that women were too weak to run races as long as men, so the longest races the senior ladies ran was a mile and a half in cross country, as well as in road racing. The sub-junior girls ran a half-mile and the junior girls one mile.

I started off my real competitive career in the cross-country season of 1970. The meets were held around Auckland, which even then was geographically a large city. Sometimes we'd travel 20 or 30 miles across the city to compete in cross-country meets.

My mum and dad came to the first race, at Homai College, a school for the blind located on farm grounds. I'm talking about cattle, sheep, real fences and real barbed wire. There was manure everywhere.

A lot of these events were handicapped, so everyone started at different times according to their past performance. Then your actual completion times would be compared and everyone's places determined according to who had actually run the course the fastest. The best runner would go off "scratch" and the rest would go off three minutes earlier, two minutes earlier, and so on, depending on ability.

Because of my success the previous track season, I was given the scratch mark, and Beverly Vercoe, the next fastest, was given a 30-second head start.

The race began and I set off trying to catch up to Beverly. A half-minute in such a short race was quite an advantage and I couldn't close all the gap. I passed a lot of the other girls along the way and didn't really get close to Beverly until near the end. Of course in those days I didn't know what 30 seconds really meant. When it came to the fences, the rules were that if you couldn't climb the fence you were allowed to go underneath. Then as now, I had a tremendous fear of jumping and landing on my feet, so when it came to those fences there was no question which route I was going to take. Underneath I would scoot, and because it was the middle of the rainy New Zealand winter, after a while I was be covered in mud.

At the end of the race some of the spectators were saying that I probably got the award for the fastest time, but my parents didn't think so because Beverly seem so far ahead. It took a while for the officials to tabulate the results, so mum and Dad went on home thinking I'd lost.

When they announced the results, I was surprised to hear that I had won after all! But the victory was bittersweet. I'll never forget the sight of Beverly there with her parents, hearing that she'd been beaten, then breaking down and crying, as her parents tried to comfort her. In all my years of competition, though I've won my share of races, I've always remembered that for every runner who wins, there are many who finish behind, and there's no shame in any placing so long as you tried your best.

In a delicious irony, first prize was a manicure set. It might as well have been a welding torch. My nails were a total wreck from my nervous picking, and no manicure set was up to the challenge. I still laugh about that.

I was still only 14 years old, a gawky, pigtailed slip of a girl, but in sports mad New Zealand I was already starting to get headlines as a new star on the scene. I became the favorite for nearly every event I entered. And I did end up winning most of them. But as the time for the Auckland championships approached, I began to feel not at all well. I was due for a lesson in humility.

The championships were held every year at a Cornwall Park, a gorgeous park in the center of Auckland that is administered as a farm, complete with cows and sheep. It's totally accessible to the public, and you can go for a walk through those fields in the middle of the city, completely surrounded by cows and the sheep the whole time.

It was an out-and-back one-mile course, and I took off and tried to lead the race. But it became obvious after a while that I was full of the flu. When you're young, you aren't very good at evaluating what's going on with yourself physically, so I had no idea what was happening. I got more and more dizzy and at about the halfway point, I just collapsed. Beverly ended up winning the Auckland championships.

It was a good early lesson, a much-needed reality check, because I had begun to think of myself as invincible. I was chastened, but didn't get down in any way. I bounced right back and decided that since cross country was over, I would redouble my efforts and focus on the road-racing season.

I began to win every race I entered.

That wasn't making me very popular with the other girls. It started causing a lot of competition outside our group as well as within it. Even some of the parents were cool towards me, an attitude that spilled over to some of the girls.

That was probably a natural reaction among teenagers in a competitive situation. You see it now, when someone's on the outside for some reason and the kids don't speak to him or her. That's what happened to me when I started winning. Of course Gordon didn't do much to help, and in fact he actually made it worse.

Anyway, when my successes caused a little distance to grow between the other girls and me, so I would go out and run with the guys for a while instead. When things got back to normal again, I'd return to running with the girls and everything would be fine. Sometimes it would make me sad, but as always my desire to run was so strong that it enabled me to overcome anything else I had to deal with.

And the social scene around the Otahuhu club was wonderful. There were parties every Saturday night that included the parents, officials and kids, 150 strong at times. There was a disc jockey and dancing, and the adults would have a drink or two. The mums did all

the catering, bringing lots of home cooking. It was a real family ori-
ented event, with the little ones running around and the teenagers
flirting, and the adults sitting around talking. These events would
sometimes go on until two in the morning, and then everyone would
help cleaning up.

We would also have our annual awards ceremonies, and they
made sure that everyone won something, a medal or a ribbon or a
cup. It was a great era to be involved with track and field in New
Zealand, not only in terms of the success of our elite athletes, but also
at the local club level. I don't know if they still have those club
evenings or not, but I certainly hope so. They were a wonderful part
of my early years.

9 ~ *Gordon's Gauntlet*

Gordon thought that the secret to success was just training hard. The harder you trained the better you'd become. He would get us doing all sorts of things, like running 100 meters 10 times, with each of them close to all out. He would time them with a stopwatch and each was supposed to be faster than the last.

When it came time to doing longer repetitions, he made us do something that has stayed with me all through the years. He wouldn't allow any of us to wear or carry watches. When we did 200 or 400-meter repetitions, he would use a whistle and blow it when we were supposed to hit each 100-meter mark. If we didn't hit the first two as he blew the whistle, he would pull us back and make us start again. He'd keep doing that until we got the pacemaking correct. That was a skill that stayed with me a long time, and I think I still have it, the ability to run lap after lap with perfect pacemaking. In later years, I could run a completely solo 10K on the track, 25 laps by myself at a perfect pace. One time I actually did just that, with every lap within four-tenths of a second of the correct pace.

Gordon taught us the patience of pacemaking, the feel of a 70-second 400 meters, or two-minute 600 meters. He was constantly teaching us about the rhythm of a distance.

He would carry five stopwatches at once. He would spread us around the track so that we were never competing directly with each other. That was to teach us not only about pacemaking but also to train independently of others. There were many athletes who couldn't handle it and far preferred to be running with their chums. But those of us who stuck with it learned to train and race independently and not be reliant on others. Because of that independence, I became self-centered in my own training and unless everyone else in a group is running the pace I want, I'd really rather be on my own.

Gordon's home in Remuera was close to a park called the Auckland Domain. There's a big museum and a glorious park up on a hill, with a wonderful view of the city and the harbor. We are blessed in Auckland to have these huge parks for everybody's use and runners certainly take full advantage of them.

Auckland is all hills. There's only about six flat miles in the whole place, and that's along the waterfront. The rest of it is either up or down. The area where Gordon lived is one of the hilliest in the city, which was perfectly all right with him. He quickly picked out some of the steepest ones for his runners to train on.

Right in front of his house there was a hill about 100 meters long, and he would have us run up that incline 10 times, as hard as we could. He'd be standing there at the top, timing every one of them.

Then he had a longer hill that usually took around three minutes to run up, an absolute monster. By the time you got to the top you were buckling at the knees. His favorite phrase, repeated hundreds of times, was "Run all out! Pump your arms!"

At the Auckland Domain he had yet another hill that took about three minutes to run, and we just dreaded it. His whole training philosophy was hill reps, hill reps, hill reps. They were the best thing you could possibly do to get strong, he felt. Once again, that's something that stayed with me my entire running career, and to this day if I want to get my feet stronger and get back in shape, I'll do hill repeats. I believe they are better than lifting weights to get your legs strong.

The Domain has a hallowed place in our sport's history. An amazing park, at any given time you'd see the Who's Who of New Zealand running out training. There is a circular road there that's about a mile long, with painted marks every 100 meters. Those marks date back to the days of Arthur Lydiard, the legendary New Zealand coach, and his most famous athletes, gold medalists Murray Halberg and Peter Snell.

Somebody repaints the marks on that road on a regular basis, and over the years many famous runners from around the world have used that mile circuit in their winter training. Runners like Toshiko Seko, the famous Japanese marathoner, and Douglas Wakiihuru, the Kenyan marathoner. American Mary Decker (later Slaney) came down for several winters to fly around that loop, and many others.

The Domain was about 10 miles away from where I lived, so we'd catch a ride or a bus, which was always a bit of a challenge, but we usually worked together to get everybody there and home again. We did a great deal of our training there.

Gordon also had a favorite two-mile hill circuit in Remuera, and he used to set us all up with a staggered start to run it as hard as we could. It was always timed, so we always knew if we were making progress. Gordon encouraged us to keep training diaries and to watch our own progress, because he felt it would give us confidence, seeing the actual evidence right on the pages of our training logs.

There were some days when you might not be feeling well, but you might still get a better result than you'd had the week before. The tiredness might be mental rather than physical, and the diary would indicate that.

I learned about mental burnout, a state in which you would not want to run at all, and could not bring in a good performance. But I learned there were other days when you didn't feel that well, yet somehow you could still run fairly well and even come up with an outstanding race. I know it's something of a cliché these days, but I certainly learned from hard experience that a lot of athletics is mental rather than physical.

I didn't fully appreciate it at the time, but New Zealand truly is a runner's paradise. On Sundays we would head up to Murawai Beach, on the west coast of New Zealand, alongside the Woodhill State Forest, which was accessible to everybody. It's a glorious forest, with pine trees and pine needle trails and sandy tracks and dirt roads. And of course there was the beach nearby.

We would go there and run through the forest, a whole group of us, and then we'd go to the beach and swim in the surf. Then we'd pile into the cars and head home, stopping off to get hamburgers and milkshakes. This was usually on Sundays when we were all relaxed, a group of light-hearted young athletes in wonderful condition, training our hearts out in this fabulous and exotic place, quite oblivious to it all, really.

Gordon would tell us stories about the renowned Australian coach, Percy Cerutty, how he got all his athletes to run up sand dunes, and that was what he was getting us to do. At times he would get us to run so hard that only the strong-willed survived. Gordon played a lot of mental games. He had studied the topographical maps until he had the entire trail system memorized. Then he would lead us off into the middle of the forest on a route we didn't know and suddenly take off like a madman, making us keep up or be left behind all alone to find our own way back. We got lost a lot.

At that time I noticed that he was starting to lose a lot of athletes who couldn't or wouldn't keep up with his intensity. Those of us who stayed tried to support each other enough to keep each other going. It's funny, thinking back on it now, I certainly understand and appreciate the controversy over various American coaches such as Bobby Knight of Indiana University or Woody Hayes of Ohio State. Gordon would fit in very nicely with that group.

During this time when Gordon was coaching Anne Smith, he would often instruct just the two of us to come to the Auckland Domain to train without the others. That's when I first saw him at his most manipulative and cruelest. He would taunt her, saying, "If you don't try harder, Anne, I've got another Anne coming up that's going to take your place."

I can only imagine the effect that must have had on her, particularly in light of their apparent physical relationship, but she endured it for a long time.

He didn't play it the other way; he never used her to taunt me. Considering the heartlessness of his taunts, one might have expected her to have resented me, but to the contrary, she was invariably kind to me and I liked her very much.

That was also the first time I saw him physically abuse someone. Up until then it had all been verbal. But one day when I had beaten Anne in a hard run, he grabbed her by the shoulders, threw her up against the wall, struck the wall, then struck *her*, screaming at her all the while.

As a young girl, it was hard to watch abuse like that, and it marked the point at which I began to distance myself emotionally from Gordon for my own protection. I never wanted to be in the position Anne Smith was in that day, being emotionally and physically battered by a semi-crazed man to whom she was apparently committed heart and soul.

With me Gordon used different tactics. If he didn't think I was performing well enough in training, he would call my mother and father and accuse them of not doing enough to take care of me, not watching my nutrition and so on. All of which was ludicrous. My mother was and is a wonderful cook and I ate extremely well, but Gordon was big on passing blame along, and once he had ingratiated himself with people, it wasn't long before he was badgering them. But my parents, like so many other New Zealanders, took Gordon with several grains of salt. As long as I wanted to train with him, they would put up with his antics.

But as easygoing as my parents were, Gordon put them to the test. He was the kind of person who would just roll up to the house unannounced, walk straight through the house still wearing his muddy running shoes, plop himself down and demand to be fed. You can imagine how this went over with my mother, who kept a clean, neat house with immaculate carpets and floors. But Gordon felt that he could just turn up at any one of the kids' houses at any time and demand just about anything he wanted. That got old with all the parents, and it finally got to the point where he wasn't really welcome to just drop by our house. My parents were civil to him, but that's where it ended. They told me that I could continue training with him but that he was essentially banned from the house.

Some of the other parents took the opposite approach when they learned he was banned from my house. They theorized that if they continued to welcome him, he might treat their kids a bit better. But of course it never worked that way with Gordon and eventually the other parents ended up paying the price as well. Sooner or later Gordon wore everyone out.

But over the years I saw him do his "Charming Gordon" routine so many times, and it nearly always produced what he was looking for: free food, free lodging, free anything. That struck me as curious at the time, because he was doing fairly well financially. He had a decent amount of money, a good job, nice car, and rental properties in Auckland. But I suppose his days as a penurious athlete had made him permanently stingy, and he was always ready to try to cash in on his reputation or his position. He could be immensely charming until he got what he wanted, then he would just mistreat people and move on.

During the 1970-71 season I continued to break records, particularly in the junior (under 18) ranks, but I began running the senior events as well, and started to win them, too.

There were some competitions when I would run the junior races and the senior races on the same day. I really enjoyed doing that. The mile race was the longest event women ran in those days and it always seemed to me that it wasn't a long enough distance. The race would be over and I would still be itching to run some more. So often I raced several junior and senior events.

The cross-country and road racing distances were approximate, anywhere from a mile-and-a-half to two-and-a-half miles. There was no need for them to be measured because there were no records kept for those events, as opposed to track events where records are meticulously kept. In those events, the only way you could tell anything about your performance was to run the same courses again the next year and see how much faster or slower you were.

My feet were holding up, but I was beginning to discover that it was the simple act of walking that caused my feet to hurt the most. As soon as I started warming up for running, in just the first few steps of jogging, the pain would go away. That's the way I am to this day. I still frequently have pain when I walk, but it goes away when I start running.

I still had problems with motion sickness, so when we traveled away from Auckland by car or bus for competitions, it was always annoying to deal this apparently inborn malady. I would often turn nearly sick at races, and that obviously wasn't conducive to good performances.

But socially my life had changed dramatically. Instead of being the loner and the target of teasing, I now found myself with a ready-made set of friends. And there were certainly budding romances blossoming all around the athletic club. We all rotated around each other over the years as we trained and went to competitions together.

As much as we would pair off, the main focus was on the club and the team effort. As I look back on those days, I'm struck by what a nice group of kids that was, growing up through our formative years together.

A lot of the events were team-oriented, with team points awarded for each event. So even though on one level we were competing as individuals, at the end of the day it was the club that won or lost. We were very proud that the Otahuhu Club was so strong and won so many events. That pride certainly fostered a great deal of camaraderie, friendship and good spirits among the athletes and officials, and I still stay in contact with friends from those early years.

High school was another matter altogether, probably because the relationship between academics and athletics is so different in Commonwealth countries than it is in the United States. Because all my friends were in athletics, and athletics were separate from school, I had no close friends in school at all.

But though organized sports weren't really a part of school, they still had inter-school competitions, which were grafted onto the school schedules like an afterthought. So athletes spent most of their time training and competing with their clubs, then one day of each season put on a school singlet and competed against other club athletes doing the same thing for their school. It was much like a post-season or all-star game in the United States.

In February every year, each school would pick a team that would represent it in the regional championships and then in the Auckland and North Island championships. Eager for any opportunity to race, I was only too happy to represent my school in this way.

During the school year I also played tennis as well as our version of basketball (called "net ball") which is played outdoors. I actually got to be a decent tennis player and ended up captain of the team at one stage. And I enjoyed net ball, too, a game Mum had played in her school years.

In the winter I often played net ball in the morning and ran cross-country or road races in the afternoon. In the summer I'd play tennis in the morning and race on the track in the afternoon. That lasted for two years, until Gordon found out, and he put an immediate stop to it.

At 15, I completed my school certificate examinations and passed. In our system a student is then allowed to leave high school to begin to work. I chose not to because I had no idea what I wanted to do. There really wasn't much discussion about it; it was all but assumed I would go for my "sixth form year," which is the fourth year of high school in New Zealand, composed mostly of students going on to college.

By the time I got to that year, many students had already left to begin apprenticeships or other jobs. The class I started with had dwindled to about 40 percent of its original size.

When I started my sixth form year we were split into two classes. One had about 10 in the academic course, and the rest were in a combination general and commercial course. That isolated the academic students a bit more. But because of the success I was having in athletics and the attention I was getting, I suddenly became a popular person in school and not only ended up on the honor roll, but was also made school house captain. When it came time for the school track and field championships, I was entered in every running event, from 100 meters through the half-mile, just to get the points for the school.

Some of the other girls at school had seen me competing and decided to try their hand as well, and some of them were fairly talented. Our relay teams were fast and we did very well as a school team. But running every event made for a long day for me. On the other hand, as I say, the emphasis was quite different than it is in the United States, and the way we looked at it was, Hey, it's just the school championships, so no need to get all worked up.

During vacations Gordon's group often traveled into Auckland during the lunch hour to train. Many of the senior athletes had jobs, so this was the best time for them to get together. This was the era of John Walker, who would hold the world record for the mile in the mid-'70s; Rod Dixon, bronze medalist in the 1972 Olympic 1500; Dick Quax, silver medalist in 1976 Olympic 5000; and Kevin Ryan, Dick Tayler and many other top athletes who would later win fame and fortune in the sport. They would all be at the Domain at lunchtime along with us kids, and we all trained in our different groups.

Sometimes I would actually hop in and train with the older guys, which I loved. They were very encouraging. I would have to modify the workout somewhat to be able to keep up. They might be running 10 miles, so I would do six with them, and they'd urge me on the whole way.

So here's this 16-year-old girl out running with these 21-24 year-old Olympians, and they certainly weren't slowing down on my account. That meant listening to all their jokes and gossip as well, something of an education in itself.

I was still dealing with the fact that my feet were still somewhat fragile. I'd get to a level of fitness and then my feet would simply not hold up to the strain. I'd have to take some time off. To an athlete impatient to find out how good she could really be, this became a frustrating process.

It's ironic, really, because I always tell other runners that I've never had any training injuries, which is unusual for a competitive endurance athlete. Most of us get some sort of over-use injury from time to time and some have their careers cut short by such problems.

But when I say I haven't had any injuries, what I'm really talking about is my professional career in the United States. I've stayed injury free during those years, but in the early going I was battling nearly daily to keep my feet healthy.

I now think much of the problem was that Gordon never did the kind of training we refer to as "base building," the long, slower runs that allow your body to become strong without risking the wear and tear of the more intense kind of training that would normally come later.

None of that lallygagging around for Gordon! His training was intense from the start, based on running hard and fast all the time. And my feet were having a tough time of it. The rough terrain of cross country particularly took its toll. I'm not talking about running on golf courses like they do in the United States. We ran on hard-scrabble farmland, with plenty of puddles, mud, fences, and all the rest.

This was the beginning of a new golden era of New Zealand athletics. Arthur Lydiard had coached Peter Snell, Murray Halberg and Barry Magee to Olympic medals in the early '60s, followed by a period of relative quiet. But then in the early '70s Walker, Quax and Dixon were beginning to be familiar names in track and field circles, and when John Walker broke the 3:50 mile barrier in 1975 it put little New Zealand right back in the forefront of the world running scene.

And we girls were starting to get some attention as well. Our track meets were well supported and we all got so much media attention we would often be recognized on the street.

These were heady days. Track and field athletics were very popular in the country anyway and it was especially so when we had athletes good enough to make their mark on the international scene. As young as we were, we knew that we were a part of something very special and exciting.

New Zealand would be hosting the Commonwealth Games in Christchurch in 1974, and there was even talk about turning Mt. Smart Stadium into an all weather track, a dream come true for runners so accustomed to slow, old fashioned grass or cinder tracks. The energy level and excitement among New Zealand athletes was high in those days.

10 ~ Bureaucrats

New Zealand had never sent a full men's and women's team to the world cross-country championships, because up until the early '70s only a few individuals were considered good enough to go. A full team would have been nine men and seven women, and the federation just didn't want to spend the money to send that many athletes to Europe. Then in 1971, all of a sudden our little country had so many excellent runners that our officials started thinking that we might make a good showing as a team.

The big goal for many of us who were developing then was making the 1973 world cross-country team. Even younger runners like me were focused on it. There were no junior world championships then; It was all or nothing.

All the athletes in contention for places on these teams knew each other from racing and training together around Auckland. Most of us had known each other from the time we were kids running around together at club night. Many of us had flown around the country to competitions and were billeted together with families or couples, nice local people who were interested in athletics.

At the time I was consistently breaking Auckland records when I raced at our club on Wednesday nights, but they were never officially recognized because no Auckland officials would attend weekly club nights or have the required three stopwatches. The officials just assumed no one would be running records at a club meeting, so they didn't give them any credence whatever. Any time I wanted to break a record I had to do it at Mt. Smart Stadium at a bigger meet.

That was the first time I had trouble with athletic officialdom and a lot of that was because of Gordon. He was always getting into squabbles with officials, verbally abusing them; they simply retaliated when they got the chance.

Gordon used top athletes like me as pawns to get what he wanted, and he often ridiculed other athletes who were not in his group. If I had been a target of his scorn, it would have just made me mad and more determined to win. In any case, his behavior didn't help our public relations within the sport, and that counts for more than one might think at that level.

In New Zealand, officials would always set standards that were *even harder* than the Olympic standards because of the expense of sending athletes to the Games. They intentionally made it more difficult because they wanted anyone who represented New Zealand not just to compete, but to make it to the finals. So they arrived at a qualifying time that would literally rank you in the top 16 in the world in your event in the previous year! And that was just to be considered for the team!

So when I refer to breaking the "Olympic standard," I mean the New Zealand Olympic standard, which was harder than the International Olympic Committee (IOC) standard. And they would sometimes change *even that* after some athlete had achieved it, making the athlete qualify again. That's what made it so psychologically difficult through the years. I was always being asked to meet higher standards, and then once met, even higher ones.

It got a bit better later, but early in my career I was constantly being psychologically bruised by our nonsensical selection process. For instance, in the 1972 Olympics the IOC standard was 4:27 for the 1500—the first time the event would be held for women in the games. I ended up meeting that standard four or five times. Then the New Zealand selectors announced that we would need to break 4:20 to be sent to the Games!

I finished second in our so-called Olympic trials of that year, in 4:24, three seconds under the IOC's standard. The head of selection committee told me that as far as he was concerned I was on the team and that it was time they sent a female to the Olympics.

Later he called back to tell me the other members of the committee thought that I was too young to go and they weren't going to select me after all.

That's the sort of thing athletes had to deal with over and over again. We'd meet the Olympic standard (and in my case become the national champion) and then not get selected for the team. The selectors would look at the numbers of athletes who had qualified in their various events and decide they needed to cut back, so they'd just make the qualifying standard harder. And it was always weighted in such a way as to allow more men to go, because women's sports were considered secondary.

That year, in order to compete in the Olympic trials, I had to miss the "Champion of Champions" school competition, which was held the same day as the trials. So I got permission to run in the trials and to skip the regional secondary meet while still being allowed to compete later in the Auckland school championships.

But when it came time later to go to the Auckland championships, the officials suddenly changed their minds and said that because I had not run in the regional competition, I couldn't run in the championships in the 800.

There were big stories in the press about the way I was being treated. When I did actually turn up at the Auckland championships on that particular day, the event that I would have run in actually had an open lane. But they still would not let me run. Strangely enough, after the competition was over, when they picked the team to go to the national meet, they put me on it. So they weren't going to let me run in their local meet because of a technicality, but they were only too happy to have me represent the city in the national competition.

This was my introduction to the kind of petty, bureaucratic infighting that would haunt me during much of my athletic career in New Zealand. There was no logic, no consistency to the rulings, and it became more childish as time went on. And, of course, Gordon's behavior with officials didn't help much either.

But despite the brouhaha with officialdom, I went down to the North Island championships to run the 400 and 800 meters, and that was the first time I encountered a gifted young runner named Lorraine Moller. At that time she was being coached by a former New Zealand Olympic 1500 bronze medalist, John Davies. The media started to sense a potential rivalry between us because she was the top athlete of that area, the Waikato Province, and I was the Auckland Province champion. The fact that we both had famous coaches probably added fuel to the fire. So the media actually started this rivalry long before we'd even met.

I was meeting Lorraine on her home track and for perhaps the first time in a competition with girls of my own age I was a bit apprehensive.

In the 400 meters we had to draw for lanes and I was surprised when the official handed me a card instead of letting me choose, as had the other girls. Naturally, "the fix was in," and I ended up in the outside lane. Lorraine was in lane two. In a longer race it wouldn't have made much difference, but the 400 is a sprint, and obviously someone was trying to give Lorraine as much of a leg up as they could.

Nonetheless, I ended up winning the 400. And the next day I came back and beat her in the 800 meters. In the 400, someone entered a protest that I had stepped out of my lane. There was always that kind thing going on.

But that did start a friendly rivalry and later a true friendship between Lorraine and me that continues to this day. She would later win a bronze medal in the Olympic marathon in Barcelona in 1992, and would become a successful road racer in the United States as well.

11 ~ *The Clay Crumbles*

I decided to go to a doctor named Lloyd Drake about my feet. He was a sports medicine specialist, well ahead of his time. There was a lot of jealousy in the sports medicine hierarchy because a number of top athletes in different sports were going to him. The Olympic officials had their own experts they wanted us to work with, but athletes are wonderfully eclectic when it comes to sports medicine. They'll go to witch doctors if they can actually help, and Dr. Drake was extremely supportive and successful in getting athletes through their various problems. He gave me a great deal of confidence in dealing with my problematic feet.

Running shoes were hard to find at the time and we had to take what we could get. We were finally starting to get some light nylon shoes from a Japanese company called "Tiger" (later "Asics") for around $3 a pair. We were also wearing a type of canvas shoe that had almost no structure to them, and they caused problems for me. Because I run up on my toes, I was pushing my toes into the fronts of my shoes, causing bruising and fluid to build up under my toenails, eventually leading to infections. This was a chronic problem for the next three or four years. I was constantly going to Lloyd Drake for help with my poor bludgeoned toes.

It was sometimes so painful my poor mum was putting me to bed at night with a shot of whiskey and a glass of warm milk. This would knock me out enough to allow me to sleep so we could get to Lloyd the next morning. He would drill holes in the toenails to drain them and relieve the pressure. Often in order to keep training, I cut holes in the front my running shoes to spare my big toe. I would do anything not to miss a single day of training.

As if I didn't have enough on my mind, I took on the job of club treasurer. An energetic 16-year-old, I was always interested in taking on new tasks, and it seemed to me that managing the books for the club would be a good challenge.

The club system was strong and well organized throughout New Zealand. There were monthly inter-club meetings at the Auckland center attended by two representatives from each club, and I was one of them. I was always involved in the administration of the sport at that level, and I suppose I became known for getting up and speaking my mind. That may not have made me very popular at the time. Even fairly tame comments may not have been particularly welcome from a mere teenager. But my parents had raised me that way, to be willing to speak out and to contribute. It won me a lot of friends, but I suppose a few detractors as well.

I continued that job for three years. My mum became secretary at one stage, so between the two of us we had all the records of the club in our house. With my homework and everything else I was trying to do it sometimes became a bit stressful to get everything done before the next meeting, making sure the books were balanced and so forth.

The other activity I started about this time was the sport of orienteering, which Gordon had become interested in. It's an event that combines a kind of rugged cross-country running with map reading. You run through a forest using little markers and a compass, trying to find the shortest consecutive route between each marker. Most of these courses are long enough that even if you are good it can take you up to two hours and often three. You can get extremely lost, particularly in the forests of New Zealand, with their dense undergrowth.

Gordon maintained that orienteering was a great way to build endurance but, knowing him, it was probably just something he wanted to do and he simply preferred having company. Most of the other runners in our group didn't want any part of it, but I enjoyed it, and as it turned out, I became pretty good at it. I ended up being New Zealand champion and even the Australasian (New Zealand and Australia combined) champion. I banged up my shins running into a few too many logs, but I was always drawn to the solitude of running in the forest. I was certainly never afraid, although I got myself good and lost a few times—occasionally because I had the map upside down! But I always managed to retrieve my position and get home.

On many of our training trips Gordon singled me out as the one he was either going to torment or encourage, depending on his mood on a given day. He would get me out in the forest and try to wear me down, running as hard as he could, challenging me to beat him. And if I couldn't keep up, he would run off and leave me and try to get me lost in the forest. He had been a gifted runner, and was still in excellent condition, so keeping up with him was no easy matter.

It was about that time that an incident happened that changed my relationship with Gordon forever. He was taking me to an event down in Waikato where I often went to race against Lorraine. It's only about an hour's drive, but about halfway down he pulled off by a small town on a country road and said we were going to just stop to have lunch.

What he actually had in mind was starting a sexual affair with me. As a sheltered 16-year-old, I was scared to death. His argument was that I was an attractive young girl, and that he had been good to me, and that I basically owed him.

I rejected him in no uncertain terms, and at that moment our relationship changed forever. He never tried again, but the fact that I had rejected him surfaced again and again in the way he treated me. I never told anyone about it, I was so embarrassed, but I resolved never to be in a situation where I was one-on-one with him again.

In retrospect, I guess I'm fortunate it happened early on and put me on my guard. But later on as other problems with Gordon made our relationship more and more strained, the memory of that incident had a lot to do with my leaving him.

&

So much of what my dad taught me has stayed with me. When I was presented with awards or honors, or any situation where I was put on center stage, one thing my dad always emphasized was that I should get up and speak. I should thank the presenters, and recognized my opponents, or make some comments about the race or the season. Dad didn't want me to be just a tongue-tied athlete with no social graces. He would even help me think of what I wanted to say, so I was always prepared before I stood up.

In October of 1972 the New Zealand Senior Road Racing Championships were in Nelson, a beautiful area on the most northern tip of the South Island. A beautiful place, Nelson is called "the Sun Capital" of the country, and they grow tobacco, fruit and other crops there. I was chosen to represent Auckland, along with Barbara Moore and seven others. Most of us from the Otahuhu club were still juniors, but we won the team championship and I ended up winning the race, with Barbara second.

That was the sort of success the team and Gordon were enjoying in those early days, and despite the incident with Gordon, it was a lot of fun training, traveling and competing together. We were all becoming good friends, particularly Barbara and I. She was a very talented runner, a beautiful girl who had 20 brothers and sisters! Her father was English and her mother was Maori, and though she was sometimes irritated when she was referred to as a "Maori lass," she was a very exotic looking and graceful runner. Seeing the way she was treated by the sporting officials was my first actual experience with racism, petty politics, and injustice.

12 ~ Belgium and the World Beyond

In December of 1972 the cross-country trials were held in Wellington to pick the New Zealand team for the 1973 world championships in Belgium. I tied with Heather Thompson for first and Barbara was third. Naturally, Barbara and I were extremely excited because we thought surely the top three finishers in the trials would get chosen for the women's team because they were taking six.

But Barbara was passed over and other women were chosen ahead of her. One was her age, so they couldn't use Barbara's youth as the excuse. What they came up with was that they couldn't send two of us away who knew each other so well, as if our friendship would somehow be a detriment to the team's effort.

I think it was actually a case of jealousy that Gordon had two girls on the team. And something I didn't think of at the time, but would later have to consider, was the fact that Barbara is half Maori and they simply felt they could get away with ignoring her. The decision made no sense at all, because the two of us had had a consistent record of finishing first and second in almost all our races.

The fact that we were trained by the same person surely would have otherwise been an asset, but the officials had it in for Gordon and they had the power, so they used it. We didn't even know the term "discrimination" then, and were probably too innocent to imagine such things, but I now have no doubt that it played a part in her shabby treatment.

But she was left off the team and I was on it, and it was a tough time for both us. At the same time that everyone was excited for me, there were also bitterly disappointed for Barbara. We had such a close friendship, and for the next few months I was training to go to the world cross-country championships and she was right there beside me, training her heart out and knowing she wasn't going anywhere. Years later Barbara would get her due.

I had finished my senior year of high school and in New Zealand you normally sit for your university entrance exam at that point. However, if you have maintained a certain grade average you're allowed to skip the exam. So my years of hard work paid off and I got accepted into college without taking the test.

I still had no idea what I was going to do with my life. My primary concern was the fact that in February of 1973 I was going to get on an airplane and go half way around the world to run a race. But that was the fantasy part of the life I was living. On a more mundane level I had make some kind of decision about my future, in particular with regard to my education. I decided to enter teacher's college, thinking that if I was going to continue running I would need employment that had flexibility and time to train. As frivolous as it might sound these days, in all honesty, that was the thinking that went into my decision. I wanted a profession that would fit in with my running.

And you would think the education establishment would have been happy to have someone who might be held up as a role model for children, but it didn't work that way. The first time I put in my application for teacher's college, I actually got rejected!

In New Zealand then they paid you to go to teacher's college, and they had a certain entrance quota each year and were very selective. Since I was still very young, they simply decided I wasn't as ready as some others. The pay wasn't very much, $13 a week, but in 1973 that seemed to me a decent amount of money for a young girl living at home, so I was disappointed.

In the meantime though, the trip to the world cross-country championships overshadowed everything. The airfare and other expenses were provided, but of course if you're going to go away to

Europe for five weeks, you need some money of your own, and my mum and dad really didn't have anything to spare. They said that if I wanted to go, I needed to get a job to help finance it.

My dad got me a job with an insurance company in the city near the newspaper where he worked. It was a six-week job, through the summer holiday. That made finding time for training very tough, because it's a long trip from Otahuhu into the city. It was two miles up to the bus or train station and then 10 miles into the city, then another mile from the bus or train station to work. I commuted in with my dad every day for six weeks, earning enough spending money for the trip, and keeping up my training back at the club in Otahuhu.

In January I got a letter from the teaching college saying they were going to accept me after all. I went in for an interview and practically the first thing they asked me about was my running. I think someone had figured out who I was, and that it might be a good thing to let a sports figure into teaching college. I was aware enough of the situation to say that I thought I could be a very good role model for children.

When college started in mid-February, I was there. But my life was becoming a constant transportation challenge. It seemed that wherever I was, I needed to be somewhere else, and immediately! But fortunately I continued to live at home and the costs of going to teacher's college weren't high. I was making it financially, but it seemed like I was always running for a bus. Both Barbara and I owe a debt of gratitude to Ralph King, a semi-retired newspaper writer who was a big fan of track and field and orienteering. Ralph helped shuttle us back and forth several days a week and probably preserved our sanity.

&

It was a very young New Zealand team that boarded the plane for Belgium in late February of 1973, and at 17, I was the youngest. I got on the plane with an infected toenail that I'd just had Dr. Drake drain the night before and I did my best to keep it a secret, fearing that at the last minute I'd be left behind or not allowed to compete.

But what an experience for a young girl! I had never realized how isolated New Zealand really is from the rest of the World. We had to fly four and a half hours to get to Tahiti, then another seven hours to Los Angeles. After spending the night, we flew to London, where we spent several days before taking the train to Dover, then a boat across the English channel to Calais, France, and another train to Belgium. I learned quickly that when a New Zealand team traveled abroad, it was always a major undertaking. Not only did we have to make such a long trip on a proverbial shoestring, we had to somehow fit our training in and deal with all the little missed connections, hotels under renovation, and all the other maddening glitches that are inevitable in such an enterprise. We dealt with all of this with typical youthful hijinks and gales of laughter. It seemed that the worse things got, the funnier we found the situation. Nothing got us down.

And of course as a wide-eyed 17-year-old I was the quintessential tourist, collecting everything I could from the plane as souvenirs, writing all my friends on hotel stationary, and in general reveling in my newfound status as a citizen of the world. In London I stayed first at the Queens Hotel, then the Crystal Palace, two of the most famous stopovers for track athletes in the world. I was in some sort of athletic Nirvana!

Here is what I wrote in my diary at the time, picking up the travelogue in London:

> On Sunday we went to church and generally mucked around. Monday morning saw us packed and ready for Belgium. We were taken by bus to Victoria to catch the train to Dover. It took 2¼ hours to Dover. Then we caught the boat and it took us to Calais up the French coast to Ostend. I slept all the way from Ostend. We caught the train to Brugges then to Ghent. The hotel we stayed in was really nice but the lady owner was a bit of a bag.
>
> I was with Val. Again Gail and Lin were together and Heather and Milly had a room on their own. The boys were on the floor above. We were the first team to arrive. Belgium is a beautiful place. The streets are all cobbled and they have trams instead of buses. Everything is old and traditional.
>
> We basically did the same things as in London like shopping and sightseeing. Two nights though we did go to a film. The first one was in English, a western and Dick [Tayler] didn't come. The second was a sex film in French but I could understand it. Dick did come this time but we were a bit late and we couldn't have sat farther apart. We had a lot of fun though. It was rest up week so none of us did very much.

Friday we went out to look at the course at Waragem. We waited an hour for the English team to pick us up. We ran two times round the course and looked it over. When we got back (12:30) we were taken by bus out to Brugges where they showed us the lace-making. We all bought some and it was a good way of relaxing, too. We got home about 7:00. Had tea and went to bed. Everyone was very quiet now and nervous. Saturday was the big day. We all spent the morning packing our stuff ready to go back to London on Sunday morning. We went out to the course and arrived at 2:30. At 3:30 after warming up we had a march past. It was really great and I felt proud.

When the race started Heather and I got well up and led for one mile, then Joyce Smith and Paolo Pigni [of Italy] moved up and I followed them in third place through the three-quarter mark. There was a bump in the course and I lost my balance and contact [with the leaders]. It was about 200 yards from the finish when the others started to pass me. Then again, there was only 30 seconds between me and the first girl.

We girls then hurried to watch the men's race. It was great to see although the fight was terrible. I saw everything, especially when Rodney got hit. [Some IRA thugs had jumped in and tried to disrupt the race.] They all ran well considering they had been upset. John got spiked and dished out. Rod (3rd), Dick (12th), Brian (14th) and Euan (15th) ran well.

There was a barbecue held afterwards in a huge hall. The food wasn't very nice though. It finished at 10:30. Busses were supposed to come every ¼ hour but they didn't, so we stood around waiting. There were a lot of flags around so Dick and Eddy got to and tried to pull them down. They got them all except one at the gate which was stuck. Then some vans came to take us back. I was waiting for Dick and the others all got in the other van. Then two policemen came up to Eddy and Dick waved for me to go in the van. I got in and was alone with some guys who were New Zealanders living in London. I was really worried about Dick. They couldn't find him anywhere. As we drove away we saw Eddy being carted off by the police, so we followed them to the station and Brian Rose got out and tried to explain. In the end we got him back and made our way to Ghent By this time it was 12:00. We went straight to the English hotel as we thought that was where the party was. But there was nobody there. We ended up in a little underground pub all smoky.

By this time I was really upset as I thought I was going

> to have to spend the rest of the night without Dick or the
> others. We were there for a half hour and I was just start-
> ing to enjoy myself when John and Heather walked in. I
> was dancing and had my back to everybody when I saw
> Dick was there, too. I was really pleased and so was he.
> He said he had been really worried, too. Anyway we had
> a terrific time. At 3:30 we went and had a Chinese
> meal...

From the short shrift I gave the race, and my ongoing concern
with the whereabouts and activities of the boys in general and Dick
Tayler in particular, it's obvious that all sorts of other matters seemed
to be on my 17-year-old mind.

But I had finished ninth in the world championships—first on
our team—and had taken on the whole field at one stage and was out
in front of everyone, leading the race! All eight women who finished
ahead of me passed me in the last 400 meters! The rest of our
women's team didn't have particularly good races and the team finished sixth. The men's team came in third and might well have won
but for the confusion caused by the IRA ruffians, who pushed John
Sheddan down and struck Rod Dixon hard in the back of the head,
perhaps costing him a first place finish (he was third).

Returning to New Zealand after that trip was a cultural shock and
I think I went through a period of mild melancholy and introspec-
tion. I had my first schoolgirl crush on Dick Tayler, who was not only
10 years my senior but, unbeknownst to me, married! It was completely innocent, of course, and poor Dick must have taken a consid-
erable amount of ribbing for the little puppy dog trailing behind him
everywhere.

But something truly significant had happened to me on that trip:
The world had been opened up to me. Not only the geographical
world, but also the glamorous fantasy world you live in when you're
part of an international sports team. The travel, the excitement of
competition, the friendships and camaraderie were like a drug to me.
My only concern was how to go about getting more of it, as is clearly
reflected in my diary at the time:

> In Hong Kong... Dick, Howard, Euan, Rod and I went
> for a walk and I've never felt so happy... But all good
> things come to an end... 6:00 found us at the airport
> ready for home. It was good to be going home but sad to
> know we were leaving each other. I sat with Rod and
> Gail till Brisbane and then between Rod and Dick. It was

the last time we would be together so we made the most of it. Seeing them go at the Auckland Airport was the hardest. Still, if I work hard enough I could possibly make the Pan Pacific and see them there. Please God.

Running now was more than my outlet and my form of self-expression, it had become my ticket into that fantasy world of travel and excitement, where I was no longer the lonely long distance runner, but was a cherished teammate and friend, where I was surrounded by soul mates who cared for me and understood what my life was all about because it was just like theirs.

So it was doubly hard for me to go back to teachers college where everyone lived such different lives. My classmates were out partying all the time, drinking and smoking dope, and here I was going about my seemingly prim and proper life as an athlete. Little did they know that my head was swimming with memories of London and Hong Kong, jumbo jets, the Crystal Palace and the World Championships! How could I ever explain such things to them?

I did what I had to do to get my work done, but I was really just treading water. My real focus was on training hard so I could get back into that fantasy world. In addition to the emotional upheaval, the trip had left me unusually exhausted, but I didn't think much of it until I woke up one morning, looked in the mirror and didn't recognize the yellow face looking back at me. Even the whites of my eyes were yellow! My training diary entry is almost whimsical: "Looks like I will be off for a while. Got Hepatitis!"

They thought I'd picked it up in Hong Kong. They classified me as contagious and I couldn't continue at college until I was cleared, so I spent a couple of months recuperating. It wasn't the really serious kind of hepatitis, thank goodness. My main symptom was terrible fatigue.

Once again Dr. Drake was keeping me motivated, encouraging me to eat as much as I could and to get a lot of rest. Naturally, I put on a great deal of weight, but that was his way of getting me to build up my strength. When I was finally pronounced well in June I had missed a lot of school and a great deal of training as well. Pictures of me in those days show quite a chubby young lady.

13 ~ Back to Real Life

I got through it all, the hepatitis and the blues, back to the routine of college classes and the hard training sessions. To this day, though, I've been told I have to be careful about the countries I visit. I have to be careful to stay away from Asia and Mexico and places where I could easily pick up certain intestinal bugs that I'm susceptible to now. Also, despite the fact that I'm in excellent physical condition, for the rest of my life I cannot donate blood.

Once I was finally back training in May, Gordon began stepping up my program. He had me getting up around 5:00 or 5:30 in the morning for a run of about two miles. Then I'd rush back, bathe and rush to the bus with my dad for the trip into Auckland. My days were getting long indeed, with training, commuting, school, and class assignments in the evening.

But my passion was still running. Barbara and I remained very good friends even though she was still in high school. We did a lot of training together and stayed close.

My feet and leg problems continued, probably because I was pushing so hard all the time, forcing my legs and feet to get stronger. When they did finally get too painful, I would take two or three days off and they would bounce back quickly.

I had to give up on cross country that year because of the hepatitis, but I did get in good enough shape to win the road racing championships later. I was still a junior racing in the senior races—they didn't have junior national championships in those days, as they do no. I somehow had managed a long, difficult comeback despite the illness, the long layoff, and the extra pounds.

My social life was still centered around the Otahuhu club, and as I began paying more attention to boys, I began to notice something unsettling: Any potential suitor that came around would sooner or later attract Gordon's merciless attention. He would pick on them until the poor boy must have wondered if I was worth it. I was having a great time, but I was beginning to realize that Gordon would be jealous of any boyfriend that I might have.

At about this time I also had a physical education instructor in college who decided to make my life miserable. I don't know whether it was because of the attention I got from athletics or if it was just the luck of the draw. But it was very apparent I wasn't going to get through his course without some hazing.

We were learning the different techniques involved in gymnastics, swimming and other sports that we might be teaching later. It came time to do a fitness test, and part of it was to see how far you could run in 12 minutes, which of course was right up my alley! I got a mark of 150 percent on that part of it. But when it came time to do the gymnastics tests, I asked not to have to jump from the beams or anything like that because I feared getting an injury. The instructor refused, and when I still wouldn't do it, he failed me.

We also had to do certain outdoor sports like sailing and hang gliding, and because I didn't want to fail any more classes, I did them. But I did them once and never again. I finally passed the course, but I continued to have a difficult time with this teacher and it taught me a lesson. Athletes sometimes get special considerations from school officials and teachers. Sometimes they're warranted because of the requirements of training or traveling for competitions and sometimes they are simply trying to curry favor like any other sports follower. But there are other teachers and officials will go so far in the other direction to demonstrate that they're showing no favoritism that they become petty tyrants. In general, teachers college wasn't a pleasant time for me. It got considerably better when I got put out on what we called "sections," otherwise known as serving an internship. We went to a real school and learn how to teach right in the classroom with the teachers. That's where I learned the most. I was lucky to get great teachers to work with, and I found that I really enjoyed the children and I loved teaching. But teachers college was another story. It was miserable and I began to look upon it as something to be survived.

In November of 1973 Anne Smith decided to leave Gordon's coaching program and go back to England for a while. There were still rumors that she had been Gordon's girlfriend and that he'd had a continuous long-term relationship with her. His wife, Shirley, was at the club many times, along with his two young daughters. They all moved together from one house in Remuera to another one nearby. But the situation became even stranger when Shirley and Gordon were living in the house with the two girls, and *Shirley's* boyfriend moved in with them!

There were a lot of times we younger athletes would baby-sit for them. We were always around the house, and Shirley was very accommodating, taking care of us all, being quite generous with her time, cooking for us and keeping up with our lives. But it was a very strange situation and though all of us were aware of it, as kids will do, we just blocked it out and rolled along with everything else that was going on in our lives.

At about this time Alison Deed (later Alison Roe, who gained fame in the '80s as a marathoner and triathlete) joined the Otahuhu club and began training with Gordon. She came from over on the North Shore across the harbor about 25 miles away, where her father was a physician. Compared to the blue-collar background of the rest of us, Alison was from a rarefied economic stratum and Gordon picked up on this right away. He had long since burned his bridges with most of our families, and now he had a prodigy with well-off parents. This made it extremely tough on all the rest of us.

Alison lived on the other side of Auckland and naturally Gordon would want us to go to her house to train. Sometimes we'd have to catch buses; sometimes we'd get as far as Gordon's house and he would take us way over to the other side of the city, over the harbor bridge to Alison's.

Used to playing the "Golden Girl," Alison didn't mind making others wait for her, so she was always late for training. Any time we were to meet at the Auckland Domain, we could never start until "Ali" (as Gordon called her) turned up. It was a frustrating time, because she quickly became Gordon's favorite, and though that was certainly not her fault, it made life difficult for the rest of us.

Ali was a tall, attractive blonde athlete, and would often turn up at training in a bikini, straight from the beach. The impact of such entrances cannot be overstated. She always rode in Gordon's car when we traveled places and her schedule and priorities were always the ones that had to be accommodated by everyone else. It was time-consuming and inefficient for the rest of us, but we had little say in the matter.

I don't think my irritation ever surfaced in my relationship with Gordon or Alison, but I'm quite sure I used it on occasion to fuel my training. In my diary occasionally I write things like "I beat Alison today" or "I beat Ali by [so many] seconds..." And that was how I dealt with it, running as hard as I could, still trying to be the best that I could.

The trials for the Commonwealth Games were in Christchurch, on the South Island of New Zealand. That was also where the games themselves would be held in January of 1974. They had built a brand new stadium for the games, called Queen Elizabeth II Park, and it boasted New Zealand's first all-weather track.

I went down with Mum and we stayed with some friends of Rita Bates, the lady who originally had encouraged me to run. I was going to run in the 1500 meters, though I wasn't given much chance of making the team. I ended up finishing second, with my best time yet at that distance, 4:19. I was chosen for the Commonwealth Games team and was absolutely thrilled.

But athletic success came at a price. I'd been failed in my first year of college. What they wanted me to do was to spend my summer vacation going back to school and passing that first year. And the very time they wanted me to do this was the time of the Commonwealth Games. Obviously some negotiations were needed because I had no intention whatever of going to summer school instead of the Commonwealth Games.

Finally we agreed that I would be given six assignments to do on my own in lieu of summer school. I remember going to my dad completely miserable because I didn't know how on earth I was going to do it. He was wonderful, as usual. He cheered me up, then sat down and started helping me do my assignments.

14 ~ Commonwealth Games; New Zealand, 1974

Any kid in New Zealand or any country in the British Commonwealth grows up aware of the Commonwealth Games and how big and important they are. In fact, in those countries, they are as important as the Olympics. So going down to Christchurch in January of 1974 was a major event, even for a "veteran" international athlete like myself. It was the first time I would run for New Zealand on the track and my first time on a really big athletic team. There would be a capacity crowd for all the events, with 67 countries from the British Commonwealth taking part, an overwhelming experience for a young girl.

Any time I got in these situations I was fired up. I never had a negative reaction to the pressure of competition or the pressure of representing my country. I guess I just didn't know any better, but for me it was just a wonderful experience and a load of fun. The bigger the event the more excited I got and the better I performed.

I was thrilled to be chosen to represent the team at a luncheon attended by the Queen, Prince Charles, and Princess Anne. So that's how I got to meet the entire royal family and how I came to have articles in my scrapbook about myself and Prince Charles at lunch, thank you very much.

I was back again in my fantasy world, living in the athlete's village, getting involved in all the mischief and pranks everybody gets up to, enjoying being with my friends once again. Unfortunately, the athletics side of things didn't go so well.

The opening ceremony was on a freezing cold day and Gordon gets the blame for really messing up my schedule. I got stuck waiting for him on a street corner in the freezing cold, and ended up getting sick because of it.

I was quite happy to make the finals but I wasn't completely over the flu and never felt right the whole way. I had no race plan except to keep up as long as I could. Still, I was happy with my performance under the circumstances. My diary records the day:

> Woke at 7:30. Went out for a run. Ran 2 miles. Felt terrible. Went to breakfast and mucked around till team meeting at 10:00. Went back to room. Got dressed and rested till 11:45. Sue Haydon and I managed to grab a lift to the stadium in a Papua-New Guinea car. Got there at 12:30. Met Gordon and rested in shade till 1:15. Due to run at 2:15. Didn't feel too bad warming up but wasn't a bit nervous. Race was fast. [My final time was] 4:21. My legs just wouldn't move. Still was first New Zealander home. Sylvia eighth (4:23), Sue (4:28). I was sixth and it was a pretty good field.

When those kinds of quirks of fate happen to athletes, we learn to accept them, of course. But you always wonder what you might have been able to accomplish had you been at your best on a given day.

These were historical Commonwealth Games for distance running. The great Kenyan runners, Filbert Bayi and Ben Jipcho were there in the 1500, and the renowned British runner Dave Bedford was in the 10,000 meters. But our own Dick Tayler (my adolescent heartthrob!) actually beat him in a thrilling race. My diary reports: "Watched everything [on TV]. The 10,000 was terrific. Dick has laid the way for the rest of us. I cried at the finish. So did Sue H. [Haydon] who was sitting next to me. It was a great day for NZ."

In the 1500 we watched from the stands as Bayi got way out in front on his way to setting a world record in the 1500, with Walker and Dixon trying to chase him down. Dick Quax, who would later join them to form an internationally known trio of Kiwi runners, was injured at the time and had to withdraw. As I was watching the race I realized that the day before I'd sat next to Bayi at lunch and hadn't known who he was. I'd asked him what event he did and he said he was in the 1500 the next day. I said, well, how do you think you'll do?

"It will be very fast," he said with a shy smile.

That was an understatement. He just went out at the gun and ran as hard as he could, getting way out in front of the rest of the field. They were coming back to him in the home straight but by then it was too late. He set the world record, with Walker second and Dixon third.

In the marathon, New Zealander Kevin Ryan got the bronze medal. And another Kiwi, Jack Foster, ran a wonderful marathon, finishing fourth, in 2:11:19. That's only astounding when you learn that he was 40 years old at the time! It was a world masters (over-40) record that stood for more than 16 years, until another New Zealander, John Campbell, broke it at the 1990 Boston Marathon in 2:11:04.

Arthur Lydiard, the famed coach who had put New Zealand on the map in the '60s, was very much a part of all this success. He was coaching Dick Tayler and Rod Dixon. Walker was coached by Arch Jelley, who was a Lydiard follower. And my old nemesis Lorraine Moller, who finished 5th in the 800 meters in an amazing time for her young age (2:03.8), as well as Dick Quax, were both coached by John Davies, another Lydiard disciple.

Looking back at it now, it's clear those Commonwealth Games in 1974 were a launching pad for many great running careers.

ଧ

I returned to my routine and life rolled along much as it had the previous year. I ran cross country, followed by the road season. Gordon was constantly challenging me, trying to provoke a rivalry among Alison, Barbara and me. It got to the point where they complained about it. He was using me because I was the strongest, but because it was Gordon, of course, he was doing it in as negative a way as he could, and no one appreciated it, me least of all.

That started to cause a bit of a strain between us, though Barbara and I continued to maintain a friendship. Alison was on the other side of the city and so we didn't do a great deal socially with her unless there was a club event of some kind.

The club was still strong, with more than 1,000 members at the time, and we won all the interclub competitions. It was still a center for a lot of our social activities.

Gordon could be an extremely difficult person, to be sure, but I don't want to imply that he didn't contribute a great deal to my career, because he certainly did. One of the things that I'm still grateful for is the way he was always looking for new wonderful places to take us to run. We went to places like Rotorua, which is the perhaps the most gorgeous part of New Zealand, with spectacular thermal pools, gigantic pine forests and pristine lakes, rivers and mountains to explore. We often went away on these training trips, and it was typically Barbara, Alison and myself who went. It was never really a large group unless there was some kind of event that we were all pointing for.

He took us to places like Mount Ruapehu in the Tongariro National Park, on the North Island in the midst of a miniature mountain range, complete with ski resorts, as well as an active volcano range. The famous masters runner, John Campbell, today runs a lodge at the base of one of the largest ski mountains. In the summer you can go there and run miles of high altitude trails at around 5,000 feet or so, with the mountain itself going up to 9,000 feet. We would rent rooms in one of the little motels, most of which were a little on the rustic side. Nothing fancy for us!

He would really push us on those little trails. I remember a couple of times when we would go out and the fog would roll in so that you could barely see the trail in front of you. Naturally Gordon would take the opportunity to lose us. We would be running along somewhere behind him in the fog, completely lost, yelling out to him to come back and show us the way. Eventually he would, but he'd leave us hanging out there for a while.

Then one day he took us to run up a really rugged mountain we hadn't tried before. It was a *very* rough undertaking. Alison and Barbara lasted literally about a mile into it and just refused to go any further. Gordon got really angry at them. Then, he turned to me and once again threw out his challenge.

"How about you?" he said, hands on hips, "How good are you *really* going to be?"

I ended up climbing this dreadful thing with him, and it really was more climbing than running. It was the most glorious view once you got up there, but it was so hard, so rough underfoot, that I was really beaten up by the time we made it. And then of course what goes up has to come down, and since I've never been a good down-hill runner, the worst was yet to come.

When we got back to the car, Alison and Barbara were sitting there, miffed. I was completely exhausted and when I got to my room, I immediately fell into a dreamless sleep. In what seemed like a few scant minutes, I was surprised to be awakened by an impatient Gordon saying, "Let's go! Time for the afternoon run!" Because Alison and Barbara hadn't completed the morning run, he made us go out and run again. And, illogically enough, I had to go, too.

But that was Gordon, constantly pushing, constantly challenging. And as I say, that's not necessarily a bad thing. But even though I usually rose to the occasion, there were many times when I simply stayed exhausted all the time.

An unusual kind of running event that was popular in New Zealand at that time was what were known as road relays. They were typically for men, and they were held over a total of 15 to 20 miles. There would be five or six runners on a team, each running seg-ments of different lengths. Of course, because of New Zealand's dra-matic topography, there were often legs on these relays that might be five miles straight uphill. Then hopefully you'd have a good downhill runner to take the next steep downhill leg.

But these were often really exciting races, which I enjoyed immensely. I was a good enough hill runner that it got to the point where the club would ask me to substitute if they didn't have enough men. I think that's really the first time I realized that I might be a road racer, and that I might be really good on a hilly course.

There were some times at the awards ceremonies where it would turn out that I'd actually finished third or fourth among the men in the uphill segments of these races. This was something of a revela-tion to me. I discovered, first, that I could run long distances; second, that I was really strong uphill; and third, that I loved the blacktop as a surface to race on. It seemed a very natural surface for me.

In the cross-country season of 1974 I got into trouble with my feet again and had to stop training before I could run in the New Zealand championships. But I'd had success early on in the season, beating Alison and Barbara consistently in Auckland, which—because they were in fact very talented runners—was no small thing.

There was going to be a national team sent away to the world championships the following year in Rabat, Morocco, and the nation-al meet would serve as the trials for the team. I asked the selectors to consider me even though I wasn't able to run in the nationals. My reasoning was that if Alison and Barbara finished well and were considered for the team, then I should be considered as well, because I had beaten them all season. I went up to Whangarei to watch, which was a difficult thing to do. Alison ended up winning, with Barbara eighth. Barbara had probably run poorly because she allowed herself to get upset by Alison's parents, who had made her feel unwelcome at the house they had rented there.

We ended up with the same sad situation we'd been in before. Barbara wasn't picked for the team, but Alison and I were chosen, and I hadn't even run in the trials. Barbara was again the one left off the team, and though I was naïve about such things at the time, I began to overhear comments by some adults that she was being treated so shabbily because she was Maori. It was shocking to me then that racial prejudice could play a role in keeping an athlete from fulfilling her dreams again, and it's shocking to me today. Here were Barbara and I, living on the same street, training together every day, but I was the one going away to the glamorous world championships. I was devastated for her, and again had not a clue what I could do about such an injustice.

We went down to the national road championships in Invercargill, way down on the southern point of the South Island. Everybody in New Zealand jokes about it, calling it the end of the earth, which is not much of an exaggeration. But that's where the championships were, and we all went down as a team. I still have photos of that trip in my scrapbooks. There we are on the island at the end of the earth, Gordon, Alison, Barbara and two of the Vercoe sisters (once again an "All-Gordon" team), looking extremely happy.

Lorraine Moller represented Waikato, and she ended up winning. I was second, Alison was third, and Barbara was fourth. Funny to think that, years later, we would all end up running professionally on the roads in the United States. But there we were in 1974, running our national road racing championships together at "the end of the earth."

I was still having to take regular breaks to allow my feet to recover. I went back to the doctors who had done my surgery and asked if anything could be done. Again they were very encouraging and supportive and gave me more exercises. They suggested that if I might want to see a chiropodist, which is like a podiatrist, and they gave me names of physiotherapists who could help with massage and other treatments.

Something else that began happening at this time were intermittent asthma attacks during training. It's all hindsight now, of course, but I look back and have to wonder if they weren't caused by the stress that Gordon was creating among Alison and Barbara and me.

I would talk to Lloyd Drake about it and he said it might be caused by a number of different things. He gave me an inhaler to use. And then a few years later after I had left Gordon, Lloyd reminded me of those asthma attacks and said, "You know, at the time I didn't want to say anything, but I knew it was the stress that Gordon was putting you under that was causing your asthma attacks. The attacks always came when he was around. When he wasn't there, you didn't have the problem. But obviously, I couldn't say that at the time."

It didn't happen for very long, maybe late 1974 into the 1975 season, around six months or so. But I did suffer from breathing attacks badly enough to need to carry an inhaler with me when I was racing.

15 ~ *World Cross Country; Morocco, 1975*

New Zealand sent a historic team to the world championships in Morocco in 1975. On the men's side were: John Walker, who would later break the world mile record and win an Olympic 1500 gold medal; Rod Dixon, who had won an Olympic bronze medal in the 1500 and would later win the New York Marathon; Dick Quax, who would win an Olympic silver medal in the 5000; and Euan Robertson, who was fifth in the Montreal Olympics in the steeplechase. Then there were Kevin Ryan and Jack Foster, both excellent cross-country runners as well as successful international marathoners; and Dave Sirl, John Sheddan and John Dixon, Rod's brother.

On the women's team were probably the five fastest New Zealand runners ever: Lorraine Moller, Heather Thompson (later Mathews), Dianne Zorn (later Rodger), Alison Roe and myself.

I don't think New Zealand or any country has ever sent such a group of athletes, and most of us at that time had still not reached our full potential.

John Walker battled through early stomach cramps to lead the men's team, finishing fourth overall, with Euan Robertson fifth, Dave

Sirl 25th, John Dixon 26th and John Sheddan 33rd. Through a great team effort, they won the men's championship. The newspaper account of the time said this about the women's race:

> Lorraine Moller drove herself to the point of exhaustion in finishing just ahead of Heather Thompson...There was some concern when Miss Moller collapsed after crossing the line. She was attended to by medical assistants and soon recovered, however. Mrs. Thomson ran a very steady, well-judged race and finished seven seconds behind Miss Moller.

Lorraine was fifth overall, Heather sixth; I was 10th, and Alison 29th. We finished second to the United States by just six points. Alison and Dianne just didn't have a good day; otherwise we would have been world champions as well.

We were all young, most of us unmarried, and as will happen in that situation, there was quite a bit of pairing off. As on previous trips, there was a great deal of camaraderie, humor, patience and tolerance, all of it put to good use because of the arduous nature of the trip. We had a manager who was so befuddled that he ran out of money to support us. So we all had to pool our money to get by, ending up moving from one place to another to try to get good training spots where we could stay cheaply.

John, Dick and Rod already had reputations in Europe by that time. Although John had yet to break the world mile record, the three of them had been track racing in Europe in 1974 and they were beginning to make names for themselves and establish contacts among race promoters and avid track followers. Because of those contacts, we finally ended up at a Swedish training camp at the Costa Del Sol in Spain, not far from Malaga. We trained there for a while, then got on a bus to Gibraltar, a boat to Tangiers, and a train to Rabat, Morocco.

No matter what mischief we got up to, we always trained together, encouraged each other, and had a great deal of fun. We ran in the Spanish championships in knee deep clay, and both teams won. I don't to this day know how we managed to pull off the performances we did with the travel conditions and the stress that were a constant on our journeys. This particular trip took us from Auckland to Australia to Singapore to Bahrain to Tehran to Frankfurt to London to Paris to Spain, then to the coast of Spain, then Morocco to Paris and then all the way back to New Zealand through Singapore.

The other thing that made it difficult was simply our hemisphere. We were coming out of the New Zealand summer into the middle of winter in Europe, so one of our most difficult tasks right away was to acclimate to freezing weather, snow, mud and ice.

I look back at that trip, the athletes, the competitive successes, the strain of the trip, and I can't help but be amused when I hear American athletes complain about the difficulty of competing in Europe. They should try doing it from New Zealand on occasion!

I think that experience helped all of us to accomplish everything we've done since, including running successfully on the American road circuit. I doubt that any travel any of us have done since was ever as bone-grindingly difficult as those cross country trips in the '70s.

While we were away, Alison and I were chosen to compete in Australia just two weeks after our return. The event was the R.H. North Cup, which pitted the Australian women's track team against the New Zealand team.

So Alison and I had barely gotten unpacked before we were off to Australia for two weeks, exchanging our muddy cross country shoes for track spikes and the snowy European clime for the delightful Australian summer sun. We competed in the 1500 meters and again my intense interval training held me in good stead. I won every event that I raced.

&

By the time I got home again, I had missed two months of teacher's college and was again worried that I was going to fail. At least I was keeping up with my assignments, and fortunately in our third year we spent a lot of time out in the schools, which I was able to keep up with.

Everything was going along on an even keel, when one evening in May I was out with Alison at a squash club. As we were leaving, I tripped and fell coming down some steep stairs. She took me to the hospital for X-rays, which showed that I hadn't broken anything, thank goodness. But you couldn't prove it by me. I'd really hurt my tailbone and I could hardly stand up straight for a week. These are the kinds of injuries athletes truly dread, because they're unrelated to our sport and thus not part of our ongoing risk/benefit calculations. They seem so random and senseless. Coaches save a special wrath for

football players who get injured wrestling in the dorm, or tennis players who hurt themselves throwing a Frisbee. Gordon was not happy
with me, but neither was I with myself. But fate had stepped in again,
and running was out for a while. That took me out of the New
Zealand cross-country season for that year.

So far I had turned out to be a good cross-country runner in the
world championships, but I never could seem to arrive healthy at the
New Zealand championships or even to complete a consistent cross-
country season.

In May of 1975 they held the opening ceremony for the new all-
weather track at Mt. Smart Stadium. To commemorate the event, our
now-famous group of milers decided to take on the world record for
the men's 4 X mile relay. It was a wonderful day and an exciting race,
but they had no competition and they missed the world record by 1.3
seconds. To most of the runners, however, the track itself was the star
of the day. We had been trying to run good performances on grass
and cinders for so long, getting access to one of these modern mar-
vels seemed like a wonderful turn of providence to us.

Meanwhile, something else was going on in my life: my first
"real" romance. I had begun dating John Walker, a relationship that
had blossomed on the Morocco trip. John was a wonderful athlete,
exceptionally attractive, and we had really hit it off, so I was about as
head-over-heels as you would expect a 19-year-old to be under the
circumstances. Of course, the media and other sport followers in New
Zealand thought this was a marvelous storybook romance, having the
two top runners in the country going together like that, and to tell
the truth, the two of us probably got caught up in the excitement
ourselves.

We continued to see each other off and on through the Olympics
in 1976, but once John set the world record in the mile in August of
1975, his whole world changed and with it our relationship. In that
one race, he became the first runner ever to break 3:50 in the mile
and he became an instant international celebrity. In retrospect it
should have been nearly a foregone conclusion that we would drift
apart. I was upset for a while, but in relationships I've always had an
ability to avoid dwelling on what was apparently not meant to be.

July 15th of that year was the first time I got a chance to run on
the new track on the Mt. Smart Stadium. I immediately concluded—
as had so many runners before me—that going from the grass track
or cinder tracks to the all-weather surface was going to make a huge

difference in our performances.

We were all truly amateur athletes then and it wasn't at all easy to make ends meet. The trips to Europe and the contacts John, Rod and the others made with Adidas allowed some of us also-rans to get to the factories where we could at least buy apparel at cost, but none of us had any official sponsorship association with any shoe or apparel companies in any way. All of us were deathly afraid of jeopardizing our amateur standing, a very real threat at that time.

On the home front I was still close to my grandmother, who had continued to live on the island right up until the previous year. Age had been catching up with Nana and one day she had an accident. She had an outside toilet that required her to regularly empty the sewage and bury it in her yard. Because her yard was so steep, it was no easy task, and on this particular day, she slipped and broke her leg as she was carrying the bucket down to the bottom of the garden. Her cottage was a bit isolated in those days, and she just sat there calling for help for quite a while before someone heard her. She was a strong, active woman, and had always been fiercely self-sufficient, but it was a bad fall, and her injury forced her to leave her beloved island.

She moved into an assisted living facility (what we call a "pensioner's flat") in Otahuhu only about a mile and a half from our house, just down the road from our school. She had her own apartment, so she was still self-sufficient there.

Throughout all those years on the island, I had visited her as often as I could. That place held so many happy childhood memories for me I went whenever I could get away. But obviously with school, training and social activities, I had a full schedule, so when Nana moved into the flats I was often able to see her on my way home from school or training or whatever. Even though it was sad she had to move off the island, in another way it was a blessing that we got to spend so much more time together in her last years. Although she never looked at it that way, life on the island was demanding; moving was really the best thing for her.

"Steadfast" is the word I would use for my parents. It must have seemed ironic to them at the time, having one daughter struggling just to make it through school, and another who's often praised in the daily newspaper. But they were never distracted, never wavered, and Katie and I got only their full devotion and attention.

My mother and father quietly reveled in my athletic success.

They were always at my races, not making a big fuss, but supporting me with their presence, my own subdued cheering section. Looking back now, I understand that they were really quite shy people, and perhaps a little intimidated by all the hoopla.

People would say to them, "Well, gosh, which one of you does Anne get her talent from?" And they would hem and haw and change the subject as best they could. Now I realize they simply didn't want to get into a big discussion about the fact that I was adopted. That seems a perfectly reasonable response for essentially private people suddenly thrust into the public eye. They were hesitant to attend too many events where they would get asked questions like that, and I certainly can't blame them.

At the time, however, I never really understood how shy they were in public or why they were so cautious about the attention and other trappings of success from my running. If Mum detected some sign that my hat size was growing, she'd say, "You know, you're only as good as the next race you win. Remember that." Dad would say, "There's no use getting a big head, there's always somebody out there somewhere working just as hard as you, if not harder." He was certainly right about that, as I found out every time I went to the Olympics. But they really kept me grounded, never letting me get an ego over anything, which was something I only truly appreciated much later.

I made it through my last year of college and, miracle of miracles, despite all my fretting, they actually passed me with honors! So I graduated from teacher's college, and picked a school in a very poor area of Auckland, about five miles from home with a heavy enrollment of the, Pacific Island and Maori children—our so-called ethnic groups. I had interned at this same school and loved it, so that's where I wanted to start my teaching career.

My professional life as a young teacher wasn't a great deal different than it had been all along: My biggest challenge was simply getting to all the places I needed to be every day. Getting to school with all my books, shoes and athletic gear, to training, to competitions, all without a car, seemed a far greater task than anything that faced me on the track.

16 ~ *Olympics Dreams*

The upcoming Olympics in Montreal cast a long shadow over 1976. It was a time of great excitement and anticipation, but in retrospect it was the beginning of the toughest five-year period of my athletic career.

The team selection process was always a psychological meat grinder. It's easy to understand why American athletes prefer the clarity of a one-shot Olympic trial race: If you make it, you make it.

On January 1st, it's obvious from my training diary that I was at a low point. Looking back, it's amazing how many times I considered myself overweight; this was one of them. I noted that I weighed eight stone 12 pounds (or 124 pounds—a "stone" in the British system is 14 pounds). My ideal competitive weight was around 118, and although it doesn't seem like a great deal of extra weight to many people, getting up to 126—the dreaded "nine stone"—was horrifying to a distance runner. My diary notes: "Going on a diet...Must not eat rubbish."

Food was a prop for me, a way of reacting to the stress. I never got into the anorexic mind set like a lot of women athletes; I went to the other extreme. I had a sweet tooth to begin with and as I've mentioned, my mum was a great cook, so the kitchen was always full of temptations. I just ate myself into trouble.

On the first day of the year our whole group went down to the traditional Tauranga Twilight meeting, a huge track meet held on a grass track, a fixture of our summer season. Tauranga boasts miles of white sand beaches. We loved to go there, even if we raced poorly, as my diary makes clear:

> Jan. 1st: All got in the van and filled in time by having a short swim and a jog. Went to a restaurant for a good meal of ham salad. Then went back to motel to sleep. Went to track at 5:00...It was raining so only went out to warm up and race. Felt good warming up but something must have been wrong in race. 16 in field. Led first 800 meters in 2:17 then I just hit a brick wall. Finished 4th in 4:35. Raced back to motel to shower. Dianne Zorn ran 4:18, Heather T. [Thomson] 4:25 and Babs [Barbara Moore] 4:29. Went to the party. Had a great time. Finished at 2:00. Great band. Very hot...
>
> Jan. 2nd: Woke at 9:00. Packed up everything and went to the Mount. Had a fantastic swim... hired some lilos [rafts] and had tremendous fun. Went for a run in bikinis, firstly around the Mount then up it. Very hard and I felt sick when I reach the top. Ran back to the beach and had another swim...

It was all great fun, but when I got home, I had a bout of stomach flu, and while I was lying around recuperating, it suddenly occurred to me that I was overweight, not very fit, and that if I wanted to go to the Olympic games in Montreal, I was going to have to knuckle down and do some work.

I got no small jolt of inspiration from that decisive loss to Dianne Zorn, who went on to run an Olympic qualifying time two weeks later. Tall, tan and blond, Dianne was being touted as the new golden girl at that stage, but she had never beaten me at anything, so losing so badly to her was a real wake-up call. I was at rock bottom and really irritated with myself.

This kind of thing happens a lot to athletes who succeed early in the tough individual sports. Through their early teen years they're able to maintain the dedication and self-sacrifice necessary to achieve great performances, but as they get old enough to begin socializing, noticing the opposite sex and perhaps get jobs and a little money, a great many are unable to maintain their focus. Swimmers, gymnasts, runners are all susceptible to this phenomenon, and those sports lose a great many athletes to the natural attrition of young adulthood. I made up my mind that I wasn't going to be one of them. I still had a lot of run left in me.

I had tests done trying to figure out why I was feeling so tired all the time. Blood tests showed there was nothing wrong. Dr. Drake took me under his charge and gave me some diuretics to see if I could drop some fluid weight. As a young woman I was considering contraception, but I noticed that the pill seemed to cause some weight gain, so I quit taking it after a month.

I did drop three pounds in about eight days, and I started watching my diet. Mum started working hard to make sure the meals were good but non-fattening, and she didn't cook as many of those wonderful cakes that I could never resist. The whole family really pitched in and helped. Looking back, I'm sure that much of my problem simply had to do with the stress of dealing with the ever-difficult Gordon as well as coping with graduation and starting a new life. But one thing I knew for certain: I really wanted that place on the Olympic team.

John Walker and I were still close. His friendship and support helped enormously. Obviously, he was now the icon of New Zealand athletics, but through those weeks, I would often see him at the Auckland Domain and would sometimes go on very hard runs with him. I think it was that kind of subtle encouragement he gave me, just allowing me to run alongside of him, was as inspirational as anything he could have said. We were often joined by others, and being able to train with top caliber male athletes like that helped restore my confidence, and convinced me that I still had what it took, that I was going to make the team.

Meanwhile all the talk was about Dianne Zorn, the new wonder girl who was going to do this, that and the other. It was a blessing really, because in a way it took the attention and pressure off me. I've always reacted to those kinds of challenges positively; it fires me up.

Gordon was putting on a lot of pressure, training me really hard with speed work. By January 20th, I'd lost six pounds. The stress was so great that I started to have anxiety attacks, hyperventilation, clinching my hands over and over, that sort of thing. That still happens to me sometimes on airplanes, usually brought on by impending motion sickness. I start feeling sick and because I don't want to throw up in front of everybody I start getting anxious about it.

Through these holidays, because I had the extra time, I tried to train twice a day consistently for the first time in my life. A lot of the top men runners did it, but it was a new experience for me and it wasn't easy. Most of the afternoon sessions were hard track workouts with Gordon at the Domain.

Despite what it was doing to me mentally, the training was getting me in shape. On the 31st of January, I ran my second fastest 1500 ever, in 4:18.2, finishing third in the event. This was only one month after the meet in Tauranga when I had run so poorly and finished in 4:35, so I had taken more than 17 seconds off in a single month. I was particularly gratified because Dianne was still running about the same, whereas I had made extraordinary progress in a month's time.

I had to give three years back to the education system after college, so I chose the school where I wanted to be "bonded." On the second of February, I started my first day of teaching at Yendarra Primary School. It was located in Otara, a suburb of Auckland. As I've mentioned, the great appeal of the school to me was the large population of Maori and Pacific Island children, and a wonderful cadre of teachers who were all so upbeat and unafraid to challenge the system to do what was right for those kids. It was a perfect fit!

It was in the suburb next to Otahuhu where I grew up, but it was a bus ride away, so my mom would take me to the bus stop and I'd catch the bus and walk the rest of the way to the school. I guess when I think about it, it would seem strange in this day and age here in the States. The typical lifestyle then in New Zealand was more like it would have been here in the '30s and '40s. Here I was, a 20-year-old qualified school teacher having her mom take her to a bus stop so she could catch the same bus a lot of her students took, then walk with them to school.

But the real challenge was getting up at 5:30 in the morning to fit a run in. Then rush for the bus. School would finish at three; I would grab all my stuff, get the bus and go up to the club where I'd sit on the track and prepare my schoolwork until it was time for training. There just wasn't enough time to get home and get changed and get back up there again. After training, I'd usually find someone to drop me home.

On February 10th, I weighed 119 pounds. I'd finally come down seven pounds to my usual racing weight. On the 14th, at the Auckland Championships I ran 4:14.9 to win the 1500 by eight seconds. This bettered the qualifying standard by .1 of a second. On February 17th I got a nomination for the Olympic team from my federation. But the Olympic committee selectors still made the final decision. In our system, an athlete's future is in a lot of different hands.

A few days later, I won the Auckland championship 800 meters in 2:05.1, leading all the way. At that time my attitude toward racing changed and I really became a front runner. That meant occasionally other runners would try to take advantage of me to set the pace, saving themselves to sprint past at the very end. But I'd gotten to a stage in my career where I was tired of fooling around. My attitude was that I wanted to run as fast as I could, regardless of whether I was beaten or not. I wasn't going to waste my time running slow performances any more. Having to meet all those standards put me in that frame of mind. If you wanted to be selected for the important teams like the Olympics, running tactical races didn't do you any good if you didn't also run fast times.

I decided to go to the national championships in March and "double," (race both the 800 and 1500) mainly because the 1500 was always held first on a Friday, and the 800 was the next day, and I thought I'd have time enough to recover and win them both.

Gordon was throwing almost all speed work at me and my feet were getting worse by the day. I started going to a physical therapist recommended by Dr. Drake, Jill Ferguson (now Henry), who proved to be a lifesaver. She was not only sympathetic, she also wanted to teach me as much as she could about how to take care of myself to avoid future problems. I still use much of what she taught me to this day.

It was around the time of the New Zealand championships that Dad and I started a tradition of having a special pre-race meal, which Dad always fixed. It was comprised of canned apricots and hokey pokey ice cream—New Zealand for pralines and cream. I doubt that modern sports nutritionists would approve!

It was always a struggle in those days to keep myself in training and racing shoes. They wore out quickly and they were expensive, so I would always push my shoes to the limit. The morning of my first race in the national championships, John Walker came by the house with a new pair of Adidas racing shoes for me. Gestures like that from your fellow athletes really mean a lot, and coming from John meant even more.

I was really pointing toward that 1500 race and had taken the day off from school to compete. My mom and dad were there, of course, and unbeknownst to me the teachers from my school had managed to get permission to bring the kids to the meet! So when I got into the stadium, I looked up in the stands and there were all these students from my school holding up banners and cheering me on. What an absolute thrill that was!

I was so inspired that I took off from the gun and led all the way, winning in 4:12.1, which was a personal best, beating Dianne Zorn, who also ran a very good 4:13.8. Heather Thomson, Lorraine Moller and all the other runners with a chance for the team were in the race.

In two months I had managed to not only take off all the weight but also to go from a 4:35 to a 4:12 in the 1500. To this day, that race is among those I am proudest of, accomplishing so much under all that pressure in two short months.

The next day I came back and did the same thing in the 800 meters, running 2:04.4. Now I had qualified for both events in the Olympic Games. The 2:04.4 wasn't fast enough to meet the New Zealand selectors' qualifying time, but because I had already qualified for the 1500, they had nothing to lose in nominating me for both, since I was going anyway.

My feet had gotten me through all the training and racing necessary to make the Olympic team, but then the day afterward they just seemed to quit on me. My training diary reads:

> Sun. 7th March, 76: Went running at Domain. Ran ¾ hour. Foot getting worse. Stopped.
> Mon. 8th March, 76: Did no running. Went to Lloyd. Will have to rest till it is fully better. Still I have done enough to qualify now.

One can almost hear me heaving a sigh of relief in that passage. I was probably having as much an emotional letdown as anything, because after a few days of rest and therapy, I was back training.

৯

Later that month I couldn't resist hopping in an event called "Round the Bays" in downtown Auckland along the waterfront. It got about 25,000 entrants even then, and as one might expect, it wasn't a very well organized road race. They have multiple starting and finishing lines and many runners join in halfway along. But at that time I noted in my diary it was supposed to be an 11.4K race (about seven miles), and I decided to just get in it for sheer fun. I finished in the top 20 overall and ran 36:25, which works out to 5:12 per mile pace, so the race course was probably measured short. But it was another early indication that I could run longer distances on the roads fairly well.

In fact, I rather found the longer distances easy to do, and somewhere in my subconscious I must have started formulating some sort of plan to return to run them seriously at some point. A little later I ran in a 10K men's cross-country race just for training and finished in 20th place, again noticing how much I enjoyed running the longer distance.

I had received a great deal of media attention from the national meet, and so did my school, which was nice because the headmaster and everyone there were so supportive. In fact, it was the most supportive school I'd ever been associated with. The kids were all excited about my going to the Olympics, and it was a happy time for all of us.

But again, the elation was tinged with disappointment. Though I had been selected in two events, my boyfriend at the time, Tony Good, was left off the team despite the fact that he had won the national championships and met the Olympic qualifying time in the marathon. This was an ongoing occurrence in New Zealand athletics. It went on for years. The selectors would set these incredible standards, the athletes would meet them, and in the end the selections would all boil down to back-room politics. Sad to say, over the years I knew many athletes whose entire careers were ruined this way. The officials always claimed these machinations were caused by a lack of money, but I don't find that a credible explanation.

The same kind of thing happened with coaches and support staff. Lloyd Drake was treating many of the top runners like Walker, Dixon, Quax, Lorraine Moller, Diane Zorn and myself, not to mention the canoeists, rowers and members of the hockey team. He was incredibly helpful and supportive of all our athletes. But when it came time to choose the team doctor for the Olympics or the Commonwealth Games, he was never picked. The athletes were so upset by this snub that we all signed a petition in support of him.

At this time of year Gordon always left on his annual trip back to Europe. He had started going back for three or four months at a time, bumming around, visiting family and friends in England and other countries. We were all simply left to train on our own, which wasn't easy. Here I was preparing for the biggest event in my life, and I was left to fend for myself. My friend Phillip Wilson, who also trained with Gordon, helped me through workouts during this period. He'd been a boyfriend earlier and we were still great friends.

On the May holidays I went down to Christchurch to visit and train with my current boyfriend, Tony Good. As it had been with Barbara earlier, this was emotionally hard on us: It was never far from our minds that I was going to the Olympics and he wasn't. But Tony was training hard because he still had some hope that he could convince the selectors to add him if he raced well enough in Europe that summer. The system, cruelly enough, allowed you to continue to try to win over the selectors right up until the time of the Olympics games. They didn't just kill your dreams outright; they tortured them to death slowly.

In fact, Euan Robertson did make it at the last moment. He had run a qualifying time and was nominated for the team by our federation, but not selected. Then he went to Europe and ran under the qualifying time five more times, so the selectors simply couldn't continue to ignore him. He was added to the team about two weeks before we left for Montreal. And he ended up finishing fifth in the Olympic finals!

If ever there was an example of how fickle and illogical our selection system was, Euan's case was it. Here was an athlete who finished within an eyelash of an Olympic medal, and two weeks before the trip he wasn't even on his country's Olympic team! Who's to say, but if it hadn't been for the stress of having to run all those races in Europe just to get the attention of the selectors, he might well have won a medal.

Down in Christchurch, while Tony was at work each day I taught myself to drive. I didn't get official lessons; I just got out in his car and taught myself. Obviously it was totally illegal, but by the end of it I took my drivers test and got my license. I was elated.

After the holidays, I started my second term of teaching. This was our winter months, and that always made a runner's schedule difficult because it was dark in the morning and early in the evening, yet we had to continue training somehow. Most the stadiums were unlit. I would try to go to Mt. Smart Stadium as much as possible, or to the Auckland Domain. It got to be a little scary when I was in there on my own. Additionally, the grass tracks, which were so wonderful for training in the summer, in the winter were flooded and muddy.

At the end of May, the Otahuhu club gave me a big farewell party, renting a rugby clubroom, and about 200 people came. They passed a hat to raise money for my travel expenses, and I was overwhelmed when they presented me with $610. They also gave me a beautiful engraved silver tray and matching goblets. I was close to tears. To this day I can't say enough about that club and the wonderful, generous people in it. They gave me such a strong foundation and continuing support through the years.

The townspeople of Otahuhu were wonderful as well. They went around to all the little shops and stores in town, collecting donations, and when all was said and done, it added up to over $2,000, an unfathomable sum to me at the time.

My mum and dad said, "Well, you can take some of that with you but really you should put some away." That's exactly what I did. And when I came home from the Olympics in 1976 I would use that money to buy a car, which simplified my life enormously. You can't put a price on the love and help those generous people lavished on me. It was really quite a wonderful time in my life.

On the first of June I had to "prove fitness," which basically means I had to run a race fast enough to convince the selectors I hadn't gone to seed since I was selected.

They told me I had to do better than 4:18. Phillip came out to Mt. Smart and paced me through a 1500 time trial in 4:15.4. These tests were an incredible nuisance and generally quite unnecessary. But even John Walker had to do one! The *reigning world record holder* had to demonstrate to a group of power-obsessed bureaucrats that they wouldn't be wasting their money buying him a plane ticket to the Olympic Games!

17 ~ European Interlude

We left on June 11th for Europe, John Walker, Dick Quax, Rod Dixon, Euan Robertson, Tony Good and Arch Jelley, John's coach. We went via Los Angeles and London to Finland, where we would be staying. There's a note in my training diary a few days later that indicates how much I was still concerned with my weight:

> Woke early. Felt lousy. Missed breakfast and went out for a 30-min. jog. Felt tired. Came back and had lunch, which I hardly ate anything of. They don't cook their fish and even the meat is raw. I won't put on too much weight."

The next day, there's this note: "Jogged slowly 30 min. Weighed myself, 8 stone 9 pounds [121 pounds]." My diary lists my weight constantly during this period, and there's a great deal of commentary about the food we were served, and the trips out to buy supplementary supplies of our own. I can certainly empathize with athletes today who become fixated on weight. It was a big concern of mine.

We went to the World Games in Helsinki where I saw Tatyana Kazankina of the Soviet Union for the first time. As I was lining up for the race, I remember looking at her and thinking, "That's the most unattractive female body I'd ever seen." She looked like that child's learning toy, "The Visible Woman." Her skin was nearly transparent; you could see every strand of muscle, every vein and all the knots in them. Her face was just like a thin layer of skin with the facial muscles showing beneath.

Later on she was banned from the sport because she would not allow herself to be drug-tested. Others may draw their own conclusions about her appearance, but at the time I was struck by how bizarre she looked. In fact, she reminded me of some kind of alien life form, a character you'd run into at the Intergalactic Café in *Star Wars*.

Before she was banned, however, she would later win the gold medal in Montreal 1500 in 4:05.48, and again in 1980 in Moscow in 3:56.6—an Olympic record.

But that day in Helsinki she won in 4:02. I was third in 4:12. 5 and was pleased with that, but it was like she was in a different race from the rest of us. But coming out of the New Zealand winter and the struggles I'd had trying to train, I was thrilled with that kind of performance. And I had never run in front of large crowds like that. It was amazing, like being in a mini-Olympics.

That meet was the first time I became aware of the under-the-table payments that the top New Zealand men were getting. Far from being upset, I was happy for them, because I knew how hard it was to train at that level and still make ends meet. But it was still quite surprising to see this well-established system of deal-making and cash payments in action. Even I was given $70 in New Zealand dollars, which was a lot of money to me.

Of course, I was with Walker, Quax and Dixon, the "big three" of New Zealand athletics, and that was like being on the road with a rock band. They were just adored everywhere they went. They had fans, groupies, and camp followers of all sorts, and why not? They were all young, good looking, and at the top of their game as athletes.

We were given the royal treatment everywhere we went and, although it was a little strange being the only woman in the group, I was grateful for the experience. It did a lot to dispel my naiveté about amateurism and really opened my eyes to the business side of sport. It made enough of an impression on me that later when I had a chance to turn professional in 1981, I had no hesitation whatsoever.

I realized then that those guys were full-time athletes and they were getting paid well. In fact, they boasted about how much money they made. I never begrudged them a thing, but I knew then that if I ever got a chance to do the same thing, I would take it.

The next stop on that trip was Oslo, Norway, for the Bislet Games, which, because it has been the site of so many world records, is a historic track and field event.

It was there that I met Norway's Grete Waitz. She had just broken the world record for 3000 meters on the track, and in her country she was a household name. You didn't have to use her last name if you were talking about sports; if you said "Grete," everyone knew who you meant. Not only did she have great times on the track, she'd won many world cross-country championships, including several in which I'd finished behind her.

But this was the first time I had actually spoken to her. I think I may have been a little awestruck, because when I think how relatively poorly I was running at that stage, she must have seemed absolutely unbeatable to me. I could never have guessed that in a few years time I would end up literally matching her stride for stride and even beating her. But I had many changes to undergo before that would happen.

In the 1500 at Bislet I was third again, and ran 4:12.3 to Grete's 4:06. The highlight of the meet was John Walker's 4:51.4 world record in the 2000 meters, a rarely run event that covers five laps of a 400-meter track, or about a mile and a quarter.

It was a wonderful experience to be part of those great historic track meets in Europe that are the very heart and soul of track and field. To this day they're exactly the same as they were then, amazing events with huge appreciative crowds, so knowledgeable about the events, so inspirational to run in front of, going crazy at the first sign of a great performance or a possible world record.

And of course we were invited out, fed and entertained, and basically treated like celebrities. We were taken to the Adidas factory and loaded up with beautiful athletic apparel and shoes, mostly in styles that hadn't even been released for sale to the public yet. For a 20-year-old, all of this was overwhelming.

We next went on to Stockholm where we met up with Gordon, who was still bumming around Europe. Although I hadn't really figured this out at the time, I can look back in retrospect and see how happy I was on these trips when he just wasn't around. As soon as he turned up, I became a different person.

Gordon could never restrain himself in any situation. He had to be the dominant personality around. He began right away sewing seeds of discontent, criticizing the guys and their training, telling them how much faster they could be running if only they'd listen to him. It was startling really, to think of him talking that way to men who already held world records and were beating the best in the world at nearly every event they entered. But that was Gordon.

The problem was that now that I was becoming more of an adult, I was thinking more independently, and I no longer hung on Gordon's every word. None of his athletes could ever really repay him for all he had done for us, inspiring us to join the group, encouraging us to consider the possibility that we could accomplish great things, herding us through all those grinding workouts. With his take-no-prisoners-devil-take-the-hindmost attitude he plowed ahead through all obstacles, refusing to admit the possibility of failure, refusing to be daunted by inclement weather, hostile officials or bad luck.

But his relentless intensity always ended up taking its toll on everyone around him. I was beginning to realize that when I traveled to events without him, I performed better than when he was there. And on the personal side, I was simply happier when Gordon wasn't there and I could just be with my friends. It's all hindsight now, but I can now see just how much stress he brought to a situation and that when he left, I felt as if I had been set free.

At the Stockholm meeting I watched Dick Quax miss the world record in the 5000 meters by one tenth of a second, and he did so because he threw his arms up about 50 meters from the tape. I remember thinking at the time that if he'd pushed all the way through the tape, he would have gotten the record. I didn't realize it at the time but watching that mistake would come back to me in 1982 when I tried for the world 5000-meter record myself. When it came time for that last lap, when I realized I was five seconds down, I knew there was no way I would let myself miss the record by a tenth of a second because of some gratuitous gesture like that.

At that meeting Gordon was introduced to the crowd and it was impressive to see that they still remembered him from his great running in the 1950's. They gave him a standing ovation in memory of all the years he'd had such thrilling races with Vladimir Kuts and Emil Zatopek. For all his difficult personality, Gordon had a huge impact on the sport during his day, and it was nice to see him get some small portion of the kind of recognition his soul clearly still hungered for. They also had Gordon present the winner's medal for the 5000, so there was a wonderfully moving moment when he got to hang the medal around Dick Quax's neck.

Next stop was Zurich and more of the same royal treatment: first rate hotels, food, service; Everything was just laid at our feet. I now joke about the fact that I toured Europe as a kind of valet for the New Zealand guys, earning tips from them for handling their mail and laundry, taking messages and so on. But if it sounds like I in any way wasn't having the time of my life, I'm giving the wrong impression. I appreciated the opportunity and didn't mind at all. I was seeing Europe with a rock band, and if I had to run some errands to earn my keep, that was fine with me.

In the races I was holding my own and never out of the top three, so while I wasn't setting the world on fire, at least I wasn't embarrassing myself.

The weather turned against us in Switzerland. I've never seen such violent thunderstorms as they had there in those mountains. I don't know if it was the humidity or the thunderstorms, but none of us ran very well. Dick was fourth in the 1500 in 3:56 and Rod sixth in 3:58. I ran 2:07 for seventh place in the 800 meters—"felt lousy" my diary reports, succinctly enough. I remember coming around the turn in the 800 and the hammer (a throwing instrument consisting of an iron ball with a cable and handle attached to it) bounced onto the track, wrapped itself around one of the girls' legs and slammed her to the track, badly injured. I left Zurich thinking, "Well, it could have been worse, I could have been hospitalized by an errant field implement."

Our pre-Olympic European tune-up tour was over and it was time to leave for Montreal. Right about then I began having problems with my lower back, so I went to a German physiotherapist, who proceeded to wrap me up in with some kind of strapping all around my waist, which seemed to give some relief. I sat next to Rod Dixon on the flight while he recounted how extremely well the boys were all doing financially on the trip. Sitting there, strapped up like a mummy, I thought to myself, "Well, I hope they're putting some of it away. This won't last forever."

18 ~ Montreal Olympics, 1976

There were only three women on our Olympic track team: me, Dianne Zorn, and Sue Jowett (later Quax), a sprinter whose father had been a bronze medalist for New Zealand in sprinting. In the same unit with us were seven swimmers and a manageress. The runners had one room, the manager had one room, and all the swimmers were strewn about in the living quarters. There was one bathroom!

But we were at the Olympics and the bathroom be hanged.

It's hard to overstate the effect of actually being at the Olympics for a young girl from Auckland, New Zealand. The village was amazing in its diversity, as every Olympic village is. And it really was a village, a whole community. It's a village that exists in spirit all the time, but then in actuality for only a few days. It's composed of people from all over the world who don't speak the same language, but who understand each other better than most of the people we know back home. We are all there on the same mission, one that draws us all together from the four corners of the earth for that one brief gentle moment.

It goes without saying that I reveled in it.

Meanwhile, on a more mundane level, personal relations got a bit strained. My boyfriend Tony had followed us to Montreal, and so had Gordon. They were staying in town, boarding with some people and it got to be a difficult situation because only athletes were allowed in the village and they had nowhere to go during the day.

Tony was still understandably bitter about not having made the team and Gordon was just his usual annoying self. And they really hounded me, wanting me to come out and entertain them and even to bring them food from the athletes' dining hall. It really became a problem for me because I just wanted to stay in the village and experience everything going on, to just enjoy it for what it was.

But then I would have to go out to do the training and Tony and Gordon would be at the training track, though they had to stay behind barriers. I continued to do my training with them, but the rest of the time they would park themselves in the park next to the village, and they would get any New Zealander going through the security gate to pass on the message that they were waiting for me. After a while it became so inconvenient to go traipsing down there that I started pretending that I never got the messages.

I've always said that sport and music are the two things that draw people together without regard to nationality, and the Olympic village was a great example of that. Even mixing with the other New Zealanders was great fun, but getting to know athletes from other nationalities was a once in a lifetime experience.

In 1976, New Zealand still played sports against South Africa, which was banned internationally from all sports because of apartheid. The New Zealand rugby team, the All-Blacks, had defied the ban and played the South African Springboks, because we've long had a policy of not mixing sports and politics. But the controversy split the country, and there were even some riots. It also brought about a boycott of the Olympic Games by all the African nations. I doubt many people remember it now, but at the time it had a devastating effect on the distance running events, in particular the men's 1500, in which our John Walker was to meet Tanzania's Filbert Bayi in a titanic battle of history's two best milers. Walker at the time held the world record at the mile, Bayi at 1500 meters (which is about 100 meters short of a mile).

But it was not to be. All those great African runners were on the sidelines as the Olympics went on without them. And for what?

To this day, when you hear that Walker won a gold medal in the 1500 and Quax won the silver in the 5000 (with Dixon fourth), how many people remember that the Africans weren't there? Who was being punished by such a boycott? New Zealand was supposedly the malefactor, yet in the distance events it was New Zealanders who got an easier climb to the victory podium.

Sadly enough, because the boycott wasn't enacted until right before the games, the African athletes were all physically present in Montreal. In fact, we were on the same floor as many of the African women because housing was arranged alphabetically, and we were neighbors with Nigeria, Morocco, Namibia, and other African countries close to us in the alphabet. We also knew many of the African athletes from past competitions in the Commonwealth Games and elsewhere. And a number of the top African runners would come down to New Zealand to train and race on our track circuit during their winters. It was awful to see them pack their bags and leave, knowing that it was because of our country's policies they were going.

But I didn't think then, and I don't now think that athletes should be used as pawns by politicians who can't think of any other way to make their points. The Olympics come around once every four years and many athletes are only at their peak for a few years, so missing a single Olympics can often mean a lifetime's work and an ardently pursued dream dashed to pieces.

No good ever comes from it. What if the United States had boycotted Hitler's Nazi showcase Olympics in Berlin in 1936? Not only would Jesse Owens have been denied his rightful place in sports history, but Hitler's theories of Aryan superiority wouldn't have been so instantly and graphically discredited, as they were by that amazingly talented black American athlete from Cleveland, Ohio.

Pulling out of the Games only hurt their own athletes. It didn't end apartheid any sooner. And of course, four years later, President Jimmy Carter did the same thing to the American athletes when he could think of no other way to punish the Soviets for invading Afghanistan. The Americans and a few allies stayed away from Moscow in 1980 and the war in Afghanistan ground on to the same inglorious end it would have anyway. The chief victims of the U.S. boycott were a generation of American athletes who will have to tell the grandchild on their knee: "I was on the Olympic team in 1980. But the president said we couldn't go. Why? No one really remembers…"

But it didn't end there. The Soviets fell into the same trap and retaliated by boycotting the 1984 games in Los Angeles. All of this started in 1976 when the New Zealand played South Africa in rugby.

It was a big controversy at the time, and when it came time for the opening ceremony, none of us knew how we'd be received into the stadium. It was my first time marching into an Olympic stadium. I look at pictures of us in those uniforms now, and my goodness, I ask myself if they *really* looked like that? Well, they did. They were pink and white, down past the knees and really quite something. Every time I show that video to school classes now, the kids laugh. And so do I.

We walked from the Olympic village to the stadium through an underground tunnel. Amazingly, the crowd gave us a rousing cheer when we entered. We heard no boos, nothing negative at all. The crowd supported us.

It took nearly seven hours by the time we got assembled, went through security, waited seemingly forever, then marched into the stadium, stood for the ceremony, then marched back out the same way. I remember getting back to the security gate by the park, and who's there but Gordon, saying, "You get your butt inside, get your gear and get out here to train." To this day I don't understand why he felt he had to push me to my limit all the time. And any time I got to enjoy the fruits of success or to just enjoy the moment, he was right there trying to undo it.

He hadn't wanted me to march in the opening ceremony in the first place. Obviously, I didn't agree and just defied him. I was not about to go the Olympics and miss bringing away all those wonderful memories.

But after the ceremony, we went to the track and again he just piled on the speed work. He was saying, "You've got to get faster, you've got to get faster." His solution to everything was simple: Sprint, sprint, sprint.

When I was in the village I was happy just being at the Olympics, but when I'd see Gordon, all the stress would instantly come back. I would get through my training as quickly as I could and then use any excuse I could to get past security and back into the village again.

I really did waste a lot of time and energy meeting up with Gordon and Tony, spending time with them, even bringing out snacks for them. I did the best I could. I certainly didn't ignore them, but it was as if my whole world was inside that village and all I wanted to do was to get back in there to experience it, and then to run well.

When it came time for the 800 heats, I drew one of the toughest groups. It had three girls who came into the Games with the fastest times of the year.

It was quite a procedure, getting ready to race. You'd be on the warm-up track and they used a series of lights to notify you about what was going on. The green light comes on and it means it's time to report in. Then you have another 30 minutes and an orange light comes on and you report in again. Finally, when you see a red light for your event, it's time to enter the stadium. Then you walk down this long tunnel into the stadium, and by that time you'd better be fully warmed up because they put you into a little room with about 30 chairs in it. You get into your competition uniform and officials come to check everything to make sure you don't have any illegal advertising on your uniform or any contraband in your bags. They check everything. They even measure your spikes to make sure they're the right length. Then you have to put your warm-ups and shoes back on before you walk out on the track.

So you're supposed to be completely warmed up when you enter the tunnel, but then you go through this whole dressing and inspection procedure, which takes about 30 minutes. By the time I got out onto the track I was already a nervous wreck, so imagine what my heart rate did when I looked up and saw 90,000 people in that stadium!

I considered myself a fairly experienced international runner. I had competed in the Commonwealth Games, I had been to the world cross-country championships, I had run in the great track stadiums in Europe. But when I walked out from the tunnel into that huge stadium, I felt like nothing so much as a very young girl from the Otahuhu Club in Auckland, New Zealand. I am not embarrassed to admit that it was fairly intimidating.

And I ran as hard as I could but I finished last in my heat. I ran 2:05.7, which wasn't such a bad time, but I was devastated. The only thing that soothed me somewhat was finding out that even John Walker failed to qualify in the 800 meters as well. That's how stiff the competition was, even without the Africans.

I was so embarrassed and felt I had let the whole country down. Here I was, supposedly a national heroine, ready to take on the world. Well, I tried, and I found out the world is not so easily taken on. I had run all those thousands of miles in training, flown half way around the earth, won or placed in most of the races I ran, and then ran right into a solid wall of reality. I suddenly realized that there's a great big world of competition out there, one I'd barely scratched the surface of. And in that world, being a national champion and a national record holder didn't mean much of anything.

My mental state after the heat was really down. I just wanted to go home. I had no interest in the 1500 at all. My diary reports:

> Felt tired. Did some sprints. Felt dreadful. Ran with a girl from Ireland. Went back to Village. Watched some TV. Showered. Had some tea and watched more TV. Bad day for NZ. John missed. Dick Quax was sick and started [in the 10,000] but didn't qualify (poor guy). Me last. Jackson [a boxer] got knocked out. Hope things pick up...

It took an effort to come back and get mentally ready for the 1500. But as my diary indicates, I had company. Dick Quax hadn't qualified in the 10,000 because of illness and John hadn't qualified in the 800. It occurred to me that I wasn't the only one having problems. Then it was a matter of pulling myself together, toughening up, and getting my head into the upcoming 1500 heat.

I went out that night and just had a good time. I even had a couple of beers. All the while Gordon is going on and on with his mantra, "You've got to get faster, you've got to get faster." During training he'd put me through these 100-meter sprints that would take two or three days to recover from. Then he'd do it all over again.

From outward appearances, the 1500 didn't go much better than the 800, but I had reasons to be pleased. I finished seventh in my heat, but my time was 4:10.68, a New Zealand record, and a faster time than the winning time in several other heats. So I consoled myself with the knowledge that had I been in a different heat, I probably would have advanced. I couldn't argue with my best performance ever for 1500 meters, and a new national record in the bargain.

Spirits were picking up all around the New Zealand quarters. Our rowers had won the bronze medal and our hockey team ended up getting the gold. As team, we were doing really well, and there was great deal of mutual support and team spirit. It was a lot of fun being a part of all that and Dianne and I decided to get up to some mischief. We loved to play pranks on the guys anyway, and that night when the rowers went out to celebrate their medal we "apple pied" (short-sheeted) their beds and put cellophane over the toilet. We then sat around giggling until they came home.

Russia's "Visible Woman," Kazankina, ended up winning the 800-

meter final in an incredible 1:54.9. The Finn Lasse Viren won a great 10,000-meter race, and later the 5000 as well. He even tried the marathon, but finished fifth, out of the medals but still impressive.

Those were great athletic events to watch and I took them in as any rabid spectator might. On the women's side of running performances, I became uncomfortably aware that I was a world behind the East Germans and Russians.

Of course, performance-enhancing drugs were a big topic of conversation amongst the athletes, and I can honestly say that it never entered my mind to try them. First of all, I looked at those women and thought, I don't want to look like that. Secondly, I always kept athletics in perspective, and that perspective was one of balance and overall good physical and mental health. Jeopardizing one's future health for the sake of instant rewards seemed perverse to me, and I never considered it.

Maybe I had been naïve, but it was a shock to actually see the Russian and East German athletes and realize the rumors that I had heard about drug taking were true. It made me realize what I was up against, so I had to come up with an attitude to deal with it. I knew that if I was going to stay in the sport I had to be able to wake up each morning and look in the mirror with a clear conscience. That was all that mattered. Whatever they were able to accomplish on the track, those women would always know they had cheated to do it and they would have to live with that every day of their lives afterward. And they'd have to live in fear that they'd compromised their own future health. No matter how many races they won, I wouldn't have wanted to be in their shoes.

Now we know from their own records that the East Germans had an extensive drug program ongoing with their athletes. The spate of unusual performances several years ago by the Chinese women was highly suspicious, and after all the attention and controversy they brought on themselves, they have dropped out of sight. You will almost never catch athletes cheating if you only test at competitions, and it is nearly impossible to implement a surprise drug-testing program when dealing with a closed society, so we may never know what the Chinese were doing, or the Soviets, for that matter.

But one memory I have from the Montreal Olympics is instructive. I was down at the training track one day and a Russian coach walked over to me. He told me that I had a lot of talent for such a young runner, and that if I were training in Russia, I would end up performing much better than I would otherwise. He might have been talking about better training techniques or nutrition or some other innocent topic, but the clear implication from his tone was that he was talking about getting extra-legal help.

At any rate, long-suffering Euan Robertson, who had been added to the team at the last minute, eventually made it to the finals in the steeplechase, and then ended up with a remarkable fifth place finish. Just think, fifth in the world, and his country almost hadn't sent him to the games at all! Jack Foster finished 17th in the marathon, a wonderful accomplishment for an athlete at 44.

In the 5000 meters Dick Quax won the silver medal, and Rod Dixon was barely edged out for the bronze. Viren won by less than half a second. My impression was that Dick and Rod were so busy worrying about each other that they let the others slip by them. To this day I believe they could have got gold and silver if they had run a different race. I wasn't the only one who thought that.

On the last day of the games, we watched John Walker burst from behind in a tactical race to win a gold medal over Ivo Vann Damme of Belgium in just one tenth of a second. I watched the finish through a veil of tears. After all that had happened, the boycott, my own races, and all the hard travel with John and the others during those early years, it was quite an emotional finale to the games. I cried again as they raised our flag and played the New Zealand national anthem as John received the highest honor an athlete can win in our sport.

All in all, it was a wonderful experience. It was a tough, eye-opening reality check, but I wouldn't have missed it for anything. I had run the fastest 1500 I'd ever run, and I had to temper my disappointment with that knowledge.

On our chartered flight home there were three women on the entire plane. You can imagine an entire New Zealand Olympic team drinking and carousing their way home after all those weeks of stress and competition. The managers walked up and down the plane, sternly threatening all of us that we would never leave New Zealand again if we didn't behave, but it was pretty much a lost cause. We were an airborne party winging our way back to the Southern Hemisphere.

An article written at the time discusses my disappointment in not living up to my country's expectations. I said that to succeed at that level it seemed to me one would have to be a full-time athlete, something I didn't think I wanted to be, because of the pressure involved.

Well, when you're 20 years old, you often say things you end up contradicting later. And I certainly ended up becoming exactly what I thought I never would: a full-time professional athlete.

19 ~ Post Olympic Blues

I had been away for over two months, and as always after a big competition there was a huge letdown after all the excitement. But I got a great welcome from the teachers and the kids, and it was wonderful to see that they had followed my trials and travails through the games and had pictures up all over the school. I had written regularly to them the whole time I was gone and they had written back, so they had a real feeling of participation in the Olympics.

When I came home and was able to tell them in person all about it, added to all they had seen on television and read in the newspapers, it made it all seem very real and personal for them. Their excitement was infectious, and that helped me get back into the swing of school and everyday life again.

I didn't get my class back right away, and then I managed to get myself sick, probably a result of the sheer exhaustion of that long journey and all that had happened. And of course I was coming from summer directly to winter, and when you do that your poor body doesn't know which end is up, but whatever the cause, I ended up really sick. I got a case of what we called "school sores," which many of the children were plagued by. I had oozing sores all over my back, which Mom had to bathe and treat every night. Then I got the flu.

One part of my life got instantly better when I bought a little Morris 1100, a tiny car that was my pride and joy. It cost $1,800, a huge sum, but gave me my independence finally. With my increasingly hectic schedule, being able to get around on my own relieved a huge amount of stress from my life.

Gordon was trying to push me back into hard training immediately. He kept saying I had to improve, had to get faster. At this time, three of the other girls training with us, Pauline Vercoe, Alison Deed and Shirley Sommerville all told Gordon they wanted to leave because they thought he was spending too much time with me, and that I was too competitive on our runs. Gordon persuaded Alison to stay, but not the others, and there was a bit of a rift for a while after that.

Was I too competitive? From my perspective I was just trying to run as hard and as fast as I could. Did I compete with the others? Damn right I did, that was the business I was in. And I had no apologies whatever for trying to get the best out of myself I could. I felt badly that the girls thought they had to go elsewhere, but it never crossed my mind to approach training with anything other than an all-out effort, every day.

But even so, it was clear I didn't have my usual enthusiasm. I was having a hard time getting back not only into running, but also teaching. I have since learned that a lot of athletes have a hard time with the letdown after the Olympics. I had a lot of medical tests done, but they didn't turn up anything suspicious. I just had the blues.

My 21st birthday rolled around on November 1st, and I had again allowed myself to get overweight. I had a wonderful party at which we roasted two lambs in the back yard and had friends from running and school over. My sister Katie wasn't doing very well then. She was so weak, she had to attend the party on a cot. Improvements in medications would later make her life much more comfortable

A few days later I was again chosen for the 1977 world cross-country team, this time competing in West Germany. Alison, Barbara, Heather Matthews, and Lorraine were also on it, along with Irene Miller, who had edged out Dianne Zorn. But it was the "old gang" back again, and everyone was happy to be part of it.

Now that I had my car, Gordon insisted that we spend even more time over in Alison's neighborhood, so Barbara and I would drive all the way across Auckland to the North Shore.

In December, after completing a year of teaching, I was trans-
ferred to Papatoetoe Central, which is located in a similar but more
middle-class area. I had really wanted to come back to Yendarra, but
the rule said one year at your first school and then two at your second.

At this time Gordon's life was becoming a bit of a mess. He now
supported himself by being a milkman! He had always held a great
variety of jobs, most of which he managed to get fired from or walked
away from.

So for a while, he would get us all out there to help on his milk
run. He also owned some old houses in a section of town that is now
rather upscale. At the time it was just starting the transition from its
more Bohemian roots. Gordon would buy one of these rundown
houses, do a mostly cosmetic fix-up job, then rent it for an astronom-
ical sum. It seemed he was always either out doing his milk run or
else running around unclogging the drain in one of his ramshackle
houses. There were many nights we would turn up to train and end
up pushing carts up and down the Auckland hills, delivering milk.

His personal life was as convoluted as ever. He continued to live
in the house with Shirley and their two daughters, but there were
times we'd turn up there for training and Gordon would have clearly
slept on a mattress in the bathtub because his wife's boyfriend had
stayed over.

Gordon just blithely rolled along this way, and Shirley did the
same. Shirley's boyfriend was years younger than her, but it must
have been a very solid relationship, because it lasted many years.
After a while, Gordon moved into one of his nearby houses. Dick
Booth, in his excellent recent biography of Gordon, *The Impossible
Hero*, writes of this period:

> Gordon and Shirley had met on the running track,
> trained and raced together and run open house for ath-
> letes for 20 years or more. The break up was painful. It
> also had an impact on Pirie's work as a coach. Dave
> Harness, who was doing a lot of training with Pirie,
> remembers: "I really felt he lost his confidence at that
> time. He began to ask me questions about what we were
> doing. It wasn't like Gordon at all."

Being so young, we had no insight whatever into his unorthodox
lifestyle. It seemed to us that Gordon's life was just deteriorating
around him like one of his rented hovels.

By now he'd sold his beloved Mercedes, and Shirley had her own job. The two girls were in high school, and Gordon was at loose ends. He had broken with Anne Smith, who went to England for a while. I remember Gordon boasting about breaking into her apartment while she was gone and burning her training diaries so she wouldn't have any record of the training secrets he had given her. That certainly put me on notice that if I wanted to keep my diaries I had better protect them.

I never saw Anne Smith again after she left Gordon. She returned briefly and taught school, then went back to England for good. She taught school and kept up her running as a masters, but died tragically young of a cerebral hemorrhage at age 52 in 1993.

In February I started at the new school with a class of 30 second-graders. I was still in something of a post-Olympic daze. In addition to school and going through the motions of training, more and more I was being asked to participate in non-running events. It wasn't hard to speak to a group, but I had a low tolerance for small talk, so I was intensely uncomfortable attending a function where everyone was expected to stand around chatting.

I was still naïve about publicity and celebrity, but after suffering through a number of these occasions it occurred to me that the only reason I was invited was because someone thought they could use my name for his or her own purposes. I began turning down such invitations, and was the happier for it.

I was still having trouble with infected toenails some thought they were caused by under-sized shoes, but I still thought it was my toe-first running style. I note in my diary that on February 23rd I was up all night. We had a going-away party at Barbara's home up the street from me and I was in a great deal of pain. So much so that I came home early, sterilized a needle and tried to operate on my toe myself. Mum gave me whiskey and milk, plus a couple of aspirin, and put me in bed. The next morning we went to Dr. Drake's and he operated on my poor toe. This time it was so painful it took four injections to numb it so I could stand the pain. The next day I got on the plane to Germany for the World Cross-Country championships. In my diary I note rather perfunctorily the trip from Auckland to Singapore to Bangkok to Karachi to Vienna to Amsterdam and finally to Hamburg. It was becoming something of a routine, flying for 50 hours halfway around the world to put on shorts and run a few miles in the mud.

20 ~ *World Cross Country; Germany, 1977*

Boy, did we land in the middle of winter on this trip. I don't think any of us had ever been so cold. We were in a very nice place, a town called Bad Segeberg, staying in a beautiful hotel right beside a lake. It was really wonderful, but my goodness it was cold! None of us wanted to go outside to run. We didn't have the clothing for it and were frankly intimidated by the weather. But we found that we were very popular in town because New Zealand was so well known in running circles.

As usual, we were in "exchange-rate shock." Our basic expenses were taken care of, but any incidentals seemed outrageously high to us. One nice diversion was that the rock band "Status Quo" was on the plane to Germany with us, and they invited us to their concert. Then during the concert, they brought us up on stage with them! They invited us to hang out and party with them afterwards, but the manager put a stop to that. Too bad. That was a particularly lively team. John Dixon, Rod's brother, was there, as he had been in 1975, and though he wasn't quite as fast a runner as his brother, he was every bit the comedian and more. He was always up to mischief and we had a great time with him.

One of the side trips we took was to Lübeck, on the border between East and West Germany. It was a somber sight for all of us, standing there in the freezing cold, staring at that cold, concrete monument to repression. It quieted even our high spirits and left an impression on all of us.

New Zealanders, being from a young country, are fascinated by all things European, and on all of these trips to London, Belgium, and Paris I found myself entranced by places with so much history.

During the previous summer when his team was training in New Zealand, Detlef Ulemann, one of West Germany's top runners at the time had become a good friend. Now that we were in Germany, Detlef and his friends would drive over and take us around, which was a real treat. Barbara had become friendly with one of Detlef's pals, and Alison with another, so it all worked out nicely and we had a wonderful time together.

As a tune-up, we ran in the West German National Cross-Country race, which was held around a horse race track, with the women running three laps around. For the first time in my life I ran hard just to stay warm and to get it over with. I finished third behind two German women, 12 seconds behind the winner. My feet were so cold and painful I was in tears. On the bus back, Lorraine Moller massaged one foot and Heather Thompson the other, with me just bawling in pain.

We ran in several more tune-up races, traveling around by bus and train, having a wonderful time. Sometimes I wasn't getting a great deal of sleep, but I always got my training in. The discipline of my earlier years always kept me on the straight and narrow even in distracting circumstances such as this.

The German club system is very strong and there were always other runners to train with. And with all the socializing at night, sometimes I had to sneak naps in during the day to stay rested. The local German running clubs were very professional and well run, with many wealthy members who made sure the clubs were well supported and that their top athletes wanted for nothing. It was an eye opener to us to see the kind of support those German athletes enjoyed. And they were extremely generous to us as well, giving us athletic apparel and other gifts and really making us feel welcome. Our usual trip to the Adidas factory ensured that we got enough shoes to keep us training for a few more months.

Finally we went down to Dusseldorf for the world championship race, and by this time the whole team had caught the flu and was miserable, trying to come around in time to race. I finished in ninth place and the New Zealand women were third in the team competition. Our men didn't fare as well, finishing fifth. My friend Detlef was third in the men's race.

After the race, as runners were trading singlets and souvenirs, I realized for the first time how coveted our famous black uniforms were. It seemed everyone wanted one, and they were willing to pay quite a lot for them, so all the Kiwis recouped some expense money by selling our uniforms at the end of the competition. Some years later they changed the design completely, tossing out not only the lovely simplicity of the design, but all that history. To this day I think those black uniforms with the little silver fern were the classiest ones in the running world.

On our way back to New Zealand we again hit Singapore and had a great time spending whatever money we had left. We boarded the plane for the final leg overloaded with luggage and had to pay excess weight penalties.

21 ~ Steve

It wasn't until I got home that I realized how close I'd become to Detlef. Then I was devastated at the thought that I might not ever see him again. We both lived in the fantasy world of elite athletes, where we might see each other several times a year at competitions, but that depended completely on how well we were running at the time. It could all be over in a heartbeat. For some reason I had a premonition then that we wouldn't be seeing each other again and strangely enough, that ended up being true.

My diary reports:

> This is the first time I can say that I wouldn't have minded staying there for lots longer. It's nice to be home but I'm afraid I'm going to miss a wonderful guy I met. Still I know I'm going to see him again, and I hope our meeting becomes more permanent. It's been a great trip, probably the best [yet] because I was happy throughout...

Then the next day, I settle back in to reality:

> Mucked around all day, tidying up and unpacking. The weather is lovely and I'm as white as a ghost. Gordon is still a bit of a mess... the family is glad to have

me home. What a life I make for myself. But I wouldn't
swap it for the world.

I started spending a lot more time at the home of marathoner
Kevin and Jeannette Ryan's, where a number of other runners would
assemble before training. Jeannette was wonderfully hospitable, and
would always have food ready for us when we finished our run. We'd
often just hang around and chat afterward.

My new school was becoming less forgiving of my travel schedule.
They had been having a teacher temporarily take over my class while
I was away, but then after a while they began using *me* as the substitute. When I finally got back to my regular class I had 31 first
graders, and with that number of such young students, they were a
handful! The headmaster was not particularly supportive of my athletic endeavors and the faculty was more or less divided into pro and
con camps. I often felt like I was being penalized because of the time
I had to take for traveling, and I can understand that some people
wouldn't be very understanding.

As I've mentioned before, I had to deal with that kind of attitude
from time to time over the years. It really is a shame that some people seem blind to the benefits of a colleague or an employee who
excels in athletics, or art or whatever. One would think the intangi-
bles of the situation would be highly prized: the attention and good
will the school received, the experience the kids had of rooting for
their teacher at the Olympics or world cross-country championship,
the national pride engendered by a fellow citizen doing well on the
world's athletic stage. But there were those who just didn't see it that
way.

I would take my kids out for physical education classes and was
told that I was wasting time and I should have them in the classroom.
So it wasn't as happy a situation as it had been at Yendarra, and I'm
sure I was bringing a lot of it on myself by just trying to do so much
in my life, as usual.

Later that year the World Cup was going to be in Dusseldorf.
The World Cup, in track and field, is similar to the Olympics, except
that it's held every other year, and it's only track and field, no other
sports. I wanted to make the team, in no small part because I wanted to see Detlef again. I had already written that we should break up
because from a practical point of view I just couldn't see how a New
Zealand girl and a West German guy living a world apart could ever
have a future. But I still had feelings for him and thought he was a

wonderful guy. So who knows what was in the back of my mind as I plotted to get to the World Cup later that summer. I dreaded asking for more time off, the school authorities were so unsympathetic. At one stage I had to go in to the education board to answer questions about what my professional intentions were.

Like a lot of amateur athletes in those days, I had a tough time making it financially even though I was living at home. I was not getting paid for any time that I was away and I also had to use up all my sick leave for those days. Consequently if I really got sick and took time off, it was unpaid. That sometimes forced me to go to school when I wasn't well. With everything going on in my life at that stage, I think my poor mum and dad must have thought of me as a boarder. I hardly saw them during the day, and on the weekends I was gone much of the time. I think they had a hard time adjusting to that.

They were also dealing with Katie's struggle with her school. There wasn't a special class or school for the deaf she could attend, so she would attend regular classes and then get speech therapy outside of school. But she was getting so frustrated by not getting enough attention, and that frustration would spill over to me. When she got out of high school, she went to occupational therapy, then got a factory job close to home, assembling safety equipment. That was a great relief for Mum and Dad.

There was always that dichotomy in the house. My life was so seemingly glamorous, going off around the world to compete, and Katie's was always such a struggle just to get through a normal day. She never came to the airport to see me off; it was such a traumatic thing for her when I left. She'd always be there to welcome me home, usually crying. Even these days when she visits me in the United States, it takes an effort to get her on the plane to go back to New Zealand. That's a holdover from the days when it seemed to her that I was constantly getting on a plane to leave.

I was putting on weight again, and as I look back, it seems when my weight went up, my feet took a beating. I was also fighting the flu all the time, probably another indication of stress. Gordon would be leaving soon on his annual European trip so I would be left to train on my own as best as I could, with the support of anyone else around at the time.

Thanks to the New Zealand health care system, I was able to get treatment for my feet every day. It was while I was waiting at the treatment center that I met Steve Audain in mid-May of that year. A football player, he was there to get treatment for a knee injury. My diary reports:

> Went to Jill's [the therapist] at 3:45. Met a nice guy
> called Steve? who I have a date with next Saturday.

Jill was playing cupid. She always knew when I would be there, so she scheduled Steve's appointments for the same time. That's how we met the first time, and why we kept bumping into each other there. But I only got to know him for three weeks before I had to leave for Europe.

The education board reacted as expected when I requested time to travel to the World Cup. They said I could go but it would of course be without pay and they couldn't guarantee anything about my job on my return.

I had been selected for the Oceana team, which included Australia, New Zealand and the Pacific Islands. They selected just one person per event, and the world was divided into eight different areas. So in some ways it was more selective than the Olympics.

Finances were so strained I had to start trying to sell some of my belongings to raise money for this trip. Mum and Dad were always willing to pitch in as much as possible but they didn't have a great deal of money, and I still had my pride (or at least as much of it as I could still afford).

I was constantly querying John Walker about the possibility of making money at some of the track meets before the World Cup, but it was hard to get specifics. He knew how much he, Dixon and Quax could expect—in fact they often bragged about the actual amounts they got—but he really couldn't predict how much a female middle distance runner might ask for. It made it difficult to plan financially for the trip. If I could count on just $100 from a race, that would just about see me through, as long the other expenses were met. My diary on May 26, 1977 clearly reveals my state of mind:

> Didn't run in the morning. Tired out. Horrible day at
> school. 28 kids are too much. Went training at 3:15.
> Gordon was supposed to come but didn't. Ran 2 mile
> warm-up, then 10 X 100 meters with a 400 jog in 14 sec-
> onds each. Never under 14. Hard as I could go, too.
> Cried. Went to Jill [the therapist]. Came home and rang
> Jeannette [Ryan] to see if they had sold my radio. Could
> only get $2.50 for it so didn't sell. That upset me no end

as I now have no money to go to Europe with.

Went round there [to the Ryans'] to get cheered up. Talked over things with Jeannette, Kevin and Philip and finally decided to leave Gordon, as he's so inconsistent. So we worked out a schedule that I am gong to stick to until I go away. (I hope.)

A day I want to forget. I hope everything works out. Please, Please!

Dr. Drake even offered to lend me some money for the trip. A number of friends understood how difficult things were and were trying to help. I obviously still wanted to run and compete, but I don't think I really understood myself how difficult it would be to do that and hold down a full-time job at the same time. I thought my situation was unusual; I didn't realize it was something all so-called "amateur" athletes had struggled with for years.

Looking back, I can see I was in a kind of no-man's land then, drifting in my life with no real direction. My real profession, running, didn't exist then, and had someone suggested to me that one day it would, I would have laughed out loud. I think my mental state at the time had a lot to do with the way I reacted to Steve Audain, the man I was seeing and would soon marry. He came out of nowhere and introduced me to an entirely different world, a world light years removed from my stresses and worries.

I am a great believer in destiny, so I don't look back and say, What a mistake I made and I wish I had done this and that differently. I believe things happen for a reason. Looking back, I can remember my frame of mind at the time, and can view my meeting with Steve in context.

Up until then I had only dated other people like me, runners. Straight-laced, obsessed with our health and fitness, we were an early-to-bed-early-to-rise crowd. We certainly had fun, but it wasn't the same kind of wild, partying lifestyle led by young athletes on rugby or football teams. So here I was just worried sick about raising travel money, about my job, and about my so-called running "career," and here came this muscular, blonde, blue-eyed football player, laughing at everything, oozing charm, and apparently without a care in the world. I can see now how I was captivated not only by the man, but by the world he inhabited, a world that would allow for such an easygoing attitude, such laughter, such *happiness*. He was only too willing to introduce me to that world.

My parents knew something was up right away.

He turned up at the house to pick me up for our date wearing huge bell bottom jeans, a denim shirt and a nearly floor length denim coat with a fur collar. On his feet were these big chunky black boots and his hair hung down to his collar. It was something out of a Beatles movie during their transcendental years, and my poor dad just about had a heart attack. My grandmother was there as well, and she was nearly apoplectic. But neither of them said a word. I tried to act casual as I made introductions, but I confess to being a bit taken aback myself. Up until then I had only seen him on workdays at Jill's when he was dressed in a business suit, with his hair conservatively restrained.

We dated for three weeks before I left for Europe. I remember crying before boarding the plane and my dad asking me what the matter was. I told him I didn't really know, and that was the truth.

Now I know it's because I didn't want to go. I don't believe I knew Steve well enough to be that upset at leaving, but for the first time in my life I was boarding a plane for a wonderful far-off place, and I wasn't excited to be going.

I was also traveling on my own for the first time in my life. I was supposed to meet up with a friend and training partner of John Walker's in Singapore, Bruce Jones. We would then fly to London together. I was still worried, because I didn't have much money, although John Walker and everyone else said to just come to Europe and everything would be fine.

I look at pictures taken at that time and can't believe how over-weight I was. I arrived in Singapore wearing these high heels that for some reason I'd decided travel in, and by the time I got to Singapore they simply didn't fit my feet. So there I was, walking through the airport in Singapore in bare feet, looking for Bruce. I was fat, stressed out, and under-trained, and I'd been crying because I'd just left behind an exciting, garrulous man who was showing me a whole new world where none of that mattered.

I was 21 years old.

22 ~ *Europe; Summer, 1977*

Bruce and I got to the Crystal Palace, keeping our fingers crossed that John Walker had set up everything and that we'd have a roof over our heads. When we got there, we had a room all right, but only one. I knew Bruce from training in New Zealand, but I didn't know him that well! Fortunately, we were able to get a suite with two separate rooms.

Almost immediately we began learning about the business aspects of the European circuit. My diary on June 24th, 1977:

> Went to lunch and spent a hilarious afternoon [over-hearing] a conversation between some American athletes and the meet promoter. I honestly never realized that it was such a business. The money that's involved is phenomenal. One guy is asking $16,000US for himself and 5 other athletes. By asking this much they are stopping athletes like me from getting any. Besides getting upset by this, I had a hilarious time trying to listen. I even sat in the toilet to hear more!

Walker was nowhere to be found. After making some calls, we found out that he was injured and not running in the meet. It began to dawn on us that we were in a bit of a jam. We had been relying on John and his contacts in Europe to get us into races, to bargain for accommodations, and possibly to get some money for expenses. Now it turned out that he was staying at some kind of golf resort as he tried to recover from his injury. When we asked him what we should do, his response was that since he wasn't sure what he was going to do himself, he didn't know what to tell us.

What we were discovering rather quickly about John was that when something went wrong in his world, it went wrong in everyone else's world as well. And it was a particularly rough season for a pair of wide-eyed Kiwis to be running around Europe without an experienced guide. My diary, June 25th, 1977:

> Everything is so cutthroat that Steve Riddick [a world class sprinter] turned up and got told to go home. Another guy who is so good has been told he can't race because there's no room. The B grade men's 1500 has all guys faster than 3:42, even as fast as 3:39 [equivalent to a 3:56-3:59 mile]. A 46.5 400-meter runner has been turned away. It's so cutthroat I feel sick about it all. John is being so inconsiderate and selfish. He's out playing golf or snooker while we're sitting worrying. He's being bloody lousy.

This was beginning to be quite an educational summer in Europe.

I had one particularly interesting conversation with a major British promoter, who made it very plain to me that if I expected to continue to get into races, I needed to be "nice" to him. This was long before the term "sexual harassment" was in common usage, and it certainly wasn't the last time I would need to turn down such a distasteful invitation.

Finally, John found a place for me to stay. It was with a New Zealand couple, Allison and David Wright. She was a runner and was coached by John's coach, Arch Jelley. David worked for a British meat company. They lived in Windsor, next to the castle and park of the same name.

I've always loved English culture and history, and London is one of my favorite places in the world. Allison and David were kind to me and Windsor was a fine place to train, but everything in my life seemed to be falling apart. Far from the good-spirited camaraderie of past trips, here I was abandoned in England, lonely, short of funds, and worried. At the absolute nadir of my existence, I had to take the train in to London to get a pregnancy test. Along with everything else gone wrong, it seemed foreordained that it would be positive. Fortunately, it wasn't. My cycle was probably just disrupted by travel and stress.

Allison and David were both intense about running and she was competitive with me on training runs at a time when I just wanted to get by. But I'm just not a quitter, so I got in a survival frame of mind: I would hold out as long as I could and run as well as I possibly could.

I needed to get into races to prepare me for the World Cup, but because of John's injury situation everything was up in the air. I felt as if I had been dumped by the side of the road and left to fend for myself. Both Allison and David worked during the day, so I entertained myself as best I could. Mom had taught me all the homemaking skills, so I bought some material and wool and started to sew and knit during the day.

Finally, John called and said to get ready to run in a meet in Dublin. We were all going, Allison, myself, Arch and the guys as well. Then, I don't know how I did it but I hit my foot on something and hurt it pretty badly, so things were starting to go from bad to worse.

On the day of the event we got stuck in an elevator in the Dublin hotel, seven adults and a child. Dick Quax and his wife, John Walker and I were in there for an hour. At first, it seemed very funny. Then, as the lights went out and the air got very stale and warm, we runners stripped down to our racing outfits. John entertained us by telling a story he once read about some people stuck on a lift who killed each other to survive. It wasn't the best preparation for a track meet.

I was still not running particularly well, though I did finish fourth in the 800 meters in 2:10.6. I felt strong, but not very fast. I just wasn't anywhere near top form.

But my biggest problem was that I was really on my own for the first time, in an unstructured situation, generally at loose ends. I would try to call Steve Audain collect to make contact with home, but with the time difference and him at work all day it was difficult. I got a bad bout of flu again and was really homesick. I called Mum and Dad to try to calm any fears that they might have and of course I had to try to sound upbeat so that I didn't worry them. Katie got on the phone and just started crying and it was all I could do not to join her.

Finally Dianne Zorn arrived—she was going to the World Cup, too—and the situation improved considerably. We had always gotten along well and having a familiar face around eased my homesickness.

We got lodging together with a running club family and began training together. The money situation eased as well, with my federation finally coming up with some expenses, and small loans from Steve and my parents arriving.

Later when we traveled to Dusseldorf my spirits were again lifted seeing so many past teammates. What a relief to finally have accommodations, to be with a team and be among friends!

My running was still disastrous, however. In the 800 meters I ran a miserable 2:11, got one of my stress attacks and to my great embarrassment was put on a stretcher and carried off the track. Before they could whisk me away to a hospital, one of our managers intercepted them and took me to one of the American team doctors, who gave me some medicine.

I tried to get myself together for the 1500 a few days later, but it was not to be. My diary describes my misery:

> Sat in the stands until 7:15, then went to the warm-up area. My leg was really sore and got worse until I had to get Russ Hoggard [a trainer] to massage my back. So while all the other girls were still warming up I was lying on the ground crying. I'd just had enough. I went down the tunnel and out onto the track. I couldn't even stride out. I ran 4:31 and last [place]. I was there at the bell [start of last lap] but just limped the rest of the way. Once again for the 2nd time in a week I got carried off the track on a stretcher.

I had hit rock bottom as an athlete.

Then I found out that Detlef was at the meet, but that he was still so upset about our breakup that he didn't want to see me. That hurt because I had had feelings for him and didn't want it to end bitterly.

So after the whole miserable summer, the homesickness, worry and loneliness, the exposure to the sleazy underbelly of the European track circuit, the relentless injury problems and the awful races, I was finally getting on a plane to go home.

And after that long, long journey from Germany to Bombay to Singapore to Jakarta to Australia to New Zealand, when we finally landed the weather was cloudy, freezing and awful. And I was never so glad to be home.

23 ~ Steve's Other World

Steve wasn't at the airport to meet me. He was down south on a business trip, so I had a day of playing the schoolgirl, nervously anticipating seeing him again, wondering what it was I was feeling. Whatever it was, I was thrilled to see him when he got back, and we picked up right where we left off. After such a miserable time in Europe, I was only too happy to be back with Steve and his fun-loving rugby cronies.

One mid-September entry in my diary sums up the lifestyle I fell back into quite easily:

> The team they played was rough. I didn't say a word until some guy late-tackled Steve, threw a punch at him. Then the only words I could say were, "Shit, you bastard." Everyone laughed. Steve played really well. I only hope he gets a game in tomorrow's final. Went to town so that Steve could have a sauna. Nice place. Then we went to the Richmond club's after-match [party]. We left there at 7:00 and went to the Te Papa Squash Club for another do... had a lovely feed. Yummy chocolate log and Pavola. [a New Zealand traditional desert, meringue covered in cream]. Danced till about 10:00. Had some lovely Kahlua's and milk. Oh, dear. No diet! Got home at 1:00.

I was taking a break from running, getting overweight again, but after that terrible summer, I couldn't work up any discipline whatsoever. I still had ambitions in running, though. My diary at one point sums up the whole experience:

> Another trip over. Not quite the best but a good experience. I know what I have to do: Get Fast!! My next aim is a Commonwealth Games gold medal.

Gordon called and in his most humble, charming way managed to talk me into training with him again. He apologized for all the confusion in his life and really acted like he wanted to make amends, and since I hadn't managed all that well on my own, I agreed.

Then Steve started to talk about house hunting! I had only been back a few weeks and all of a sudden he announced that we were going to start looking for a place together. And at that stage of my life, I just went along for the ride. In the runner's world, such an idea would have been too impulsive, too extravagant. There would have been dozens of questions about expenses, about commitment, about the wisdom of such a precipitous decision. But I had been in the careful, staid runner's world for too long, and Steve's world was irresistible to me. To him, it was full speed ahead, all things are possible, devil take the hindmost.

We had a lot of late nights, drank far too much, went to the rugby club too often. He belonged to a sauna and I would often meet him there and we would go out to dinner. Of course, I was trying to fit too much into my life and I got ill. This time it was cystitis, a bladder infection so painful I wouldn't wish it on my worst enemy. I took strong antibiotics, but had to keep teaching because I had no sick time left and couldn't afford to stay home.

I know my father was aware of this new lifestyle and was really concerned about my relationship with Steve, but he didn't say much about it. For my part, I felt that I was in love and being carried along by this exciting, carefree new life. Possibly it was a matter of needing to sow some wild oats after so many years of striving and self-restraint. So I doubt it would have done much good to talk to me about it anyway, but I could tell my parents were concerned.

My weekly take-home pay as a school teacher each week was $91, which in 1977 seemed to be a great deal of money. At any rate, so long as I was teaching and not traveling, I was at least able to make ends meet. I was still on the club committee and attending the monthly meetings, but with the back and leg injuries I was battling, my new lifestyle, and my weight going up, running had certainly slipped as a priority in my life. Though I proclaimed to myself that my goal was nothing less than a Commonwealth Games gold medal, one couldn't have told it by the way I was living.

Steve and I bought an apartment in a building called Shortland Flats in the middle of downtown Auckland. In those days New Zealanders just didn't live in apartments, and apartment buildings were rare. But this building dated to the 1920's and was very nice.

Steve had lived in London for three years in his early twenties so he knew all about urban apartment life. When he asked me whether I wanted to get a place with him and I said yes, he said, "Well, I can't see living in a house in the suburbs." That sounded fine to me. I couldn't see myself living that way either.

Since it took all the money we could beg, borrow or steal to buy the place, naturally we had no furniture. Steve's father made us some chairs out of bottle crates, and we bought some old furniture and recovered it. Then, after several months of living like we were in a college dorm, I just walked into a store and bought some furniture on time.

Officially, it was Steve's place. I could never have simply moved in with him and set up housekeeping. It would have been too much for my parents to absorb, and after all I had put them through, I wasn't about to add that to the list.

So we lived this dual existence, with me teaching all day, going into the city to train, then meeting Steve at the apartment. From the apartment we would walk down to the city, where we had several friends who owned or managed restaurants. We would be there until three and four in the morning, with the guys drinking Irish coffees, which were certainly more Irish than coffee. There were so many lost nights, nights when Steve would get into fights, nights he shouldn't have been driving. And much as I was convincing myself that I was happy, that I was having great fun, there were some miserable, miserable times when we would get back to the apartment and he would just pass out inside the doorway. I would get him to bed and get in my car and drive the 11 miles home, crying most of the way.

There were too many late nights and too much alcohol, particularly for an athlete. I had never seen drinking like that, not in my family, and didn't know how to deal with it. Steve's father and brother both knew they had problems, and Steve always said that he was a potential alcoholic himself, but that he "had it under control."

It never entered my head that something was wrong. In hindsight it's easy to see the problems, but back then it never occurred to me that I was in over my head, that things were out of control.

And despite my $91 paycheck and Steve's salary, between paying for and furnishing the apartment and keeping up our lifestyle, we would often get to the weekends with 70 cents between us. So we would go to his parents for one good meal one day, and my parents for another good meal the next day.

One Sunday morning before anyone else was around, Dad asked, "Well, what is this place that Steve's bought?"

"We've bought an apartment together," I said. I knew they'd find out sooner or later, but didn't know how they'd take it.

"Does that mean you're going to get married?"

I told him I didn't know, and I didn't. I suppose it was in the back of my mind, but it wasn't like I was operating from some grand design. Then one day Steve and I for some reason were in the garage of one of his friends' houses, and he looked at me and said:

"Well, do you want to get married?"

I said okay.

That was the extent of it. He never bought an engagement ring, I never had a party. We just called our parents and said we were getting married next March 18th. He was 27, I was 22.

Over Christmas holidays I got pneumonia. So I started on really strong antibiotics again, and the only good thing about it was that it was during school holidays so at least I could try to rest and get better.

Then I was out running alone in the Auckland Domain the day after Christmas, and a car full of kids came around a bend and veered right towards me. I jumped off the path and fell down an embankment, hurting myself badly. I had cuts, bruises and a badly twisted ankle. It took a long time to heal, and in fact cost me nearly the whole of 1978.

Gordon met Steve right after the New Years, and my diary says they hit it off. In fact, it soon became obvious that Gordon was extremely threatened and jealous of Steve. Though he played team sports, Steve didn't really have much understanding of what it took to run competitively, and Gordon would have been absolutely shocked at Steve's lifestyle. There's no reason to think they would have had any common ground at all, but I managed to convince myself at the time that they did.

We got our two sets of parents together after the first of the year. Steve's folks, Frankie and Kitty, were wonderful, and though his dad has since passed away, I'm still close to Kitty. In fact it was Kitty who first warned me about the health consequences of my new lifestyle. She was all too familiar with Steve's habits.

My poor parents were also disturbed by our late nights. One particular night I had been at the apartment late and had driven the freeway home and gone to bed. The next morning I woke up and Mum and Dad had already gone to work. Then I got a phone call from Steve.

"I had visitors last night after you left," he said.

"What do you mean?"

"Well, around two o'clock in the morning your Mum and Dad turned up. I was fast asleep, and they turned up looking for you."

We must have passed each other on the freeway, so I was in my bed asleep as they were out in the middle of the night looking for me. I woke up the next morning thinking that I'd had a bad dream in which Mum had come in and shaken me, asking where I'd been, that they'd been looking for me. But it obviously was no dream. They never said a word about it and I certainly never brought it up. I guess they felt embarrassed about it, but they were concerned about me. And with good reason.

My ankle was getting worse and worse, and while I couldn't get any consistency in training, I somehow managed to keep up my hell-bent-for-leather social schedule.

On February 11th I ran in the Auckland Championships 1500. After I led the whole way, Heather Thompson and Allison Wright passed me in the last 200 meters. I was third in 4:22. My diary says, "I have gone back to being mediocre." A week later I was second in the 800 meters in 2:08.2. My ankle was so painful, I don't know why I was still trying to run.

Several weeks later I went to the Nationals and was just pitiful, getting third in the 1500 meters in about 4:30 and 4th in the 800 meters in 2:11.7. My ankle was really bad now and I was performing so poorly I had X-rays and blood tests. Nothing showed up, but I decided to quit running altogether until I was healed up. My diary indicates my frustration: "Gave up running until foot completely cured... looks like I just need to rest it...Well, that's the Commonwealth Games down the drain. I'm really disappointed.

Once again I have to hope it's a blessing…"

I didn't want to get married in the Catholic church I'd attended, and didn't want a large wedding at all, which was fine with Steve. To keep everyone happy, we chose a little Catholic Church out in a little township called Mangere. We were married on March 18th, 1978.

I remember getting out of the car at the church and Dad actually asking me if I really knew what I was doing. Although I didn't hear about it until later, apparently a number of people who knew Steve had talked to my father. In fact, Steve's own father had called my dad to express concern. Steve later joked that his father took him aside on our wedding day to tell him it was time to get his life in order, or words to that effect.

But for better or worse, as they say, we were married.

We couldn't afford a honeymoon, but Steve's company was donating a trophy to the winner of a power boat race down in Christchurch, so one of his friends suggested that the firm send Steve down to present it. I went with him on that little junket and it was a kind of honeymoon for us. Dad came out to the airport the morning we were leaving and gave me a bit of money, snuck it into my hand surreptitiously, and wished us well.

Gordon did not come to the wedding. He still had his milk run and that was his excuse. He showed up as we were about to leave the wedding breakfast. Then he just sat on the stairs outside and behaved childishly. I should have known earlier, but it was now all too obvious that he was extremely jealous.

24 ~ Trying to Come Back

On April 9th I tried to start running again but my ankle wasn't strong enough. I began getting therapy on it daily. Then, during the school holiday I spent eight straight days in the dentist's chair, getting wisdom teeth extracted, among other things. The apartment was not heated and it was the middle of winter, and at one point I had to move a mattress out into the living area where we had a wall heater. Dreary, dreary.

I started back training with Gordon again in May. The ankle finally seemed strong enough and I needed the structure. The problem was that Gordon suddenly had come up with some dramatic changes in his training program. He decided I needed more mileage and because it was Gordon, he decided the way to do it was to run all these miles in one day. So we had some very strange, long training sessions during this time. At one point he had me run four separate one-hour runs in one day. That had to have been more than 30 miles! Thank goodness he got off that kick quickly.

Our married lifestyle continued along the same twisted path. We were still socializing quite a bit, entertaining others at our apartment or going out. I would often cook, and we'd have people over, and there was always, always, too much drinking. I was an amateur among professionals. Whether it was the training, or my metabolism, or whatever, I was way out of my league. It didn't take much to put me out of commission. Once I got violently ill on wine and liqueurs after dinner and to this day I don't touch either. That year, 1978, was the last time I ever drank wine or hard liquor at all. That's how bad it was.

Like a lot of his friends, Steve kept marijuana around and used it regularly. I tried it a few times, and all it did for me was make me ravenously hungry, which was the last thing I needed. Food was already a pretty good friend to me. Sometimes the behavior got risky. There was the dangerous driving, of course, and there were several times Steve was so drunk I stopped him just before he got into a bath of scalding hot water. Another time we had a guest over and Steve put a pie in the oven and forgot about it until it caught fire.

Then he starting staying out late on his own. When he would come in and I confronted him, we would end up in awful fights and he would get physically violent. There were times I would turn up to training in a long sleeve shirt to cover the bruises on my arms. The smell of alcohol and pot in our bedroom was sometimes overpowering. I would try to get a few hours of sleep in the living room before getting up early to head for school.

He still had his membership in the men's sauna club next door to our apartment building. I could see the parking lot from our top floor window. Many a night I would stand there and watch him drive in from work, park his car, and instead of coming upstairs to even say hello, immediately walk over to the sauna and not come home until nine o'clock or later. I remember standing at that window, the new bride, crying. I couldn't understand why anyone would want to get married, but then continue to live his life the way he always had. But the culture was still very macho then and I was just supposed to fit in.

At the time I was probably in denial, and since I had so little experience in the ways of the world, I had little to compare my life to. In retrospect it was certainly a stressful life. We had so little money that I would go to the supermarket with a calculator, adding up items as I put them in the cart so that I didn't go over the exact amount I had. Steve's mom saw me doing it and confronted him about it one day.

We were struggling to pay off the property within two years and that had put us under a great deal of pressure. I still had a key to my parents' place and I'll never forget having to stop by there and pilfer some change from my Dad's dresser for gas money to keep me going for a few more miles.

I really needed help, but didn't have anyone to turn to. It would have just worried my parents more if I had confided in them. Gordon was such a mess himself, he was no help. Every time I tried to confront Steve I always chose the wrong moment and ended up making things worse.

I finally did go talk to his parents at one point when I was really struggling. His father, Frankie, urged me to hang in there, that things would change and get better. I guess he thought Steve would outgrow it.

So, like most women who find themselves in such a situation, I put on a happy face and just muddled through.

I was still having problems with my weight, and one little incident really opened my eyes. One day I ran into Rod Dixon as he was coming out of a shop. Now this was a guy I traveled with on many international trips, a guy I'd trained with, spent months at a time with. I walked up to him and said, "Hi, Rod, how are you doing?" He just looked at me with a blank look on his face. I couldn't figure out if he was mad at me or what. Then it dawned on me that he didn't recognize me! I was so out of shape, so fat and unhealthy looking that he didn't know who I was! That was a shock.

But the ankle seemed to be strong finally, and at least I was back training. Still, I had gotten so far out of shape that it must have been sheer native ability that allowed me to beat Alison Roe in a road race on September 2nd. There was a picture of me in the newspaper from that race and I look absolutely terrible. But I not only won, I set a course record. I was surviving on sheer genetics, tenacity and memories of better times.

My diary from this period reports attacks of diarrhea, sore feet, sore back, bouts of bronchitis and the flu, and really, really inconsistent training. Gordon had taken off on his European trip through the winter months, so I was left to try to puzzle all this out on my own. On the 14th of October I started the New Zealand Road Championships but had to pull out after less than a mile. I just couldn't breathe. I had the flu again and took two more weeks off. Ten days later my diary reports that I was still sick and planned to stop training until I was well. I was consistently inconsistent. I was also getting extremely frustrated. My body, which had always responded so wonderfully to training, was no longer capable of doing what I wanted it to. At one point I write: "I'm not going to set any [goals]—It seems to be bad luck."

However miserable the year was, there was a bright spot. In November we got a Rainbow Lory, a medium-sized parrot, whom we named "Fella"—mainly because I have a tendency to call animals the first thing that comes to mind and that's what they're called forevermore. He was so funny and such good company for me in the apartment when I was there on my own. I taught him to talk and he eventually developed a good vocabulary.

In December of 1978 I finally got back on the track to race. I wasn't in the best of shape, but tried to run as if I were. My diary reads:

> "800 meters, second in 2:13.3. H. [Heather] Thompson won in 2:13.0. Led all the way and she went past at finish. Brassed off. Told her so."

I was still out there leading everybody, but then getting passed on the home straight. That wasn't very smart, but for so much of my career I hadn't needed to be smart. And now I just figured that sooner or later I would be so good that it wouldn't matter: Nobody would be able to go by me at the end.

On the 10th of December that year Mum had a mild stroke. She recovered quickly and to this day she hasn't had any further problems, but at the time we were all concerned. Dad disliked hospitals and was a natural worrier anyway, and Katie couldn't cope with the idea of Mum being sick, so there were some dark days until we knew for sure that she was all right.

Papatoetoe Central invited me back for another year, and by this time Steve had secured a good sales job with Xerox through his friend Terry Eames, and our income situation improved some.

In early 1979 I noticed that Steve had begun to enjoy running, and was doing more of it. As he got into better shape, he was able to run with me more regularly. We would get up in the morning and run from the apartment at about 5:30. That kind of regimen was exactly what I needed and it was good for him as well.

As my life became more orderly and I settled in training with Gordon again, I started to lose weight and to train more consistently. In January of 1979, I ran the best 800-meter time that I had run in three years, 2:06. Later that month I ran a 1500 meters that was won by Natalia Marasescu of Romania, with Grete Waitz second. I was third in 4:18.3.

A few days after that Marasescu set a world record in the mile of

4:22.1. I was second in 4:44, way down the track. It was a little discouraging, but then a few years later Marasescu was banned for life from the sport for taking steroids.

I didn't know it at the time, of course. The drugs hadn't affected her like they had the Russian, Tatyana Kazankina. Marasescu was really beautiful and in great shape and I dreamed of looking and running like her. But obviously she was a cheat, and she got caught. Small, but real, consolation to the girl in all black 20 yards down the track.

25 ~ World Cross Country;
Ireland, 1979

At the end of January I was back teaching, back to regular training and back to the daily fatigue. I noted in my diary on February 10th that Gordon had turned 49. At the top of that page is an underlined notation: "9 years with Gordon."

I won the Auckland Championship in the 1500 meters leading all the way in 4:14.8 with Allison Wright second. I was relieved and happy to be back running decently again.

It was pouring rain the night I was to run the 800-meter finals at the Auckland Championships. The downpour was so heavy they called off the race. But because I had been chosen for the team for the World Cross Country Championships in Limerick, Ireland, the officials wanted me to "prove fitness," so they asked me to do a 3000 meters fitness trial right then and there. I went out in the pouring rain and ankle-deep water and ran a time trial in 9:20.1, which is comparable to about a 10:00 two-mile. Although I still make reference in my diary to too much socializing and drinking, we must have been cutting back a great deal, because I was obviously running better than I had in a long, long time.

A few days later when they finally held the 800 finals, I won in 2:05.1. I was chosen for the New Zealand Championships in Christchurch and decided to run both events.

By this time I had finally regained my old strength and obviously some confidence as well. On March 2nd, in the 1500 finals, my diary notes: "Led all the way as usual" to win in 4:13.7. In the 800, I complain: "Legs tired. Stiff... Very hard." But it also notes perfunctorily: "Won in 2:07.7."

What fun it was to be back running well again!

Our team made a stop in beautiful Milan to compete in the Italian national cross-country championships on our way to Ireland. I managed a third place and we had a wonderful time exploring. Then we went by train to Paris where we spent several days, and got to meet Michel Jazy, the Frenchman who had broken the world mile record when it was held by our own Peter Snell.

Old friends Barbara Moore, Lorraine Moller and Heather Thompson were on the team, along with Mary O'Connor of Canterbury, so it was a familiar and spirited group and we made the most of it.

Coming out of our summer into the ice, snow and cold of a Paris winter was again a shock to our systems, but we were able to get to an indoor track, which really helped.

We ran a tune-up race in Paris in ankle deep mud and water so treacherous that several runners lost shoes. Lorraine pulled away from me at the end, but I wasn't particularly disappointed as I've never been much of a mud runner. As usual we kept ourselves entertained with games and pranks, getting up to mischief at every opportunity. Steve and my first wedding anniversary passed with little fanfare while I was in Paris. We never got sentimental about such occasions, and considering my schedule, it wouldn't have done much good anyway.

The world championship race in Limerick was held in a driving, freezing rain and the team finished a disappointing fifth. I was 14th overall and first on the team and felt a little let down after having been 9th in the '77 race. But it was a difficult and intimidating race that I was only too glad to have behind me. My diary captures some of it:

> Sunday, March 25th. Woke at 9:00. Had a little breakfast then went out for a short run plus strides. What a miserable day!! Very cold, raining, etc. It's now rained

for two days so the course will be muddy. Left in the bus at 1:00 and when we got to the course just one look told us it was going to be shocking. We sat huddled under a blanket in the changing rooms before going to the warm-up at 2:00. I wore socks, two sweat pants, three tops to keep warm. It rained the whole time. We had to march past at 2:45 through a ton of mud in pouring rain in our spikes... I got a good start and stayed in relatively the same position throughout. Honestly it was hopeless trying to run any faster. I passed a few girls at the end... Poor Lorraine lost her shoe.

The men's team, which had won the event in 1975 and was fifth in 1977, was bitterly disappointed to finish in 13th place, with Euan Robertson's 17th place finish the best they could muster. But cross country is like that, and arduous conditions can play havoc with expectations.

Ireland had been beautiful but miserable, raining nonstop the whole time, and we were all tired of wearing all of our clothes at the same time. It was a happy bunch of Kiwis that landed in the summer sunshine at Auckland at the end of March.

I went back to my school and found that I had again lost my class while I was away, so I was back to being a substitute.

Healthy and back on track, I was training well again. In early April, I ran in a hilly road race called the Owairaka Ten Miler, sponsored by the well-known club of the same name, which boasted such past members as Peter Snell, Murray Halberg and many other Lydiard runners of the early '60s. With about a mile to go in that race I desperately needed to make a bathroom stop and I spotted a house with the front door open, so I just ran full bore into that house, into the bathroom, used the facilities, and ran back out again without ever seeing anyone. To this day those people don't know they had a visitor! Even with the unscheduled stop, I finished 10th overall amongst the men, another indication to me that longer distances and road running might both be in my future.

In May I finished at Papatoetoe Central and decided not to go back. I wasn't getting much support from the school and I just wasn't very happy there. Instead, I got a job as a substitute at Remuera Elementary School. I had now gone from a poor school to a middle-class school and finally to a rich one, all public schools in different areas of Auckland. Interestingly enough, my most miserable time would be spent with the rich kids in Remuera. I found that dealing with the parents and the egos and the problems of those kids was more difficult than any I'd encountered in the poor or middle class areas.

I was having good moments and bad. I was still trying to stay healthy and the good news was that Steve was still into his own running. But he also tried to keep up his old lifestyle, and just couldn't understand that I needed a great deal of rest and recovery time and that if I didn't get it, sooner or later I would break down.

Gordon was becoming frustrated and even angry that I wasn't running better, and it was obvious that he was still extremely jealous of Steve. He was argumentative all the time.

Although I had lapsed into survival mode and certainly was not in shape to be going anywhere, I was chosen for the 1500 in the World Cup in Montreal in August.

When I got to Montreal, I was essentially manipulated out of the competition by one of our own coaches, Arch Jelley, who also coached Allison Wright, a reserve on the team. I certainly wasn't in the best shape, but I had been chosen for the team and had earned my right to be there by being the double national champion. I was out on the training track doing a very hard workout the week before the games, and when I came off the track Arch announced that I had to run a fitness trial against Allison to see which one of us would be in the 1500 meters!

Of course I had just finished an exhausting workout, so I refused to do it. The next day at the team meeting it was announced that I was being replaced in the 1500 meters. So here I had taken all this time off for no pay, traveled all the way to Montreal, and I was summarily replaced because one of the coaches would rather see his own athlete competing in the event I had been chosen for.

It wouldn't have been so bad if the trial had been set up fairly, but I had just finished a hard interval workout and Arch knew it. Arch has coached John Walker and many others and I have great respect for him as a coach, but he was stooping to tactics more befitting the sport's bureaucrats. I'm sure he knew better, and in fact we later patched things up. When I retired from running years later, he sent me a wonderful, moving letter, which I still have.

Nonetheless, I returned to New Zealand in August of 1979 without having run a single race at the World Cup. I wasn't happy about being sent off on such a wild goose chase.

"The thing I remember mostly was how big and rough his hands were. And how stained from the ink. . ." My dad at the Linotype, in the '60s.

Mum ruled her half of the backyard domain, the flowers. Dad was in charge of the fruit orchard.

"Katie was such a beautiful baby, with a head full of blonde curls. . ." She's on the left, with me, circa 1962.

Palm Beach on Waiheke, New
Zealand, my "South Sea Island."

From left: Katie,
Annie, Nana.

In our own little backyard world;
Katie and me, 1966.

Annie, left, Katie and
Mum, circa 1966.

Jack and Rita Bates in 1978. Scion of the Otahuhu Athletics Club, Rita got me interested in running competitively and took me to my first races.

The unforgettable Gordon Pirie, who coached me for 10 years. Shown here in his "charming mode," at age 45, 1975.

First day of high school, age 13, This was after the surgery, and both of my legs are in casts and wooden "rocker" shoes, to teach me to walk correctly.

Photo by W.A. Austin

Me, leading the 1971 Auckland
Cross-country Championships.

Photo by Tim Chamberlain

From left: Alison Roe (nee Deed),
Barbara Moore, Gordon and me,
off to the world cross-country championships, 1977.

My best friend, teammate and neighbor
Barbara Moore, left, leads in the 1980 3000-
meter New Zealand Championships. I ended
up winning in a national record.

New Zealand's Cross-country team for world championships in Morocco in 1975. From left: Alison Roe (nee Deed), Dianne Rodger (nee Zorn), Anne Audain (nee Garrettt), Manager Pam Kenny, Heather Thompson, Lorraine Moller. We were second in the world!

Diane Zorn (Rodger), Sue Quax (nee Jowett), and me relax at opening ceremonies of the 1976 Olympic Games in Montreal.

Me with world mile record holder John Walker, London, 1977.

Students at Yendarra School were my most enthusiastic supporters for the upcoming Olympic Games in Montreal in 1976.

Lisa Weidenbach and I had some real knock-down-drag-out battles on the roads, but we were always the best of friends. We finished one race in a dead sprint, giggling the whole way. This shot was taken in 1990.

I had to get used to the idea of lining up with thousands of others in the same race. What I soon realized was that I was still really just racing the same handful of top competitors I always had. This is the 1981 Cascade Run-Off (I'm above the arrow).

Post race reverie with long-time training partner and fellow professional runner, Jon Sinclair, 1990.

Dave and Jenny Kyle, 1981, our good friends and housemates from Colorado. I was so grateful they were in New Zealand for my world record.

My coach, John Davies, and I talk over a training session, Edinburgh, Scotland, 1986.

Setting the world record at 5000 meters in 15:13.22, Mt. Smart Stadium, Auckland, New Zealand, March 17, 1982.

Afterward, tearful congratulations and a hug from Mum, with Katie at right.

It begins to sink in that I've just run 5000 meters faster than any woman in history.

"If ever I had to choose one snapshot of my life, this would be it. . ."

The Commonwealth Games 3000-meter gold medal race, 8:45.4, October 4th, 1982.

Photos courtesy New Zealand Herald

Celebrating my gold medal in "the world's shortest parade," Otahuhu, New Zealand, 1982; From left, husband Steve, the mayor, a young athletics club member and me.

Thanking the crowd with long-time friend and teammate Lorraine Moller, who won a bronze medal in the same race.

"All the solitary hours of my childhood, the taunting of other children, the endless pain of my feet, the training runs in the dark and the rain, the hills that demanded your dignity before they relented, the mean struggle to earn a living while trying to be an athlete, it had all been worth it . . ."

Opposite page: The Audain running style: On her toes and out in front. Sixth victory at the Revco 10K, Cleveland, Ohio, 1990. →

Photo by Victor Sailer

The "Who's Who" of Road Running in the New York L'eggs 10K of 1988, from left: Anne Audain, Margaret Groos, Joan Nesbitt, Joan Benoit Samuelson, Susan Tooby, Lisa Martin, Mary Decker Slaney. I was only able to manage a fifth place.

A training trip to the New Zealand South Island, near Christchurch, 1987. From left: Anne, Jon Sinclair, husband Steve, Coach John Davies.

Training on the Royal Mile, Edinburgh, Scotland, 1986.

Kim Jones on the left; we met sitting on the curb after the Bloomsday race in 1981, when she had no idea she was talking to the winner of the race. She later became one of the best marathoners in America.

The Idaho Women's Fitness Celebration, 1999, saw more than 16,000 women fill the streets of Boise. ➤

Training on One Tree Hill, outside Auckland.

A man who's comfortable in his own skin: husband Chuck Whobrey, who won my heart by sending tapes of Jimmy Buffet, John Prine and Hoyt Axton.

The two families: from left: Annie, Katie, Mum, and birth parents Margaret and Johanes (Jan) Oosthoek.

26 ~ *Full Time Athlete*

In September of 1979 I resigned from teaching. Gordon had been putting a lot of pressure on me to be a full time athlete. He argued that if I wanted to make the 1980 Olympic team and really see what I could do in the sport, I had to devote everything to the effort. I thought it over and talked about it with Steve, and decided I was willing to take the chance. Steve, to his everlasting credit, was very supportive of the decision. By that stage we were beginning to get our finances in order and had enough breathing space that we felt we could manage. Still, it was going to be tight. I sold my little car for $1,400.

In hindsight, I may have been just clutching at straws. The Olympics were coming up and I probably was using the occasion to try to formulate a goal, to get some structure in my life. At any rate, in September of 1979 I became a full-time athlete, and I remained one for 13 years!

Gordon saw this as his chance to push me even harder than usual, but he still had no overall plan. He hadn't changed his methods a bit. Everything with him was based on intensity and emotion, each day's workout a test of will and body. If I had put a gun to his head at the end of a training session, I doubt he could have told me what the next day's workout would be.

In about November of 1979 Steve and I bought a little cottage on Waiheke Island at a beach called Onetangi. It was a tiny cottage, in decent shape, only a quarter of a mile from the beach, and it cost us $9,000. I was just thrilled because I had such an emotional attachment to the island from my days there with Nana, and it was a gorgeous place to train.

I started going down there often to get in some good training as well as to get away from Gordon. He was becoming more and more erratic and abusive, and he seemed to be on some new kick every other day. One day he announced that he had come to believe in biorhythms and would begin to monitor our biorhythms so he could tell us why we weren't running well.

"I don't care what your chart says, I don't want to hear about it," I told him, "You look it up and if you think I am having a bad day because of something on the chart, that's fine. Just leave me out of it."

Steve and I were still having problems. One November weekend, I was to run an 800 meters on Saturday. My diary reports:

> Fri. Ran 2 miles. 6 X 100m. 1 X 400 in 58:9. Felt good. Went to a wedding [that evening]. I left at 9:00. Steve came in at 1:30 a.m. I was really upset, tired, angry. Up all night.
> Sat. Cried all morning. Really upset. Lost a lot of nervous energy. Had a cold, too. Race was good till last 100 meters. Died terribly.

Gordon had me doing two hard workouts a day and I began to notice that whenever I raced on Saturday, it didn't matter whether I ran well or badly, the next day he would have me back out there doing double speed workouts. One December weekend I ran a tough 800-meter race on Saturday, then Sunday morning he had me do a warm-up, an exercise circuit, then 20 X 50 meters hard, then a hard mile in 5:00 minutes flat. In the afternoon I did two miles, 4 X 100 meters, then 2 X 150 hard. My training diary notes: "Beat legs. Will be tired tomorrow and sore."

That was an understatement. The next day I record: "Tried to do more 50's but legs tired. Couldn't run. Left leg really sore. Jogged 3 miles at night." Gordon's philosophy was that you just pushed yourself brutally until either your body gave in or it improved. I think mine was giving in most of the time.

On Christmas Day of 1979 we had both families, as well as

Gordon and some athletes to our apartment. Nana was there, too, and it was lovely to have everyone together like that, even though it was an extremely hot, humid day and the apartment wasn't big enough for that many people.

Steve was out in the kitchen blending all these tropical drinks that he had discovered on a trip to Fiji. He had to be careful not to hand his father one that had alcohol in it. And my mum makes the most amazing Christmas cakes that contain a half bottle of brandy, so that we had to watch which cake Frankie got as well. There was always good humor and understanding about Steve's dad's problem with alcohol and everyone was very open and supportive about it.

After New Years, I started working at a little pancake parlor that was within walking distance of the apartment. I would work from 11 a.m. to 2:30 p.m., through their busy hours, as cashier, waitress, even cook. It brought in a little extra money for groceries and got me out of the apartment in the middle of the day. I could still train twice a day but at least feel like I was contributing.

The Olympic qualifying times came out and once again the New Zealand qualifying times were much harder: 4:07 in the 1500, and 2:01 in the 800. I had never run anywhere near that fast in either event. My national record in the 1500 was 4:10.68 and my best 800 was 2:04.4.

The great American middle distance runner, Mary Decker, was going with Dick Quax at the time and had come down to New Zealand to train during our summer (her winter). On January 26, 1980, she ran a world mile record of 4:21.5 and I finished a very sad and distant fourth. Her time was roughly equivalent to a 4:02 1500 meters. Once again, I had been in the vicinity of true excellence and had found myself wanting. I wrote in my diary: "Too fat!!"

But somehow by the time the Auckland Championships came around in February I had myself back down to a decent weight and was in much better shape. I ran 4:15.7 in the 1500 heats and 4:15.1 in the final, leading all the way.

In training one day I ran a 400 meters in 56.4, the fastest I had ever run. Then in the Auckland 800-meter finals I ran 2:04.1, my fastest ever and under the IOC standard. A few weeks later at the national meet I won the 1500 meters in 4:11.3, the fastest ever run by a New Zealander in the country. In the 800-meter finals I finished third in 2:05.9.

The full-time approach to training was paying off; I was able to rest and recover much better. All through the early months of 1980 I would go out and run solo 1500 efforts, trying to meet the New Zealand Olympic-qualifying standard, but coming up short. I met the actual Olympic standards over and over, but not my own country's. It was getting to be frustrating.

I was planning to run another 1500 meters on March 21st. Several days beforehand, however, I read in the newspaper that Arch Jelley was going to have his athletes run in a 3000-meter race at the same meet to try to make a team that would compete in Holland later in the summer. It looked as if the 3000 for women might be added to the Olympic schedule in 1984.

This event in Holland was called the Inaugural World Championship for 3000 meters, and the qualifying time to make the event was 9:07.

This article said Barbara Moore, Christine Pfitzinger, Lindon Wilde and some of Arch's other runners were going to go for the qualifying time. So we made some calls and found out all the details and decided that instead of running the 1500 meters I would get in the 3000-meter race and see if I could qualify for the trip. I had always liked longer events anyway, and in the back of my mind I was thinking that I rather owed Arch a favor anyway. Gordon, never one to miss a chance for sweet revenge, encouraged me to do it.

We kept the change a secret, so when we were all warming up together, Arch's girls were wishing me luck in the 1500. I just smiled and said, "Thanks, you too."

Then when I lined up on the starting line for the 3000 meters, everyone got all upset, saying, hey, you can't do this! I said, sure I can.

It was interesting that Lorraine Moller had also heard about this 3000-meter race, and had called Arch up to ask about it. He told her the wrong starting time and she arrived almost too late to run. That's one way to defeat an opponent, I suppose. Unfortunately for them, I wasn't in the least bit tardy. I was warmed up and standing on the starting line.

The other girls had a pacing plan already set up, so I was content to follow along until the last 600 meters when I struck out on my own. I led the rest of the way to finish in 8:59.0, a new national record, breaking Heather Thompson's old mark by 8.4 seconds. It's wonderful being a runner when everything is going well. My diary says it all: "Ran to win. Just followed. Easy!!"

Obviously my time was well under the qualifying time for the Holland trip, and I was the one selected, which didn't make me very popular.

By this time squabbles with officialdom were commonplace. On March 28th I tried to run another 1500-meter qualifying time, and had four independent watches on me, each reading 4:10.6, which would have been a new national record. The only official there, however, had me timed in 4:11.1, so that was recorded as the official time. That was the kind of thing I was up against much of the time. I had the fastest times in the country over the 800, 1500 and 3000 meters and was nominated by my sport's federation for the Olympic team, but of course wasn't selected.

Politics on a much larger scale soon made it all moot anyway. U.S. President Jimmy Carter, unable to think of any other way to punish the Soviets for invading Afghanistan, announced a boycott of the 1980 Olympics in Moscow. My Olympic dreams had been dashed anyway.

27 ~ Kidnapped!

In April Gordon left for Europe and was soon putting a great deal of pressure on me to join him there. I had a strange feeling about going; I didn't want to do it.

Steve thought I should go. He thought I wanted to and was trying to be supportive about it, but in my heart I knew I didn't want to do it. I was so tired and mentally beaten up and my desire to run had pretty much evaporated after the Olympic fiasco. And I just didn't want to be around Gordon that much. His behavior had become so erratic and difficult to deal with that I almost couldn't bear being around him.

But he persisted and Steve kept saying, well you gave up your job and this is your opportunity, you should go and try it. I was going to have to go eventually to run the 3000-meter race in Holland anyway, so I finally relented. On the 16th of June I left for Oslo, where Gordon was living with a friend, Rob Davies, in a little hut out in a forest outside the port town of Dramen. They both had jobs on the wharves, driving imported Japanese cars off the boats. This was typical of Gordon, whose lifestyle was forever like that of a college student on summer break.

When I arrived at the hut Gordon asked for my passport. I asked why.

"I'm going to take it and hide it somewhere it will be safe," he said.

I thought it curious, but no more so than much of his behavior, so I gave it to him. Gordon and Rob had the loan of a van and would drive in to town each day to work at the wharves. I would stay behind at the hut. It was a rustic kind of living, no running water, no indoor plumbing. We had to hand wash clothes, and used an outhouse. It was primitive, but our little cottage on Waiheke wasn't much better, so it was no great shock to my tender sensibilities to live that way.

Gordon had immediately decided that I was too fat, so he began watching how much I ate. Then he decided that it was a fluid problem so my intake of liquids was restricted. He became more and more inconsistent in what he was telling me to do, more and more abusive, with constant yelling and screaming. On training runs he would pull his old trick of taking me out into the forests to get me lost if I couldn't keep up.

His Jekyll-Hyde personality was in full flower. We'd go into town and see people connected with the local running scene and he was as pleasant as could be. He was always lining up a free meal, the loan of a vehicle, whatever. But when we'd get back to the hut he'd be right back to his usual abusive self.

I was so miserable anyway, so homesick and lonely, it would have been tough under any circumstances. But to have to put up with Gordon's abuse on top of everything else just made it a terrible situation.

On one sad day in July we went down to Bislet Stadium to watch the Bislet games. It had been four years since I had run in the same meet and had competed well, and now here I was sitting in the stands, watching, a spectator who lived in a hut in the woods.

To have to sit there and watch everyone else perform was excruciating, particularly knowing I was in such bad shape. But Steve Ovett broke the world record for 1500 meters and it was amazing to sit in the stands and watch that. The experience of being in that famous stadium for a great track meet was always moving, but it was tinged with nostalgia and sadness for me because I felt so far removed from something I loved so much, from my own sport.

There was no phone in the hut, of course, so during the day I would run through the forest to a nearby house owned by some local running club friends. I would use their phone to try to call back to

New Zealand. I had to do all the housework, the cooking and the cleaning in the hut, doing everybody's laundry by hand, but I often got the use of the car to go down and run errands for them, so I was able to get away occasionally.

I raced over 3000 meters in a local event and ran 9:32. Things were going from bad to worse with my running. There was no consistency from Gordon. I didn't know from day to day what he was going to come up with next. At one point he decided that I needed to essentially starve for three days! The threat of verbal and even physical abuse was ever present. One time he threw me in a sauna all day to make me lose weight, a ludicrous idea for someone who was supposed to understand physiology.

I finally got through to Steve on the phone on August 6th, and just broke down crying, telling him how bad things were. Of course he could do nothing, so it just worried him, but I was so beaten down, I had no emotional reserves.

At one point Gordon decided that I needed to contribute more to the household income, so he had me go down to the wharf to apply for the same work they were doing. Women didn't do that work, so I had to dress up like a man, with my hair tucked up under my cap and baggy clothes and so forth. So for several days, I was going down into the holds of those container ships, breathing all those fumes, driving cars off the ships. And keeping my head down and keeping quiet so no one would know I was a woman. I had been going so stir-crazy at the hut that I told myself that it was kind of fun. That's the kind of thing I did to survive.

But I had already decided that I would endure the situation as best I could, then get back to New Zealand and that would be the last I would have to do with Gordon Pirie.

In early August we went to Holland for the 3000-meter event. At this stage I was an absolute wreck. I literally hated the man and I didn't want to have anything to do with him. When we checked into the sports center where everyone was staying, I asked for my own room. Naturally Gordon didn't like that. He wanted me under his thumb 24 hours a day.

When I finally got to my room, I locked the door behind me and just shut down emotionally. I refused to talk to him, wouldn't open the door for him, wouldn't answer him when he called to me. I didn't want to have anything to do with him. When I did go out, I made sure there were other people around. He started to get angry with me, asking what the matter was, why was I acting that way. At that stage I had nothing left to say to him. My intention was to get through the next few days, run the event and just get the hell out of there.

In the race I finished second to last in my heat. Suffering from severe diarrhea, I raced off the track and into the bathroom. Unfortunately it was the men's bathroom, so there I was trying to clean myself up and all these guys start walking in.

That had to be the lowest point of my entire running career, standing there in a men's bathroom in a foreign country, a complete captive of this madman who had dominated my life for more than a decade, a domination that had led to the point where I was just a physical, emotional, and literal mess.

We went to Amsterdam and I had to share a hotel room with Gordon just to have a place to stay because I had no money left. I was barely speaking to him. He took me to the airport and as I was about to board the plane, he said good-bye. I said, "Good-bye, Gordon."

He said, "I'll see you back in New Zealand."

I never spoke to him again.

28 ~ *Starting All Over*

When I got back to New Zealand I went straight down to our little cottage on Waiheke to try to pull myself together. I walked a lot, totally quit running, and was very, very depressed.

I now believe I was been on the verge of a nervous breakdown. I had no desire to run and was exhausted, nervous, and shaking uncontrollably. I didn't need a doctor to tell me I was in a bad way.

The trip to Europe had cost a lot of money and our finances were strained again. Then the dentist told me I needed more work done. We actually took a lot of our belongings to a flea market and sold them. Steve's mother sewed and repaired our clothes for us, and at one point his father took my last good pair of dress shoes and re-nailed the heels so I could continue to wear them.

I went to Lloyd Drake to see if I needed to have any tests done to find out what was wrong with me. He just shook his head.

"Anne, everything that is wrong with you and everything that has ever been wrong with you is the stress that you've been under with Gordon," he said. "All these years I've watched the situation getting worse and worse and worse. All of that's over now."

Steve saw that I was at rock bottom, that I had given up on everything. He proposed that we leave New Zealand and go to England.

He had spent three years there in his early twenties and liked it. He thought the change would do us both good.

I would have gone anywhere. I was so distracted I didn't have a clear thought in my head. England didn't sound like such a bad idea at all. I had always loved London and I thought, well, if he got a job there, I'd get work waitressing and maybe join a running club. It sounded like some kind of plan, and getting away from New Zealand seemed very appealing to me right then.

So we moved out of our apartment, which we decided to rent furnished, and put it in the hands of a real estate agent. We had refurbished a lot of nice antiques that Steve had managed to find on his sales trips around the country, so the place was actually furnished nicely by this time.

At that time we thought we'd be gone for a few years, so we moved some of our clothing to his parents' house and lived in the little cottage on the island on the weekends and came up to the city during the week. Steve continued at Xerox and I did substitute teaching.

Gordon came back from Europe and, when I wouldn't meet with him, essentially began stalking me. He would find out where I was substitute teaching and would sit outside the school and wait for me to come out, then try to talk to me. He would leave phone calls at the schools, at Steve's parents; he would write letters and leave them in the letterbox at their house.

One day Steve and I were running together at the Auckland Domain and Gordon began driving alongside of us in his car, yelling out the window at me. Finally, Steve had had enough. He went over and told him in graphic detail what he was going to do if he didn't leave me alone. Steve's a solid guy physically and for all his bluster Gordon was a real wimp when it came to any kind of confrontation.

This went on for a couple of months after his return, then Gordon finally got the message that I wasn't going to have anything to do with him again.

I did finally start running again, but I really was rudderless. At one point I was trying to run three times a day. I don't know where my head was, but that's the kind of madness I was up to.

We went to Australia in September, to Sydney, a place I dearly love. Steve had brought some Dale Carnegie tapes with him, and I remember at one point Carnegie said something to the effect that if you had a God-given talent, it was your responsibility to work as hard

as you could to develop that gift. As much as I've never been one for
self-improvement schemes or inspirational lectures, that one thought
stuck with me. I went out to run around Centennial Park and was
thinking about that tape. Before I knew it, I was really flying, just
floating along in that beautiful park with the sun shining on me, feeling so totally free and alive. I thought, I've got to try to continue running. It's what I love to do, it's my talent and my passion and I have a
duty to do it as well as I possibly can.

I came back from Australia rejuvenated. I knew I still wanted to
run, but I didn't have a clue as to how I should go about it on my
own. It was Steve who came up with the idea of talking to John
Davies. John was one of those well-known Arthur Lydiard runners of
the '60s, an Olympic bronze medalist and Commonwealth Games silver medalist. He coached Lorraine and a small group at the Domain
when we were there. He had always been very cordial and friendly.

Steve said, "You know, John has always been really nice to you
and has always complimented you when you've run well. Maybe you
should have a talk with him."

It was true. John would say "Great run, Annie. You did great yes-
terday." He had a most pleasant nature, not at all competitive or
aggressive. In fact, he and Gordon were total opposites in that
regard. That was exactly what I needed.

So I thought about it and finally called him. I asked him to consider coaching me. Of course, he knew exactly what he was up
against. Not only was I in bad shape, but Gordon was still lurking
around in the background. He knew what he was getting into, and
didn't call back for quite a while.

Steve's mom said, "You know Annie, any good coach ought to
welcome the challenge of trying to revive your career." Which was
kind of a backhanded compliment, but she was right. When John
finally called back, he said that was what appealed to him, the challenge of bringing me back. So in mid-October John and I went for a
run at Cornwall Park. He asked me what I really wanted to accomplish, and I said I just wanted to get better.

At that time, Dick Quax, Rod Dixon and Lorraine Moller had all
run on the roads in the United States that year and had done very
well. Lorraine had won the first Avon women's marathon, and both
Rod and Dick had won races. So some of the runners were starting to
talk about road racing and the possibility of actually make money at
it. It sounded exciting.

I told him Steve and I were leaving for England, but maybe we could go to the States first and run some road races. John said, well, don't get sucked into the idea that there's going to be a lot of money in it. I said, no, I just want to see if I can improve, I want to see how good I can be.

Which was big talk if you could have seen me that day. I had turned up for the run wearing Steve's big football shorts and a baggy jersey because I was so embarrassed about the state I was in. I didn't even *look* like a runner.

John told me that he used to watch me training at the Domain and he couldn't believe what Gordon was having me do. He said he knew I had so much ability and always wondered what it would be like to coach me and see what I could really accomplish.

So now, here I was, presenting myself to him at my lowest point, athletically.

"Well, it's not going to be easy," he said. "And you'd better get used to the idea: I'm going to have to take you completely apart and put you back together again."

And that's exactly what he did. He turned my whole training program upside down and inside out. As a follower of Arthur Lydiard, he believed in philosophy of developing a "base" of many miles of long, strength-building runs before doing anything hard. He believed in taking your time, training consistently, and building strength and speed gradually. It was all very positive and encouraging, and I was excited to get started on the program right away.

The first order of business was to begin building an endurance base, so I went down to Waiheke and started doing long runs, training twice a day, building up to 70 or 80 miles a week, something I'd never done before. Training on Waiheke was wonderful, I could sense that it was making me very strong. And I loved being there anyway, so it was a wonderful time. After a few weeks, Steve left his job with Xerox in preparation for the trip to England, so he stayed on the island and we only ventured back to Auckland every now and again.

It was getting to be summer and after I had done some base work I came back up to Auckland to train with John. We went to the grass track at Auckland Grammar school, and John said, "Okay, now you're going to learn how to do the next phase, repetitions." So we started doing an interval workout. Unfortunately the track was rough, with a lot of holes, and sure enough, on my first workout with John, I sprained my ankle badly.

So it was back to the drawing board. I had done so well building the base mileage and now here I was with an injury. I went back to Waiheke, where I swam and walked, and we spent time working on the cottage, trying to make it more livable. I spent the rest of 1980 just trying to heal that ankle.

One might think that I would have been discouraged, but quite honestly, I had been through so much in the previous five years with Gordon that something like that didn't particularly get me down. In fact, considering that I'd been right up to the edge of my sanity, the fact that I survived left me so mentally tough that no challenge I ever faced again would seem so daunting to me.

&

My ankle didn't seem to be healing fast enough on its own so I finally admitted that I needed some help and made a trip back up to Auckland to get some physical therapy. When it got better, John took me on a 45-minute drive up to Woodhill Forest, a place where I had trained with Gordon many times.

It's a beautiful place, right on the ocean with pine forests and lots of dirt roads and pine needle trails to run on. There was a well-known story about the place. It happened when I was very young and training there with Gordon and some other girls. We were running along and came around a bend and ran head on into Walker, Quax and some others all running along in their underwear! It was such a hot day and it was so isolated they never thought they'd see anyone out there.

So John parked the car by the gate and told me we were going to run for an hour and a half, something I had never done before.

"It's a circular loop," he said, "So you're going to have to make up your mind to do the whole way round. There's no shortcut back."

The finish was a mile and a half up a steep hill. I was fine all the way around until we got to the bottom of that hill. John said that I had to run all the way to the top as he wasn't going to let me stop nor could he bring the car to me. We ran up with him holding his hand on the middle of my back pushing me so that I wouldn't stop.

So I was finally learning to do the kind of base work that John wanted me to do, the long slow miles of early strength training that Lydiard had developed and which had been used so effectively by Snell, Halberg and so many other famous Kiwi runners of that earlier era.

My weekly mileage count was much higher than it had ever been before. I was doing two workouts a day and was gradually getting stronger, while continuing therapy on my ankle. I went back down to Waiheke and continued to pile on the miles.

In mid-January I overheard Dick Quax talking to John Davies about running road races in the United States. Dick was still dating Mary Decker and was spending a lot of time in the States, working with Nike's elite runner program, Athletics West, in Eugene, Oregon. He told me about newly emerging road-racing circuit and how Rod Dixon, Alison Roe and Lorraine Moller had been winning races there. He thought there might be an opportunity to win some prize money or at least some running gear. It was all very exciting, not only the possibility of winning prize money, but also the idea women could run longer races on the roads than we ever had the opportunity to run on the track: 5000 meters, 10,000 meters, even marathons.

I wore the same sizes as Mary Decker, so when she left at summer's end to go back to the States that year, she left me a lot of her Nike, clothing and shoes. Nike was making special shoes for her at the time and they worked perfectly for me. I was grateful to her because it had been a long while since I'd visited the Adidas factory and most of my gear was getting fairly worn.

We had placed the apartment with a real estate agency with strict instructions: no children and no pets. We had taken out renters insurance expressly to protect our investment in the furnishings. We heard that the apartment had been rented, and assumed everything was fine. Then one day while we were down on the island we got a call from the real estate company to tell us that we had been robbed and our tenants had absconded.

This apartment was on the top floor with one small old French-style elevator and the thieves had managed to get everything out under the noses of all the other residents without anyone asking any questions. Steve's brother had actually welded our old bedstead together, so they would have had to break it down into pieces to get it out. They even took the houseplants.

Some neighbors even told the police that they had watched them load it all onto a truck in the parking lot. Still they didn't think to call anyone just to check. The only piece left behind was an antique coffee table made from an old butcher's "pig table" from England. It had been cut down into a coffee table, and because it looked like an old piece of wood they must not have known how valuable it was.

The neighbors thought we were putting things in storage in preparation for leaving New Zealand. Some days after the crime, the real estate agent had gone to check on the place and found it empty, the walls covered with food and excrement, and the tenants gone. It was a terrible experience and we learned later that our tenants were possibly drug dealers who had fled to Australia.

It was heartbreaking because we had put so much effort and money into getting the place fixed up. Now we had to go through the whole process of cleaning up and re-renting it, this time unfurnished, of course, and through a different agent.

But the really tough part was when the insurance adjuster suggested in his report that we might have sold everything to finance our trip, because none of it was ever found. On that basis, the insurance company refused to pay.

The timing couldn't have been worse. We were due to leave soon and obviously had no time to fight the insurance company. So we decided to cut our losses and just leave. But being treated like that stuck in my craw, and I vowed they hadn't seen the end of me.

My training with John was still going well. I was starting to feel much stronger, with much better endurance and greater consistency in my workouts. I was still carrying too much weight, but I was content to let it come off naturally from all the miles I was running. I wasn't trying to diet and John never pushed me in that direction.

In early February I ran a mile time trial in 4:49, the equivalent of a 4:30 for 1500 meters. I was stunned to learn I could run that fast in the midst of all that long training, with no special preparation. My diary says: "Felt great! Couldn't believe it!" I had run 75 miles the week before, and 72 miles the week before that. I had done almost none of the kind of speed work that Gordon preached was so essential and I hadn't taken any kind of rest break to get ready for the test. Yet I found I could easily go out alone and run a national-class performance just based on all the strength training I had been doing.

A few days later I was at the Trenthem Horse Track in Wellington for the trials for the World Country Championships to be held later in Madrid. I had to finish in the top six to make the team, and the competition was fierce. It had been a long time since I had raced, and I really struggled, barely slipping into sixth place a second ahead of the seventh runner. I hoped my past record would help in the selections, but I was nervous waiting for the announcements. I over-heard some people calling me "fat" and saying I shouldn't be on the team. But I knew with the progress that I had made so quickly that in a few more weeks I would really be rounding in to shape.

It was not a popular choice, but the selectors chose me and I was a happy young woman! At the function that evening when the team was announced I felt the eyes on me. I had tears in my eyes because I knew how far I had come in such a short time. And I was so over-joyed to be starting all over again!

After laying a base of the longer, slower runs, Lydiard followers like John believe in moving on to the much faster training of interval sessions, "tempo" runs, and time trials. He also believes in discipline and consistency, and he likes a training program to be carefully planned, which is just what I needed. After the chaos of Gordon's ad hoc approach, I thrived on John's structure and stability. It was great to know ahead of time what my workout would be so that I could get mentally prepared for a hard session. It allowed me to focus on my training and at the same time to plan my non-running life as well. John's quiet nature was so welcome after years of being yelled at and abused.

From the moment I made that cross-country team, I knew John and I would be a great team. At long last, I had a true partner in pur-suing my goals as a runner.

&

I was now consistently up to over 70 miles a week and improving very quickly. In early March Steve left for London. Our plan was that he would go back to work for the company he had worked for years earlier, and I would leave later for Madrid for the world cross-country meet, then head to England myself. We had no idea when we would be back to New Zealand so it was tough saying good-byes at the air-port.

On that trip I was teased unmercifully by some of my teammates because of my weight. Even the manager of the team was obnoxious to me. He never missed a chance to insinuate that I didn't belong on the trip. At this point, such harassment had little effect on me. I'd been through a lot worse. All I cared about was running. It had become a protective barrier, a brick wall against a lot of things that might otherwise have hurt me. I would later forgive my tormentors, but I wouldn't forget. And in athletics, there are often opportunities for a comeuppance or two.

Rod Dixon was on the team and he stayed in a hotel far away from our hostel on the outskirts of Madrid. This was when I first became aware of how much the sport was changing. Rod had always been a great ragtag team member roughing it with the rest of us, but now he had the money and the status to live better, so he did. I didn't blame him a bit. But I could sense a definite lack of the kind of team spirit we'd had in years past, an absence of the fun and camaraderie that had made those early adventures so much fun. Lorraine Moller was on the team, along with Dianne Rodger and Barbara Moore, so some of the old crowd was around. We had always enjoyed training together and we got along fine.

Then one evening the team manager got drunk and broke into my room. He was too drunk to be a threat but not drunk enough to be entertaining, and it was not a pleasant experience. However, my "brick wall" was up and it didn't bother me.

My running was improving almost day by day. And though the stress and fatigue of travel were as hard as ever, it was so old hat by then that we were well accustomed to it. That would stand us in good stead later on when we traveled and raced for a living on the American road circuit.

In the world cross-country championships, Dianne Rodger pulled out ahead and ran with the leaders, while Lorraine, Mary O'Connor and I stayed close together for the whole race, finishing almost in a dead heat with each other. Dianne was 11th overall and the three of us finished in the mid-20's, giving the team a fourth place finish. And while I still wasn't back to the very top of my game, I was more than gratified to have come up with a complete and unequivocal answer to those who said I didn't belong on the team. Only the four top women on each team count in the scoring, and I was one of them. The race had been won for the fourth year in a row by the incomparable Grete Waitz, and I was again in awe of her, of just being in the presence of such excellence. I was still dreaming of attaining it myself, but though I was healthy, strong and confident for the first time in years, it seemed a distant goal indeed.

29 ~ *American Road Trip*

I went to London and joined Steve for a few days. We discussed my going to the United States and running road races for three months. Dick Quax had talked the race directors of the New Orleans Crescent City Classic 10K into extending me an invitation for the race in early April. And an excellent example of the persuasive arts that was, too, as I had never really competed in a 10K and had no competitive time to offer. Unbeknownst to me, Dick told them I had run 34 minutes for the distance and they snapped me right up!

We managed to get tickets on Laker Airlines, a discount outfit operating out of London at that time. We flew from London to Miami for $400 each, or $800 in New Zealand dollars—which seemed like a relatively heavy investment in my road running ability. We stayed in a hotel close to the airport and just slept for a day. The next day we flew to New Orleans, which cost $300 each. We were really eating into our savings.

We must have been a sight, arriving at the airport in New Orleans with one suitcase and a big old backpack. We were met there by Mac DeVaughn who was one of the race directors then and still is today. He was very warm and welcoming and brought us to the New Orleans Hilton and installed us in this beautiful suite up on one of the top floors. I took one look around at the wonderful view and the accommodations and turned to Steve and said, "Gosh, I wonder who they think I am?"

They truly made us feel welcome. I soon found out about my alleged 34 minute 10K performance, and since that was a relatively good time for women back then, I began to understand. I had some kind of fantasy reputation to live up to.

They took us down to the running store owned by Mac and George Owen, where we met the American Olympian, Jeff Galloway, who was starting a chain of franchised running stores called "Phidippides," after the original Greek marathon runner. We were joined by Canadian star Jackie Gareau and all went out for a run. They presented us with lots of gear from the store and I was beginning to be overwhelmed by it all.

It was so exciting, a whole new world where runners were honored and treated royally! Just trying to absorb it all was a challenge. I attended the clinic the night before the race and met Patti Catalano and Joan Benoit, who were among the best American road runners at the time. Then I witnessed all the hype surrounding the press conference and I knew for certain that this was a whole new world.

On the day of the race I went to the starting line at Jackson Square and saw the most people I had ever seen on a starting line of a race ever, 8000 people. Seeing all those people filling the street for as far as the eye could see, it seemed inconceivable to me that I should be entitled to start on the very first row.

The gun went off and I was so anxious about being in the front that I was probably not concentrating and I suddenly found myself down on the ground along with some other unlucky souls, being trod on by the galloping hordes as they raced right across our backs. It all happened very quickly and I was shaken up. I lost my watch and necklace, and had my skinned knees and elbows. Fortunately, some Good Samaritan grabbed me by my left arm and hauled me up and over the others and got me on both feet and moving forward.

I often think about the choices we can make in such circumstances. I was so mad to have started off so miserably I considered my options: I could have easily chosen to step off to the side of the road and called it a day, or I could pull myself together start running down the people who had just run over me.

So I just ran as hard as I could, passing other women and having no idea how fast I was running or where I was in the race. I had no frame of reference at all.

After 6.2 miles of racing along blindly, I finished third in 33:18, behind Patti Catalano, who ran a new U.S. record, and Joan Benoit. I must have lost at least 30 seconds in the fall, so I could have easily been under 33 minutes in that first road race. But of course the important thing was that I had broken my fantasy PR by quite a lot! I still have my trophy from that race, a beautiful glass statue of a runner.

TV commentator Toni Reavis says he has a taped interview of me that day, standing there with bloody knees and elbows, obviously flushed with excitement, saying, "You know, I could really get to like this road racing."

After all the post-race hoopla and celebration had died down, the question became, well, where do we go from here? Jeff and Barbara Galloway were going to catch a train back to Atlanta and offered to put us up there if we wanted to come stay with them. We had dinner with them and Jeff was a fountain of knowledge about the road-racing scene. He also knew Creigh Kelley, who owned one of Jeff's franchise stores in Denver and was starting an agency to represent runners. Jeff started to educate us about all the things happening in the sport. On the train trip, Jeff told us who we needed to know and what we needed to do. It was just the kind of education we needed, because we were totally naïve about everything.

Jeff told us there was a powerful group of people who wanted the sport to go professional. It couldn't happen soon enough for me. With the exchange rate at 2:1 New Zealand to U.S., we were going through our reserves very quickly just on everyday living expenses.

When we got to Atlanta, Jeff called Creigh and introduced me over the phone. He was just starting his agency business, and had already signed Jon Sinclair, a successful American road runner. Creigh asked if I was interested.

It sounded great to me but of course it was still an amateur sport, so the rules were going to have to change at some point if all these wonderful dreams were to come true. I will always be very grateful to Jeff and Barbara for their kindness and generosity in those early days, initiating me so quickly into to the American running scene.

On the 18th of April we headed to Eugene, Oregon to stay with Dick Quax, who was still training there and operating Athletics West for Nike. He was now living with Sue Jowett, the sprinter who had been my roommate in 1976 Olympics in Montreal. I had just finished my biggest training week ever, 93 miles, and continued getting stronger and losing weight. Dick would drive up to Beaverton to the Nike headquarters and bring back loads of Nike gear, which the company was only too happy to have competitive runners wearing. I was beginning to feel really spoiled. We runners were so used to being the paupers of sport, just scraping and begging our way along. Now that the "running boom" was starting in the United States and there suddenly there was money in the sport, the top runners were now being courted and treated royally. I have to say, it didn't take long to become totally accustomed to the idea.

While we were training in Eugene, we got word that our own Alison Roe had won the Boston Marathon, beating Patti Catalano and running 2:26, a first-rate time.

That was quite a shock to me because, despite her obvious talent, Alison had always been a relatively lazy athlete. Now she had a new coach, Gary Elliot, who was spending all his time with her to make sure she trained. He even ran beside her or just ahead of her in her races, which you could see on the race videos.

I couldn't help remembering all the grief Gordon inflicted on us because of her, and it took all my self-control to congratulate her.

Dick kept me up to date on what races were going on so that I could start getting some more road experience. One was a women's-only 10K in Eugene that had as a first place prize a trip to the L'eggs Mini-marathon in New York. So I entered the Eugene race and easily won in 34:24.

We stayed in Eugene for about five weeks and trained with the Athletics West runners, which helped my running a great deal. Being settled for a while was helpful, too, after all travel we'd been doing. Another event Dick persuaded me to enter was Bloomsday 12K in Spokane. He said the more visible I could make myself on the road scene, the more interest Nike would take in me. He called up Don Kardong, an Olympic marathoner who founded and directed Bloomsday, and asked if I could get into the race. Don said as long as I got myself there and ran well they would reimburse some expenses.

So we caught a train to Spokane and got checked in at race headquarters, then went for a van ride around the course. As we were riding around, the runners were talking about how bad the hills were. I leaned over and whispered to Steve, "Gosh, if they think these are hills, they ought to come down to New Zealand!"

That gave me a lot of confidence and I got excited about my

chances. The favorite in the race was Cathie Twomey, a Nike-sponsored runner coached by Peter Thompson. Bloomsday had 12,000 entrants back then, so it was a huge starting line with more people than I had ever seen at a race. I was still a little nervous after my experience at Crescent City, but then I discovered that they started the elite women on a separate street from the rest of the race so everything was spread out by the time we merged with them at the two-mile mark. Wonderful!

I just trailed Cathy. Her coach had been given permission to ride a bike with a flag on it to alert the TV people where the top woman was, so it was very easy for competitors—me!—to keep track of her as well.

Everyone was convinced she was going to win. Watching her coach riding along beside her giving her encouragement the whole way was only feeding my fire. I have always looked askance at these arrangements where a female athlete is paced by a male coach, husband or boyfriend. It's not fair and it's lousy sportsmanship.

I just ran side by side with her for most of the race, and when we finally came to the so-called "Doomsday Hill," I found it fairly easy to just pull away from her. At this point Peter, her coach, was in a quandary, as he was duty-bound to go with the lead woman. But what he really wanted to do was to stay back and try to motivate Cathy to catch me. I found it very amusing making him come along and keep me company.

When I got to the top of the hill I kept pushing hard and won by about 10 seconds. My prize was a medal, as there was no prize money yet. I ran 41:54, which turned out to be the slowest I ever ran on that course. At the awards ceremony people were shocked when I went up to get the first place prize, at least according to Jon Sinclair, who was in the crowd. By that time I had showered and changed, so I was dressed in street clothes, had on makeup and was still carrying a few extra pounds and no one could believe I was the winner. In fact I overheard Cathy say, "I got beaten by her?" Jon said, "Here you were with all these other women runners and you looked like a China doll."

Something else amusing happened right after that race. Steve was running the race, too, so after I finished I sat down on the curb to wait for him. I hardly knew anyone there, so I was just sitting by myself. Steve had hooked up this fellow and his wife in the race. She was a pretty blonde named Kim and I started chatting with her. She told me she was very pleased to finish in 56 minutes, as she hadn't trained at all. It turned out she had been a track runner years before in high school in the 400 and 800 meters but had quit the sport in college. She told me what her times had been and I told her that I had run similar times in school, and considering her performance that day, I thought she could be pretty good if she trained.

She said she wanted to, but had a baby and it would be a struggle. She had no idea who I was and after going on for a while about how pleased she was with her race, out of politeness she finally asked me how I had done. I said, "Oh, I won."

She looked stricken. "I've never been so *embarrassed*," she said. But later she would say that it was at that moment she decided to start training seriously again.

That woman turned out to be Kim Jones, who soon became one of America's best and most consistent marathoners and road racers during much of the '80s and '90s. In fact, she *won* the Bloomsday race in 1997! She's a good friend to this day, and never tires of telling this story.

30 ~ Blossoming in Colorado

We went back to Eugene and stayed a few more weeks and then headed to Denver, where Creigh had found a British couple, Jenny and Dave Kyle, to put us up until we found a place. Creigh wanted us close by to facilitate working together.

Creigh had entered me in the Bolder Boulder 10K that weekend and of course I had no idea what running at altitude was all about, so I blithely hopped in the race and just about died trying to race in the thin air. I finished third in 36:20, which I thought was terrible until I heard everyone going on and on about what a good performance it was. But I was disgusted because I thought something was wrong with me. Ellen Hart won the race. She is now Ellen Hart-Peña, wife of former Denver mayor and former secretary of the U.S. Department of Transportation.

I still needed to lose some weight but it was coming off quite naturally with the training, and without dieting. After staying in Denver a couple of weeks I was getting used to altitude and getting to know some of the people involved with running around the Denver-Boulder area, all of whom were extremely supportive and generous.

I flew to New York with Jenny Kyle for the L'eggs race, which was run around Central Park. It took all day to get there, and visiting

New York for the first time was quite a cultural shock. I attended the press conference at the race headquarters, where all the current stars of the running world were asked about the race. Patti Catalano certainly didn't lack confidence and both she and her husband-coach, Joe, were occasionally very loud and obnoxious. You would have thought she was the only woman in the race.

I guess I got caught up in all the hype and hoopla surrounding the race, and when the gun went off I went out with the leaders.

It wasn't a good idea.

I took off with everyone else and blew myself up in the first mile. At mile three I was really struggling, so I started to walk. Then I thought I could take a shortcut to the hotel if I cut across the park. Of course by now I was totally disorientated and started to ask people for directions. New Yorkers are a wary lot and no one was of much help, so I climbed over a rock wall and found myself in Harlem, in the opposite direction from where I should have been going. I had grazed myself from the wall and was really tired and upset and I finally remembered what street my hotel was on. I eventually got the right directions and ran back to the hotel. After all that I would have been better off just finishing the race.

I was probably just tired from all the recent racing, as well as adapting to altitude, but after my early successes on the roads, this race left me angry and disappointed. It did get me fired up, however, and at that moment I swore that I would never come back until I thought I could win the race.

To salvage something from the trip, Jenny and I went out and had a wonderful time sightseeing. New York is amazing the first time you see it.

I went back to Denver and started training hard again, but it's so flat there, after a while I started worrying about losing the strength I got from running hills. Jenny and Dave suggested we go run Lookout Mountain, about 20 miles away, which they had run before. A group of runners would start from the bottom and run five miles up where someone would meet them with a car, saving the pounding of a downhill leg. It started at 5,000 feet and went to 7,000 feet, and you get a spectacular view on the way up, but it was very hard work. I started doing this run every Wednesday. I really started to improve, not only from the uphill, but because I was breathing so hard in the thin altitude that it was building my lungs too. I thought of that mountain workout as my secret weapon. Most runners wouldn't do it because they wouldn't want to do the downhill portion. I had a great support group; they never made me drive the car up.

After that mountain, everything else was a breeze. The people at the Cherry Creek track near Creigh's store were also good to train with and I began to do my track workouts there. I look back on those early days in Denver with great nostalgia. They were great times with great people and there was so much joy in my running. Creigh was as supportive as he could be. He would get Jon Sinclair to come down from Ft. Collins and we would put on training seminars and clinics right in his store. He would slip us $100 or $200 from time to time and that was what Steve and I were getting by on. We were still living with Jenny and Dave, though paying rent now.

Creigh would also pay us to participate in any local races that he put on. In the days before prize money became a reality, those $100 payments from time to time kept us going.

I ran in a local 10K qualifier for the huge Peachtree 10K in Atlanta, and was able to get my airfare paid to travel there. The temperatures in Denver were now reaching 93 degrees and Steve and I had never experienced anything like that before. I was having to learn about training in both altitude and heat. My next race was the Garden of the Gods 10-miler in Colorado Springs. I had never really raced for 10 miles before and this was over a very hilly course on a hot day. I really struggled, but I became the first woman to break 60 minutes on the course, winning in 59:56.

I was not a pretty sight at the finish, but I beat Ellen Hart by quite a distance so I knew I was back on track. I was very inspired and motivated by this new world of running I found myself in. Everything and everybody seemed to be on my side, and I kept thinking I should pinch myself. After all my struggles trying to train, teach school, deal with Gordon and with Steve, the kind of atmosphere I found in Colorado was all I needed to run well.

31 ～ Showdown with Shamateurism

J eff Galloway kept me informed on all the political maneuvering going on in the sport. It appeared that a critical mass had been reached and a number of top runners were ready to defy sports officials and openly take prize money, and some of them had organized into a group named the Association of Road Racing Athletes (ARRA). They were being egged on by the athletic shoe companies, primarily Nike, who wanted to be free to sign runners to endorsement deals.

At the end of June I flew to Portland for the Nike Cascade Runoff and the big showdown. Creigh agreed that this might be a historic confrontation and decided I should take one of his business partners, Ken Buckius, a lawyer, with me.

I had every intention of turning professional. If it meant leaving behind any further Olympic or Commonwealth Games aspirations, then so be it. I had seen firsthand the kind of money the male athletes were getting under the table in Europe, and while I didn't begrudge them anything, I understood now that I had some real economic value as an athlete, and I wasn't going to miss the opportunity to be compensated for my skills and efforts.

In the Cascade Runoff, Nike had put up $50,000 in prize money to be split between the top male and female finishers, with $10,000 going to the winners and smaller portions going to the next nine. The race director was Chuck Galford, a lawyer who was also helping Don Kardong organize the athletes in ARRA.

The night before the race we all assembled in a room at the Portland Hilton to talk about the situation. The Who's Who of the sport were there: Patti Catalano, Joan Benoit, Alison Roe, and Lorraine Moller, who had just broken 2:30 at Grandma's Marathon in Duluth, Minnesota. Among the men were Jon Sinclair, Herb Lindsay, Don Kardong, Bill Rodgers, Benji Durden, Frank Shorter, Greg Meyer and others. Most of the athletes there had been chaffing for years under the paternalistic thumb of officialdom, eking out a living from sub rosa payments and secret shoe company deals. Their anger and frustration was obvious. They were tired of being told that their dedication to their sport required a vow of poverty. There was a lot of big talk and outright bravado as nearly all the runners proclaimed their willingness to stand up to the threats of their national federations and the International Olympic Committee.

I didn't say anything. There were not enough chairs for everyone so Ken and I sat on the floor in a corner and just observed, fascinated by the interplay of all those egos and personalities. There were some very cocky people there who thought they were going to get rich the next day. In fact, I remember Patti Catalano stating, "We are all going to be millionaires tomorrow!" which I just thought was stupid.

Patti as arrogant an athlete as you'd ever find on a football field or basketball court. She was the favorite going into the race and was behaving like she had that $10,000 in her pocket already. It seemed to me that many of the runners hadn't truly thought the consequences through and weren't really committed to defying the authorities. Pure road runners like Patti had little to lose, but the more track-oriented runners, or those who had Olympic marathon ambitions, were being asked to put their dreams in jeopardy. It was obvious that some of them were just riding along on all the excitement and hype.

There were some serious people there who knew what they were getting involved with and meant business. Don Kardong, Chuck Galford, Frank Shorter, Herb Lindsay, Benji Durden were the ones who had thought through the legalities and logistics involved in changing the sport. They were fairly certain about what would eventually happen, they just couldn't tell us how long it would take or how much sacrifice would be required from individual athletes. They emphasized the strength we had in solidarity, and how loathe our federations would be to sanction and jettison so many of their country's top stars en masse.

They asked us to sign documents confirming that if we won prize money we would accept it and would deal with the consequences. As I say, I had thought this over long and hard and I had no hesitation at all. My diary for the day says simply: "Felt good. Signed to go professional." At that time I thought I was perhaps good enough to finish fifth or sixth and win $1,500, a sum that would help keep Steve and me in the States a bit longer.

The next day I lined up for the race calm and confident in my training. I had been putting in a lot of miles at altitude and many of them had been on serious hills. The Cascade course then ran by some railway yards in the first mile, then headed uphill for five miles. The field was huge, another one of those multi-thousand mass races. But by this time I was used to the idea, because I had come to realize that I was still only really racing against the same handful of women at the front anyway.

I stayed with the lead group of five or six women until around the two-mile mark where I found that my rhythm going up the hill was just stronger and more comfortable than the others, so I just went for it. I ran exactly the pace that seemed comfortable for me going up that hill and it just carried me away from the others like I was floating on air.

I crested the hill and turned to look behind me and couldn't see anyone! But I also knew I had four miles of downhill running ahead of me and that is where I am not so strong. I also knew I had two excellent downhill runners behind me in Alison and Lorraine and that they would certainly be thinking the same thing and would come after me.

So I ran down that hill like a woman possessed, never looking back. As I came into the finish area, I heard some people calling out "It's Rosie Ruiz!" referring to the woman who faked a victory in the Boston Marathon. I might have still been carrying a little extra weight, but I was beginning to realize that because I always ran in makeup and with my hair fixed up that I often just didn't fit the traditional mold of an elite female runner.

Watching the tape of that race now, I guess I was still bigger than many of the others, but I was incredibly strong from John's program and all that hill training in Colorado. I won by 30 seconds over Lorraine, with Alison third. I had run a 15K in 50:30 and had won $10,000, triple what I would have made teaching school in New Zealand for a year!

I was also in a lot of trouble.

I was in the United States on a visitor's visa, so I wasn't supposed to be earning any money. There were tax issues involved, in addition to the reaction of the sport authorities. Within hours I received two identical telegrams from the New Zealand Athletic Association informing me that I was banned from the sport for life. That was the quickest response I had ever had from them on anything! It's a pity they couldn't process my national running records as quickly.

I knew one thing: I wasn't going to give the money back. In the first place, I needed it! Secondly, I was tired of bureaucrats who led comfortable lives telling me if I wanted to run, I had to live in poverty. I was prepared psychologically for a battle with them.

Greg Meyer, an American, had won on the men's side, but I was one of the least-known athletes in the race. I immediately sensed that the dissidents would have preferred a better-known American woman as a standard bearer. Having three foreigners in the top spots on the women's side wasn't as good for public relations as having well-known Americans. Interestingly enough, Patti Catalano wasn't nearly as defiant and arrogant after finishing fourth.

So some weren't thrilled that I had won, but I certainly was! Not only because of the money; I had soundly beaten some great athletes and I felt there was no stopping me now. My diary reports: "Race went perfectly. Went in front at 2 ½ miles uphill. Beat them on the hills!! Doors flying open now!!" I felt more confident than ever that I had a chance to make running a career.

Alison almost immediately backed down in the face of threats from officials. Her advisors told her not to risk her future, as she had just won Boston and was really making a name for herself. She knew, as we all did, that she could still take money under the table, so she could still make a good living as a technical amateur. Lorraine took a middle course, putting her winnings in escrow to wait it out and see what happened.

But I took mine and put it in the bank and said, essentially, "Okay, what are you going to do about it?"

Having even a few top runners openly take money was a blatant challenge to the sports authorities. For years they had maintained their control over athletes by the "contamination rule," which mandates that if any banned athlete competes in an event with other "pure" athletes, then all the athletes in that event become "contaminated" as well. And if those newly contaminated runners compete against other pure athletes, they contaminate the third group, and so on. It was the sports bureaucrat's version of a viral epidemic.

But now that American road races were lining up tens of thousands of competitors at a time, the consequences of the contamination rule were farcical. For one thing, who could ever hope to keep track of hundreds of thousands of banned athletes flying around the country and world, hopping into road races every weekend? It was a joke to even contemplate such a thing, but the athletic federations were going to bluff it out a while longer.

I went to Atlanta to run the huge Peachtree 10K, and ran into heat and humidity such as I'd never experienced before. There were some athletes there who protested my running because of the contamination rule. It wasn't pleasant, feeling a persona non grata to some runners, but the race director didn't care a fig about the ban and welcomed all of us. Most everyone involved in road racing was so positive and forward looking, I was confident I was doing the right thing.

The race itself was somewhat frustrating, because there were still a few athletes out in front of the starting line warming up when the gun went off and when they saw what had happened, they turned around and started racing. The starter tried to call everyone back but with 10,000 runners surging up Peachtree Street, it was like trying to send rain back to the heavens.

Alison was one of the runners who was still out in front warming up, and she got an 80-meter jump on me because of it. She ended up beating me by about that distance, so I was angry about it.

From some of my experiences with her, it probably sounds like I really have it in for Alison. The truth of the matter is that over the years I arrived at the view that she was not an "honest" athlete. By that I mean she used people and situations in whatever way would benefit her personally. She didn't for a second acknowledge that she had gotten an unfair advantage in that race. And her equivocating on the prize money issue was another example of her all-for-me attitude. Her selfishness didn't help the sport and I believe it ultimately led to her career being so brief.

Within a few days, I sat down with Charlotte Lettis (now

Richardson), who was director of Nike Women's Promotions. I signed a contract to represent Nike for $400 a month and all the shoes and apparel I could use. I am fairly sure that I was the first female athlete to sign such an agreement with Nike. Of course, Patti Catalano and Mary Decker had agreements to receive shoes and gear, but I've since discussed it with Charlotte, and she agrees that I was the first to sign an open, paid endorsement deal.

Now I had enough money to stay and continue racing in the states, so we hired an immigration lawyer in Denver to begin straightening out our immigration status. Some athletes expected others to help them *gratis*, but we paid the going rate. I thought of myself as a professional and I never hesitated to pay for professional services, a philosophy that I believe stood me in good stead throughout my career.

At this point I was trying to do some serious, long-term thinking about my athletic career. Jeff Galloway invited us out to his camps at Lake Tahoe in July, where Arthur Lydiard would also be coaching. I was delighted to accept. I was really on a high. I had never had so much joy from my running, nor gotten so much help and support from so many people. The newspapers in New Zealand were full of stories about our challenge of "shamateurism" and there was an outpouring of support from other athletes, coaches and journalists, all of whom had long detested the hypocrisy in amateur sports. They had seen our athletes struggling for years to make a living while training, and then go off to do battle with eastern bloc athletes who were amateur in name only. Lydiard spoke out publicly, as did my former teammate Heather Thompson and Olympic medalists Murray Halberg, and Barry Magee.

The second day at Lake Tahoe I felt so sick I told Steve I needed a doctor. I was hot and cold at the same time and felt pain all over, as well as a splitting headache. In the morning a doctor told me I had a combination of sunstroke and altitude sickness. The day before we had gone for a run and then climbed up to the top of one of the ski lifts. It had all been too much.

With two days of rest I was fine. It was great fun being there with Arthur, who always took credit for any New Zealand athlete doing well, myself included. Of course, since my coach, John Davies, was a Lydiard prodigy, he had a pretty good case.

I did one seminar with him where we talked about hill workouts, which all of us were trained on. There are many famous spots in

Auckland where at one time or another every top New Zealand distance runner from the '60s to the '80s has trained. Then I spoke about my tactics in racing when it came to hilly courses, and said that I always tried to push up hills hard and then to maintain it right over the top to break away from the pack. Arthur said, "You will never win many races that way!" Well, of course, I already had! It was just the technique I had used at Bloomsday and Cascade.

At the camp we met a couple from Boise, Idaho, who owned a Phidippides store there. They put on an all-women's race there in October and asked if I would run it. I agreed to. Then our friend from New Zealand, Terry Eames, came through Lake Tahoe and he and Steve went down to San Francisco for a week while I stayed to keep training.

On our way back to Denver we flew to Portland where I visited Nike headquarters for the first time. At that time they had a small group of offices on Murray Boulevard in Beaverton, about 20 miles south of Portland. There was a great bunch of people working there and you could sense the excitement about where the sport was going and a real pride that Nike was right in the middle of it all. Everyone was very friendly and welcomed us with open arms. They took us through the warehouse and just loaded us down with gear. This was in the very early days and they still made running shoes right there instead of in the Orient, so it was interesting to see how it was all done.

I always joke that I knew Nike "before Michael," and in fact was sitting at the same table with Phil Knight the evening Jordan was introduced as a new Nike spokesperson. I'm pleased that I was associated with the company in those early days when they were so running-oriented and everyone involved seemed to come from a running background. My association with the company would last for many years, and it seemed to me that once it got involved in other sports and started making money by the basketfulls, it began to lose its way, if not its soul. But it was nice to have been there at the beginning, when we were all young and excited about running.

We headed back to Denver and I noted in my diary that I opened my first bank account in the United States. The lawyers were dealing with my immigration problem and I was having to file all sorts of paperwork on a regular basis. I can understand why so many foreign athletes got into trouble when they neglected to deal with this, as it was time consuming and costly. But I've always been the type of person who tackles challenges immediately, even though they can be a headache. Steve was the type who thought you could let things slide and get away with it.

The problem was that the INS did not have a visa status that really applied to my situation, because most people coming to work in the United States were sponsored by a company. Finally, I was able to get an H-1 status, which finally came through in February of 1982 when we were back in New Zealand.

My visa status meant I was only allowed to earn money in the United States through running, no other kind of work. Steve was given an H-4 status as well, which allowed him to stay as long as I was in the country at the same time. I had to do something about my tax situation, and because New Zealand had an agreement with the United States that allowed me to choose, I began paying U.S. taxes in 1981. I know some athletes who never handled this properly and tried to hide their income from both countries, but eventually it caught up with them.

Chuck Galford, Don Kardong and others were working with Nike behind the scenes to come up with some sort of accommodation with the sport's governing bodies. They were confident it would happen, but no one could say when. I was just in limbo. There was talk about having the money go into some kind of trust fund. I thought that was a ludicrous half-measure, but since I wasn't directly involved, I just had to wait until it was worked out.

We were back in Denver and I resumed training. We got the chance to house-sit for the American marathon star, Tony Sandoval, so we had our own place for a while. Jenny and Dave, generous as ever, gave us one of their cars to use.

I continued to do Lookout Mountain as often as I could, and I noticed I was getting to the top faster and faster. I ran in a local 15K in Broomfield, a suburb of Denver, and won in 52:00 at altitude. I was still improving.

The next race I entered was the Lynchburg 10-miler in Virginia, probably the toughest course in the country and certainly the roughest I ever ran. Creigh had negotiated with Rudy Straub, the race director, for an appearance fee. It seemed I was now good enough and well known enough to be paid just to show up! There was prize money as well.

At Lynchburg they housed the invited runners with families, and that began our relationship with the Dillard family. We stayed with them every year for many years and I remain in contact with them still. In fact they have visited New Zealand and have met all the family down there and gone sightseeing with Mum.

It was while I was out on a run a few days before the Lynchburg race I had a little lesson in human nature. I was running along and suddenly came across Rod Dixon. I stopped to say hello and was amazed to find that he was very angry with me about my stand on professionalism. He said, "You've just screwed everything up and will ruin it for everyone!"

I couldn't believe the hypocrisy, after boasting about all the money he had made on the European circuit, money that I never begrudged him at all. Now that I was seeking the same opportunity, he was upset with me for rocking the boat. Maybe he was really upset because the old system benefited a tiny handful of athletes who took their money unofficially and probably never reported it. Now that everything was going to be above board they were going to have to play by the rules like everyone else and they weren't happy about it.

At any rate, I won my first Virginia 10-miler in 53:54 over the hardest course I had ever run. It goes downhill steeply for the first mile and a half and you have to run back up the same hill at the finish. Slow as it was, I was thrilled with my time. Rod got over his pique well enough to win the men's race, so it was an all-Kiwi day. I could hardly walk afterwards because I had for once run the downhill hard and the pounding really got to my legs.

A couple of days later my legs were still so bad I had to use my hands to lift them over the side of the bed to get up in the morning! Then I had to do the same to get in and out of the car all day. I was wondering how in the world I was going to run the Freedom Trail 8-miler in Boston the next weekend.

We flew north and met up with Bill Rodgers at his store, then stayed with his brother, Charlie, at his really neat old three-story house by a reservoir. Unfortunately they put us in a room on the top floor, with a narrow, steep flight of stairs to negotiate. It took me a long time to get up and down those stairs, and the whole time I was trying to not let anyone see how sore I was. I was really worried that I would not be recovered in time for the race. I pretty much stayed up there on the third floor for two whole days, resting my legs. That's what I always did when I got in that kind of trouble. I figured I would just do more damage by trying to run. We were trying to keep my situation quiet. Charlie would ask Steve if I had been out running and he would say, "Oh, yes! You just missed her!"

Finally on the third day I made it down the stairs and went out for a run around the reservoir. It wasn't pretty! It also hurt. I wasn't worried about missing the training, but I certainly wanted to be able to run the race without pain.

Because of those sore legs, by the time the race rolled around I was about as well rested as I had ever been for a competition. I beat Lorraine, who was running very well at the time, by two full minutes. My time was 41:50, which works out to 5:13 per mile pace. I was very pleased.

Rod Dixon again won the men's race for another all-Kiwi finish, and I guess he must have gotten over his pique somewhat, because he gave me a little congratulatory peck on the cheek before we went into the post-race press conference.

Over the years I often watched competitors continuing their training mileage run up to race day and I knew they could not be well rested. It's such a simple concept to rest properly for an important competition, but runners get so focused on their training and their mileage that they can't bring themselves to break away from their daily routine. Ironically, they're afraid to change their training pattern even if it makes them too tired to do their best in competition!

At this stage I knew that I had found my niche as an athlete. I loved competition, loved running on roads, and loved the distances, especially when it was good and hilly.

We went back to Denver and then on to Boise for the women's 10K I'd agreed to run. I won it in 33:01, almost going under 33 minutes for the first time. We spent 10 days with our friends there, taking a trip up to Sun Valley and really getting an appreciation for the beauty of the area. Little did I know I would have a connection with Boise and with women's racing for many years to come.

Back in Denver I got to see what it was like to live with heavy snow in a city for the first time in my life. I had no idea how to run in those conditions. Jon Sinclair would sometimes come down to run with me, and sometimes I would drive the hour up to Ft. Collins where he lived. In addition to the snow, training the cold was new to me. I always hated wearing socks, and I had to get some bigger shoes so that I could wear them. The bad circulation in my feet often left my feet feeling frozen when I was out running.

I celebrated my 26th birthday in Denver and we moved back to

Jenny and Dave's after having the Sandoval's house for the summer.

In mid-November we flew back to New Zealand and back to merciful summer. Glorious! We stayed with Steve's parents, and we had our little cottage on the island to retreat to. Everyone was still very positive about our stand on professionalism. My coach, former athletes, and the media all were behind us. Both Lorraine and I were still banned from racing in New Zealand, so my plan was to do a big training build-up and then go back to the States in the spring and continue to run road races.

But with the Commonwealth Games coming up in 1982 John was trying hard to persuade me to run them. He was convinced the officials would come to their senses and reinstate me. The problem was that my head was elsewhere. At that point all I wanted to do was run more road races. I had found my calling, and it wasn't on the track.

In January John and I went down to Christchurch to a track meet where Grete Waitz was attempting a world record for 5000 meters. At that time, New Zealand was holding some very good track meets that attracted crowds of 15,000 or more. There was still a great deal of interest in track and field because of our successes in the '70s, and also because there were so many great athletes training in New Zealand to escape their winters.

Grete missed the record by about 20 seconds but I was still impressed by the kind of time she could run for that distance. I still thought of her as an athlete on a different level, that I didn't have the same kind of "stuff" she did. I was in awe of her as she clicked off mile splits that I could only dream of.

After her race, John turned to me and said, "You know, you could break that record."

I was flabbergasted. The world record then was 15:14. I broke that down in my head to mile splits and said, "John, there's no way."

But he insisted that he could train me to do if we set up a program right then and I completed it by March, 1982. With everything else going on, trying to deal with the ban, worrying about our visa status, I didn't think I could cope with the effort, but I agreed to try. After all, John's training had clearly paid off spectacularly for me; who was I to question his judgment in these matters?

Steve and I went down to Wellington to talk with the New Zealand officials. Lorraine had already been there with a lawyer and her then-husband, an American marathoner named Ron Daws. We sat down with the president and secretary and they proceeded to tell

me what a bad thing I had done. When they had finished their dia-
tribe, I said "Fine, I will just go back to the States and run road races
and New Zealand will have lost me as an athlete."

With the Commonwealth Games coming the next year, I knew
they wanted Lorraine and me to be part of the team. The secretary
brought out a list of events coming up in the next few years and stat-
ed that they would love me to run in them. I said, "Fine, but what do
we do about it?" They said that they would consider lifting the ban in
New Zealand, and they would work harder on our behalf with the
international officials to overturn our worldwide ban. They had complete authority to overturn the ban on New Zealand soil, and we did-
n't realize it at the time, but the international officials had no particular interest in banning athletes that were approved by their own federations.

Alison Roe was back home training. She had just won the New
York Marathon in an alleged "world record" that was never ratified
because the course was found to be short. But she was getting a lot of
attention, and justifiably so. This was making it somewhat harder on
Lorraine and me in our struggle to be reinstated because she was
considered the superstar and that took away some of our leverage.
The athletic association figured she was still in the fold, so they
weren't quite as motivated to deal with us.

The frustrating thing for us was that we knew very well that
Alison had under-the-table deals of all kinds, and here we had put
our careers and reputations on the line to try to bring some honesty
to the sport. Naturally, if we succeeded, our efforts would only benefit
her, but she wasn't willing to lift a finger or risk anything herself to
aid the cause.

But Lorraine and I were making a lot of the right people in
"amateur" sports uncomfortable. One incident was instructive. I was
at one of the big international meets in Auckland as a spectator and
one of the New Zealand television stations had asked me to do some
commentating. As I was standing by the track, waiting to do so, who
should pop up out of nowhere but the British promoter who had
wanted me to be "nice" to him to get into races in Europe. As he
managed a number of so-called amateur athletes, he was quite upset
with me. He was in such a rage it was comical.

"You've ruined the sport," he shouted, "Just destroyed it! You
shouldn't even be in this stadium! You're a banned athlete! You
should leave immediately!" I just let him rant and rave. Some specta-

tors actually booed him. It was actually quite satisfying to know that I was such a thorn in his side.

I continued to train through all this and was making great progress, gaining confidence as I learned more about John's program. I had been consistently running 70, 80, even 90 miles per week, and I had never been healthier or run better in my life.

Lorraine and I were anxious to get the ban lifted at least in New Zealand because we wanted to be able to race in some track events to qualify for the Commonwealth Games, which would be held in Brisbane. And now that John had convinced me to try, I wanted to attempt the world record for 5000 meters. So after a few weeks of hearing nothing, Lorraine and I announced that we would run in a 3000-meter event at the end of an official track meet, and thus get some media coverage. We were confident of running the qualifying time, 9:12, and felt we had such great support from the public and media that it would force the New Zealand officials to act. Steve called them and told them what we were doing and within two hours we got a call back informing us that we were reinstated to compete in New Zealand!

We ran that 3000-meter trial on February 1st, 1982 in Auckland. It was my first track race since the debacle with Gordon in Holland in 1980. Without tapering much from the hard training I was doing, I still ran a qualifying time, 9:05, and though I was second to Dianne Rodger, it felt wonderful to be back in the familiar world of track and field.

I was still slowly losing weight the right way, through training and hard work. Food was not a fixture or crutch in my life anymore, which is evident as I look back over my diaries. Gone are the ecstatic references to fabulous rich meals and yummy desserts. Steve's mum made good old-fashioned home-cooked meals just like my mother, so I was eating heartily and healthily and not worrying about weight.

Now that the ban had been lifted at least in my home country, I was happy to get back into my old competitive patterns. In mid-February I won the Auckland Championships 1500 meters in 4:13, only a few seconds off my best, despite the volume of training I was doing. Excitement began to grow for possible Commonwealth Games medals.

Jenny and Dave Kyle came down to New Zealand and as a thank-you gesture, Steve and I paid for them to go to the South Island to do the Milford trek, our country's most famous hike. So they happened to be in Auckland staying with us at the time of the world record attempt, which was really gratifying to share with them after all their kindness.

Now that my life had changed so completely, I found that being a professional athlete wasn't all fun and games. Our family income now came solely from my running. We had decided it would be better that Steve not get tied down by a regular job because if we were able to get the visa situation cleared up, we'd be heading back to the States quickly.

That was all fine, but I quickly found that I could no longer live the same kind of social life I had previously. My success depended on how well I managed the daily structure of my life to get the best training and rest I could. I could not go out partying until all hours. I couldn't go places where there was cigarette smoke. And I needed sleep and lots of it. Steve went back to his old social life with the rugby crowd, often staying out overnight. I had to get used to this. But my life had changed and now I had a great deal of responsibility. I knew that this window of opportunity might be small indeed, and I had better make the most of it.

At that time I thought if I could run at that level until I was 30, I'd be happy. But I knew it would all come down to how disciplined and focused I could be. I couldn't go sailing, lie on a beach, or even take long walks. All of this was no small sacrifice, because we New Zealanders love the beach and the outdoors! When Jenny and Dave were there, Steve would take them out and I would have to stay home.

It took a while to work all this out. My father-in-law smoked and when we were staying at their house I would occasionally just have to leave the room. The house was always open to visitors and I often had to just go to my room to get some peace and rest. This is not a criticism of others, just the facts of life for an endurance athlete. It was what I simply had to do to run well.

John was still encouraging me to go for the 5000-meter world record, so we planned it for March 13th in Auckland. The city gets strong winds in the early evening, so we scheduled the event for the end of a meet, between 9 and 10 p.m. We were accustomed to racing and training in severe winds, so the occasional calm night was a blessing. Often you could lose as much of three seconds a lap to the wind! So to go for a record, one really had to get lucky with the conditions.

Steve's parents' house was high on a hill overlooking Mt. Smart

Stadium, so I spent all day on March 13th traipsing out to the porch to check the wind situation on the track. On this particular day it just got worse and worse. In such situations, what makes it hard is that you have got to get yourself mentally ready for an enormous task that from all appearances you won't even be attempting! Roger Bannister wrote about dealing with this same phenomenon before his historic attempt on the four-minute mile in 1954.

Holding out hope to the very last, we went down to the track for the start of the meet, but the conditions were worsening and it wasn't long before the whole thing was canceled. It was so frustrating; all I could do was go home and brood.

32 ~ World Record!

They rescheduled the 5000-meter attempt for the following Wednesday night, which put me in a bind. I had agreed to run a 10K road race for Nike on Sunday, and I was loathe to back out on a commitment. I called up the race director and told him I would still run the event but couldn't afford to race it. He was agreeable, but I was worried because this race, called the Nike Rollercoaster 10K, lived up to its name and I was worried about what the downhills would do to my legs.

Lorraine and I ran it together and I tried to go easy, but she is a great downhill runner and I knew I was braking too much. My legs came out of it a bit sore and tight. This worried me because I knew I was in great shape for the record attempt but might have blown my chances! I got massages and plenty of rest, but on Monday had to fly to Wellington with John Walker to meet with the Prime Minister for a press conference to unveil the Commonwealth Games uniforms, which they always make a big deal of. Not only was it a distraction, as it turned out, the uniforms were fairly ugly, too.

But on Wednesday evening the weather was perfect!

Lorraine and I had agreed to share the pacemaking chores at 73 seconds per lap, and to alternate the lead every two laps. This was the first time I had ever run 5000 meters on the track, and our plan called for going through the 3000-meter mark in just about my best time for that distance, so this was really going to be new territory for me. My old friend Barbara Moore was in the race, along with Debbie Elsmore, Gordon's latest contender. He was there, too, and I was just praying he didn't do anything to upset me.

We lined up in the still evening air and I had just the right combination of calm and excitement. I knew I was ready. The gun went off and Lorraine took the first two laps in around 74 or 75 seconds, which was too slow! I took over and ran two laps in 71 each to catch back up to the schedule. When Lorraine took over again she did the same thing, 74-75 seconds!

At this point I got anxious. All distance runners know how inefficient it is to run an uneven pace, and you don't set world records by being inefficient. So I took the lead on my own and tried to get the pace back on track single-handedly. When they rang the bell for the last lap, I was still five seconds down on the record. I knew I would have to dig deep.

In these situations I always redouble my concentration. I had watched Dick Quax miss the 5000 world record by a tenth of a second in Stockholm by easing up in the last 10 meters, and I wasn't going to let anything like that happen to me. Things like that went through my mind as that last lap went by in slow motion: all the training, Mum and Dad in the stands watching, Jenny and Dave from the States, John's wonderful coaching and his faith in me, the small screaming crowd that had now poured down out of the stands to the edge of the track. All that played through my mind through each of those last 400 meters as I ran out the rest of the life in me.

When I finally parted the finish tape I had broken the world record by 1.29 seconds.

&

Everyone around me was jubilant, I could tell that even through my tears. The crowd was small and there were only a few sports writers there because few had taken our record attempt seriously. But they were ones who had followed the sport religiously over the years and it was only fitting that they should be the witnesses.

A television crew had arrived late and actually put the last lap on the air live, so quite a few people at home got to see it. The station had called John Davies and asked him if there was any chance we'd actually get the record, and he told them: Yes!

And it wasn't just a one-woman show. Barbara was second, well under the previous national record, in 15:29.65, a performance that would have ranked her fourth in the world the previous year. Lorraine was third in a very good 15:40.23.

I was in shock. This was the kind of achievement I thought other runners like Grete Waitz accomplished, not me. I felt privileged to have even witnessed many such hallowed moments in running, some by my own New Zealand teammates, and now I was having a hard time realizing that I had created one myself. Once I began to accept the fact that I had actually done it, I was so happy that it had happened on my own home track and in front of my family and friends. I couldn't stop the tears; they flowed and flowed.

My Mum and Dad told me later there was an old man in the crowd who said to them during the race, "There used to be another girl called Anne who ran just like her—I wonder what ever happened to her. They were very happy to tell him that I was the same girl!

We all went back to Steve's parents' house, Lorraine and her husband, too, and celebrated—for once—until all hours. The next day, Jenny, Dave, Steve and I went down to Waiheke. It was our fourth wedding anniversary, and I took a short break and just enjoyed a few days away from the city. I didn't stop training—in fact, I ran 13 miles the next day!—but getting back to the island was always a great mental break for me. Meanwhile, I don't think it really hit home to a lot of New Zealanders that this really was a world record. The 5000 meters for women wasn't run in a lot of competitions then and I don't think many people realized how good the time was. In fact, that performance would have ranked me in the top 10 in the world each year for many years afterwards.

Naturally, the New Zealand AAA would get their two cents in. They issued a statement saying the record would not be accepted because I was still an internationally banned athlete. That put something of a damper on it. At the same time everyone at Nike was delighted with the record and immediately gave me a bonus, plus some really nice custom jewelry pieces they had made up for such achievements.

Our visas hadn't come through yet, so our trip back to the States was delayed. This was the just the beginning of what turned out to be a lengthy immigration hassle that caused no end of worry and stress. It was also tough on my agent, Creigh Kelley, who was trying to schedule events for me without knowing if I would even be allowed in the country.

If I had been able to get a work sponsor somehow, a company that would vouch that I had a job with them, I could have easily gotten a green card. Nike was in a logical position to do that, but wouldn't. They said if they did it for me they'd have to do it for a number of other foreign athletes. I was disappointed because I felt that if anyone deserved their support right then, it was me.

33 ~ *Dream Season*

We finally got our visas and flew back to the States, first to Portland to visit Nike. We bought a 1971 Cadillac from some friends there for $900 and drove it back to Denver, feeling as though we were piloting a boat. We stopped in Boise to visit our friends there and then drove on to Denver, where we continued to stay with Jenny and Dave.

On March 15th, 1982, the runners' representatives and athletic officials agreed to allow runners to accept cash prizes so long as they were willing to deposit the money into a trust fund account, from which they could withdraw reasonable living expenses until such time as they retired from amateur sports. Then they would have full access to the money.

In other words athletes could take money so long as they didn't appear to enjoy it too much, and officials could tell themselves the purity of amateur sports had been essentially preserved. It was a shell game, of course, but it allowed everyone to feel as though they had accomplished something.

I never agreed with the principle of the trust fund or its rules. I felt that as a professional I had the right to earn and invest my own money. I certainly did not want the American athletic governing body, The Athletics Congress (TAC), to keep it until I retired.

But this was the ruse commonly agreed upon, so I was the first one to sign on. I never ever did put any actual prize money into it. I had earned about $22,000 in 1981, but it was long since invested or spent on expenses. So we took out a short term loan, placed it in the trust fund, then claimed legitimate expenses totaling that amount, and got it back out almost immediately. A number of other athletes did the same thing. It was infantile, but it kept the officials off our backs and allowed us to continue to compete in our sport. After a year or so, nearly everyone just ignored it altogether.

&

On April 15th, 1982 I filed my first U.S. income tax return. I was beginning to feel like an American already.

At this time Alison Roe was being represented by a friend of Creigh's named Drew Mearns of International Management Group (IMG). Drew would often call up Creigh with race offers that Alison and her husband, Richard, had turned down. It seems she was playing the prima donna and was very demanding. So Drew passed along some wonderful opportunities to me through Creigh.

One of them was a 5-mile race held at the end of April in Cleveland, Ohio, commemorating the opening of Playhouse Square, an old playhouse that had been refurbished. It was held downtown in a section called "the Flats," which has since been gentrified but was then a rough area.

The road was full of holes, and I collected bits of broken glass in the soles of my shoes, but I ran well, winning in 25:50. We then attended the opening night at the playhouse, which was the most elegant affair I had been to in my life—and one I certainly wasn't dressed for. I returned a few weeks later to win my first Revco 10K in 31:45, which made me at least the second woman to run under 32 minutes! At the press conference the day before the race, I had predicted my time to the second! Thus began my long and happy relationship with Cleveland. Race director Jack Staph put on a terrific event and was a pleasure to work with. Over the years I would return to the Revco race many times.

Between the two Cleveland races, I flew back to Spokane and won the Bloomsday 12K again, this time in a course record 40:02, almost two minutes faster than the year before. Lorraine was second, almost three minutes back, so all the signs were pointing to continuous improvement under John's program.

At that point I thought about returning to get revenge for my previous year's humiliation in the L'eggs race in New York, but when I called to ask if Grete Waitz was going to run, I was told she wasn't. So I decided to run the Bolder Boulder 10K again to see what I could do at altitude. I found out later that Grete had in fact run L'eggs, and had won it.

But I won the Boulder race in 32:38, and was immediately accused by some of the local Boulder crowd of cheating. They didn't think anyone could run that fast at altitude without cutting the course. Fortunately, three of Jon Sinclair's friends had run near me throughout the race—jokingly saying they were having a hard time staying in front of me—and they guaranteed that I had indeed run the whole course. That silenced the critics, but suspicions apparently lingered.

I was so hurt by the accusations that I never raced there again. For years they put up all sorts of bonuses and appearance fees to attract the best runners to beat my record, but it didn't happen. They even tried to rewrite history and declare a new record of 33:00 flat when they switched to a women-only race.

They finally re-acknowledged my record some 14 years later, but only after Kenya's Delilah Asiago broke it. Those holdout non-believers in Boulder should have taken note that she also broke my Bloomsday record that year by 10 seconds. There was no real reason to doubt that I was capable of such a performance. According to all the altitude experts, my Boulder performance was comparable to my "sea level" Revco time the same year, and later in the year I ran 32:50 in Denver, which is about the same altitude.

Creigh was trying to find some local appearances for me, just to earn living expenses. On one occasion we went to the opening of the Snowmass ski resort near Aspen, where they were having 10K at 9000 feet! Jon Sinclair and I raced this course, which was half uphill and half downhill. I don't think I have ever breathed so hard in my life.

I continued racing through the summer, often getting appearance fees that Alison had turned down. I always gave the race directors as much in the way of interviews and promotional activities as they wanted. I was appreciative of the opportunities and wanted to establish long-term relationships with these races. So I did dozens of pre-race clinics, television interviews, autograph signings, whatever they asked. This was the beginning of my education in the business and marketing side of sports. One interesting aside: CBS Sports sent a crew to Denver to interview me about the upcoming Cascade Runoff, and the interviewer happened to be John Tesh, who was a sports reporter then. For some reason, he never mentioned his musical aspirations.

At the end of June, I won the Cascade Runoff 15K again in another course record, 49:20. Then it was back to Atlanta for Peachtree, and this time everyone started at the same time. It was so incredibly hot and humid that to this day I don't remember running the last mile. I won by a minute and a half in a course record 32:35, a time I was elated with under such conditions. The picture of me being half-carried away from the finish line says everything about the effort of that race.

Seeing how hard on me that race was, I made a decision not to try to run Cascade and Peachtree on consecutive weekends again, so I never went back to the Atlanta race. I think I made several sensible decisions like that early on that helped me to be much more consistent on the road circuit over the years.

But I was having a dream season so far. I had run 10 races and set 10 course records. I was not only winning, I was usually winning by several minutes. After Atlanta, Steve and I took a two-week holiday and went to Los Angeles and Disneyland. While we were there we occasionally ran an easy half-hour around the streets of Anaheim just so my body didn't forget what running felt like, but I think I needed a mental break more than a physical one.

We then went up to Ft. Collins and stayed with Jon for a while. He had a team of guys he trained with there who called themselves "the Maniacs" because of their super hilly initiation run. Everyone had to run it to get into the group and win one of their coveted purple and black T-shirts. So naturally, I did the run, but was only made an "honorary Maniac," because I was a "girl."

It was great fun training with the guys in Ft. Collins. We would all pile into our big Caddy—10 of us!—and drive up to 9000 feet and do a long run. Then we'd stop for fresh hot cinnamon rolls at this little café on the way home. Some of the maniacs later made a trip to New Zealand and camped out at Steve's parents' for a week. Jon started coming down every year for winter training.

In July I flew to North Carolina to a Nike-sponsored running camp, where I met a young brash guy named Keith Brantly, who was just out of high school. He would later become one of America's best road runners and marathoners. I also got to be friends and training partners with a fellow from Virginia named Randy Cook, a good regional road runner who later had to retire because of hip problems he jokingly said were caused by our hard workouts.

In our regular transoceanic phone calls on training, John Davies began talking about the Commonwealth Games again. I had qualified but was still not convinced I wanted to do it. John was using all the persuasive ability he could muster over the phone to convince me that it would be a great thing to do, that I could win a gold medal.

Because John wanted me to do it so badly, and because I owed so much of my success to him, after going back and forth about it for several weeks, I finally said yes. We got Nike to put a bonus in my contract for a gold, silver or bronze medal, so that made it monetarily attractive, too. John asked if I would agree to cut back on the road racing. I said that road racing was how I was earning my living, so my preference would be to carefully combine the Commonwealth Games training with some selected races. He came up with a three-month training program that specified what I had to do every single day right up to the day of the finals in the 3000 meters. On that day he wrote: "Win gold medal." For the day after the race, he wrote: "Polish gold medal."

The program worked wonderfully. My weight was now down to the lightest I had ever been in my running career. A lot of that was Jenny Kyle's influence. She was very disciplined herself and inspired me to start doing upper body workouts with free weights three times a week with her.. She also made sure the house was stocked with good, healthy food, and that there was no rubbish around to tempt us.

John's program was working so well that one blustery day at the Cherry Creek track I did a mile time trial in 4:35, completely on my own into a strong wind. I could not believe how easy it was. All this time I was training at altitude, which we never made any allowances for in our program. John trained me the same as he would have at sea level.

The Denver area was a great place to train during those days. There were a lot of athletes around who were serious about running, and everyone was supportive and encouraging of my goals. I made a trip to another running camp at Pike's Peak in Colorado Springs just to show support, and found myself in yet another absolutely beautiful spot for training. I trained on the track that has now become the U.S.

Olympic training center track. A number of top runners at the time took the road racing circuit for granted, but I felt extremely fortunate to be experiencing so many great places and people. Obviously there was a lot of travel required, but somehow it wasn't arduous. It all seemed new and exciting then.

Not only did the training go well, but later in the summer I also won the Nordstrom's 10K in Portland in 33:30, and the Septemberfest 10K in Omaha in 32:31, both in course record times.

Once again, John's training program was right on the money.

34 ~ Race of a Lifetime

In mid-September, I flew to Australia to meet up with the rest of the New Zealand team. We would train in Melbourne for two weeks before going on to Brisbane for the Commonwealth Games. When I landed, there was no one from the team to meet me, and I hadn't received any information before getting on the plane. I spent hours randomly phoning colleges and universities from the phone book, because I knew they would likely be at one of them, and sure enough, I finally found them.

Three days after arriving, I ran a 1500 in 4:14, only four seconds off my best ever. So soon after that long plane trip, I was delighted. It was surprisingly enjoyable being part of a team again after being solo on the roads for more than a year. Brisbane is a sunny coastal city, and the Games' village was spacious, clean and quiet, and training went very well. In fact, I started running PR's in all my time trials. My fitness just seemed to get better and better, and with it my confidence. It was a lovely feeling.

The experts didn't share my enthusiasm. Despite my world record in the 5000 meters earlier in the year, I was ranked only ninth in the British Commonwealth at 3000 meters. Wendy Smith (later Sly) had the Commonwealth record and fastest time of the year at 8:46, more than 10 seconds faster than my best time.

A couple of other British women, as well as several Canadians, were also in good shape. I would watch them at the training track and think, Gosh, this is going to be tough. But though I did not underestimate the competition, in my mind a thought began to take shape: I did not come this far not to win a medal.

One really nice thing happened during this time. In a ceremony in front of the entire New Zealand team, I was presented with the World Record plaque for my 5000-meter mark. They had waited until I was officially reinstated by the International Amateur Athletic Federation before presenting it.

The plaque was wonderful, but my mind was now on nothing less than a gold medal. My time trials were going so well that I knew I was going to run much faster than I ever had before. Just the thought of it was thrilling. I had to concentrate to keep my emotions under control. Just thinking about the upcoming competition would set my heart to racing.

After the opening ceremonies they put on a preliminary track meet. As they sometimes did for such tune-up meets, they set up the race events at odd distances, including a 1200-meter race for the women. We tried to get them to change it to a 1500 meters to no avail, so John suggested I run the race, but continue on to the 1500-meter mark alone. So that's what I did. On a hot, windy afternoon, I ran 1200 meters with some of the best runners from around the British Commonwealth, getting to the finish line of the official race in second place, then continuing on for another 300 meters, where I ended up running a PR of 4:10.03. That also would have been a New Zealand record, but obviously would never count because of the screwball nature of the race. By this time, I was so confident, my training diary notes coolly: "Really pleased."

But the opening day of the Games was very cold and windy and I started to get a sore throat and signs of a head cold. I was really upset at the prospect of all this hard work and planning going down the drain at the last minute, but I said nothing to anyone about it. In fact, in all my interviews with the New Zealand media I spoke confidently, telling reporters that I hadn't come this far to lose. Some people even called me cocky and arrogant, but I was really just trying to talk myself through it.

No New Zealand woman had ever won a gold medal on the track in the Commonwealth or Olympics Games, and now the whole country seemed to sense that it could finally happen. There was a palpable excitement in the air. And not only for me, but for Lorraine Moller and Dianne Rodger, who were also in the 3000. We were all feeling the pressure and excitement. In fact, some journalists were calling for a sweep!

John Davies was in Brisbane as a commentator for New Zealand television along with announcer Keith Quinn, so they were going to call the race live back to New Zealand. Mum, Dad, Nana and Katie would watch from there. Steve had stayed in the United States. I knew there would be a lot of people glued to their television sets, hanging on John's every word that day.

I went to spend one day with Don and Brenda Thompson and their two boys, who now lived in Brisbane. They were the couple I had stayed with in Wellington in 1981 when I had worked so hard to barely make the cross-country team. When Don dropped me off at the gate to the village that evening, his last words were, "Annie, I really feel you are going to win a gold medal. You're in great shape and a good frame of mind."

His words brought a sense of closure to my preparation that was reassuring. When he had last seen me I had just started my comeback. Overweight and struggling, I had just squeaked onto that cross-country team. Now the transformation was complete and he saw me in a completely different light, so much fitter, happier, and more confident.

On the day of the race, October 4th, 1982, I went down to the practice track and started my normal warm-up routine. The cold I had felt coming on had not progressed. In its place was a feverish excitement. I had always said the more nervous I was before a race, the better I would run. In this case I was almost sick with nerves, physically shaking. I was miserable. I just wanted to get it over.

John walked out to the track and we chatted for a moment. He was relaxed and confident, and spoke to me in soothing tones, keeping me steady and calm. It was exactly what I needed from him then. The last thing he said to me was: "Annie, it's a windy day. Whatever you do, don't lead the race." And I thought he was exactly right. I didn't argue. After all, I was in terrific shape, I had good speed, so I was confident that if the race came down to a "kick," I would stand a very good chance. What my coach told me would have been entirely sensible and logical to any runner. It just wouldn't work out that way.

When at last it was time for the 3000 meters, they introduced us to the spectators one by one. I was the last one to walk onto the track.

The huge New Zealand contingent in the crowd went crazy.

There was a big field, 24 of us, and we had to draw for our starting places. I drew the pole position, number one, on the inside of the track. I knew that if I didn't get out fast I would be in all sorts of traffic, with the other women bunching up all around me, trying to stay close to the inside of the track.

We stood around nervously shaking our legs and hopping up and down to stay loose as the starter gave us our instructions. I barely heard anything over the roar in my head.

"Conditions are blustery and certainly we can't expect a really fast time," said Brendan Foster, the BBC color commentator, up in the television booth.

"Take your marks!" the starter called. We trotted quickly up to the starting line and assumed the half crouch stance that distance runners use. We remained frozen like that for what seemed an eternity. One official's red foul flag went up.

"Stand up!" the starter called. Something was improper in the line-up. We backed away from the line and started the nervous milling and jiggling again. This was torture.

"New Zealand, feet off the line, please," said the starter. One of us had put a toe over the starting line. I was fairly certain it wasn't me, but I was so dizzy with anxiety, who could say?

"Take your marks!" he called again. We trotted back up and crouched. Thirteen years of my life had come to this. All the pre-dawn runs and the gut-wrenching intervals on the track, the miles of forest trails, Gordon's insane abuse, the maddening officials, the cross-country races in freezing rain. It had all come down to seven and a half laps, two miles less 200 meters. Please just let it be over, I prayed.

Crack! The gun went off and I shot out so quickly I ended up five yards in front. It wasn't meant to be any kind of bold move, just a tactical precaution to stay out of the kind of leg-tangling trouble that can trip you up at the start of a crowded track race.

I slowed down to see if anyone else wanted to set the pace. No takers. Right away I had to make a decision. I had always abhorred the slow tactical races on the track, with everyone tripping over each other lap after lap, and the winner determined by a mad sprint to the finish. My philosophy had long been that if I was going to lose a race, then I wanted to lose it running as hard and as fast as I could.

So despite my coach's warning, I found myself out there in front, challenging everyone in the race to run with me. Once I discovered that no one else was willing to help with the pacemaking, I just took off. My attitude was, *To hell with them, I'm going to run hard.*

Up in the BBC booth, the commentators were convinced that the race would sooner or later belong to runners from Great Britain, primarily Wendy Smith and Ruth Smythe. Their only comment about me at the outset was, "On the inside is Anne Audain, who used to be trained by Gordon Pirie…"

At the end of the first full lap, I was in front with Ruth and Wendy right behind me, followed closely by three Kenyan women. I did not pay attention to the split times as we passed the lap marker. Everything was going by in a blur, but I could glance up at the stadium's big screen and keep track of the rest of the field. After the second lap it was obvious that Wendy Smith and I were dropping everyone else behind. The race was going to be between the two of us.

"Audain has really taken it on," said the BBC man, She's done every bit of the work so far." I learned later the laps were going very fast, 69 seconds each.

Wendy was using me skillfully, running on my shoulder, allowing me to set the pace, then dropping back directly behind me on the back straight to be sheltered from the wind. I was in control of the pace, but the smart money would have been on her. Round and round we went, pulling further and further away from the rest of the field, me in an almost Zen-like trance, running the race of my life, with Wendy on my shoulder, ready to pounce and take it all away.

"There's a fair old battle developing here," said the BBC announcer, noting that despite the windy conditions, we were on record pace. The tension in the stadium was mounting, from both the pace and the anticipation of Wendy's move.

I knew she was doing the smart thing letting me lead, but I didn't care. There was no way I was going to let her win. Like me, she had run the shorter, faster distances earlier in her career and I knew she had very good speed. But so did I. I was waiting for her move, mentally preparing myself to match whatever she threw at me.

We circled the track, now running evenly at about 70 seconds per lap, leaving the rest of the field far behind. I felt no pain, almost no sense of exertion. I was detached, as if having an out-of-body experience. It was as if I had set my body to running, and it had just continued on its own.

"Audain's been out in front, taking the pressure, taking the wind.

Surely Wendy Smith will have to wait to attack, because of the wind on that back straight. You can see them actually bending into it!" said the BBC commentator.

"The time at the bell is 7:38, so it's fast!" he said excitedly.

As they rang the bell for the final lap, I was gathering myself, steeling my will. I knew the challenge would come soon. So did everyone else in the stadium.

"They're all ready for this lap battle," said the BBC's Foster, "Wendy Smith has run intelligently in the conditions. She's had a willing pacemaker in Anne Audain, but now it's a question of judgment..."

Coming out of the first turn I could feel her move up to my shoulder. No question now, she was positioning herself for the move. I sped up slightly, putting some pressure on, testing her, trying to get her to lay her cards on the table. She wasn't going for it. She hung right on my shoulder all down the back straight, for once taking the wind head on as I had been doing the whole race.

Now I knew what she was going to do.

Right before the final curve she surged and tried to go by. It was the classic kicker's strategy, trying to take the lead before the last turn, forcing your opponent to run wide if she wanted to recapture the lead, making her use up precious resources right before the final straight.

But I was ready for her. As soon as she made her move, I surged, too. I held her off as she strained to go by, then began my own kick going into the curve, pouring it on all through the bend, trying to take out any spunk she might have left in her legs, trying to break her resolve.

Coming out of the bend, for the first time in the race, I sneaked a look back and knew I had won. Concentrate, I told myself, don't lose your focus until the finish line is behind you. In the back of my mind again was Dick Quax losing that world record by easing up too soon.

All down the last straightaway, I bore down, pulling further away from Wendy, who was now visibly faltering. Though I was running as hard as I could, everything was happening in slow motion. Every inch took minutes, every meter hours. The stadium was pandemonium, but inside my head it all seemed far away, muted. To my eyes the world looked faded, whitewashed, as though I were seeing things through a cloudy windowpane.

When I finally hit the tape, the spell was broken and all the noise poured in on me. My arms went up as if in supplication, and an immense sense of joy, of serenity, of *relief* flooded through me.

If ever I had to choose one snapshot of my life, that would be it. It's the one on the cover of this book, and it shows a transcendent elation that I wish everyone could experience at some time in their lives. It seemed as if everything I had ever done had led to that moment, and my life made perfect sense.

All the solitary hours of my childhood, the taunting of other children, the endless pain of my feet, the training runs in the dark and the rain, the hills that demanded your dignity before they relented, the mean struggle to earn a living while trying to be an athlete, it had all been worth it.

I had won.

35 ～ Afterglow

The sheer joy of that moment was only heightened as I turned and saw that the next runner finishing was Lorraine. We embraced on the track for a long time, shedding more than a few tears together. Then to our great delight, Dianne finished fourth and joined us. What pride we felt as New Zealanders then, holding hands and circling the stadium in a victory lap in our all-black suits with the little silver fern on the chest! The Kiwis in the crowd were going quite mad, of course, as we trotted around the 400-meter oval, waving and blowing kisses.

Then as we were coming off the last turn, to my surprise, Lorraine and Dianne scooped me up and carried me down the home straight as the crowd roared its approval. Distance runners are not known for their upper body strength and I was afraid they would hurt themselves!

The ceremony went by in a blur and only by watching it on tape later could I truly appreciate it. There was general pandemonium all around us wherever we went. Among the first people to congratulate me were some of the New Zealand officials who had tried their best to sabotage me over the years. How strange, I thought, after all these years of skullduggery and cheap shots, that now they want to be best friends. My time was 8:45.5, a Commonwealth record, a Games record, and a New Zealand record.

After the mandatory drug testing, a team manager told Lorraine and I that we were expected at a posh function that evening on board a New Zealand Navy frigate anchored in the harbor. The guests were mostly New Zealand dignitaries, team officials, and Olympic and Commonwealth Games officials. We had nothing appropriate with us to wear to that type of affair, so we went in jeans. When we stepped on the ship, we saw that everyone was dressed in glamorous evening-wear, drinking pink champagne. We would have felt outrageously out of place except for one fashion accessory: We each wore our medals around our necks! We tried to be good sports as everyone made a big fuss over us. At one point we were taken up to the Captain's table, where some were smoking heavily, and after a short time the small, closed room became just unbearable.

After a respectable interval, I slipped out to find a phone. I wanted to be out celebrating with our teammates and friends, not with this crew. One drunken Olympic official had even grabbed me by the haunch as I was ascending the steps to the captain's table! I still had not seen my coach, or called my parents or husband. We had been rushed off to this event willy-nilly. I called John at the TV studios, where he and Keith Quinn were still doing follow-up interviews. I said, "Please come get me!"

He said they would be there in 20 minutes and told me what kind of car to look for. I went out onto the deck and waited by the gangway, trying to look nonchalant. Sure enough, a car came screeching around the corner and slid to a halt at the bottom of the gangway. I ran down and jumped in and we sped away, just like in the movies!

We went to a Chinese restaurant where Keith had to put up with the two of us sitting around grinning like monkeys all evening. I made John wear the medal around his neck as if he had won the race. He didn't protest that much. He had been so instrumental in my success, I was overjoyed that he was there to share the moment with me.

We left the restaurant to find a phone booth, and all three of us crowded in to call Steve in the States. We woke up everyone in the house. Jenny, Dave, then Steve. A police car pulled up to the curb and asked what was going on and if I was OK. When I started laughing, I guess he figured we were just on a bender. A funny moment.

My parents were thrilled, of course, and it seemed the whole country had been watching the race. Mum and Dad said they almost couldn't stand to watch as the race progressed. Dad kept repeating the whole time, "Please let her get a medal, please let her get a medal..." I guess I had the whole country on edge the way I ran the race—I even had people on the street tell me later how nerve-racking it had been to watch.

I was scheduled to leave early the next day for Boston to run the Bonne Bell 10K, which I wanted to win to ensure a number one road race ranking. The New Zealand selectors wanted me to stay and run the 1500 meters because they had an empty spot and had visions of another gold. But I took my road racing commitments seriously and at that moment I did not think I could get "up" for another all-out track effort again so soon. As it was, Lorraine went on to get another bronze in the 1500 meters, so who knows what might have happened.

I left Brisbane and flew through Auckland where, unbeknownst to me it had been arranged for Mum, Dad and Kate to come and visit with me privately for an hour while they boarded the plane. I got to show off the medal and we traded stories. It was wonderful to get some time with them because I wouldn't be back to New Zealand for six weeks.

Air New Zealand gave me first class seats through to Los Angeles, my only time ever in first class to this day, and it would have been the most restful that flight had ever been, except that I was too wired to sleep. In California, the New Zealand crew sent me off with boxes of chocolates and bottles of champagne. I met Steve in Denver and we flew on to Boston. It was one heck of a trip, Brisbane to Boston in 40 hours! I arrived still on a high but sorely in need of sleep. I had to come down before I could get rested to get back "up" again. Fortunately, I had four days to do it.

If I could pull it off, this race would complete an undefeated year for me, as well as a string of 12 straight course records. It was important to stay focused for a few more days if I wanted to wrap up this dream-like perfect season.

The race went like so many others that year. I took the lead at the one-mile mark and ran 31:42, my fastest 10K yet and another course record. "Just relaxed and enjoyed it," my diary says.

My perfect year was over!

We went from Boston up to Exeter, New Hampshire, where exercise physiologist Jack Daniels ran a laboratory for Nike. Although I don't like treadmills because the running motion seems so unnatural to me, I got on one and submitted to a battery of tests. Dr. Daniels wanted to measure my VO2 Max, which indicates the body's efficiency at using oxygen, and is generally considered the best single predictor of endurance sport capability. He said I recorded a 74.8, one of the highest he had ever seen in a woman. He did some other tests, and concluded that, physiologically speaking, I had the capacity to break 2:20 for the marathon! I got off the treadmill and thanked him for the prophecy.

"There's just one factor you didn't take into account, Jack," I said, "I don't want to run one!"

I hated the idea of racing such a long distance. And there were aspects of marathon training I didn't like as well. I enjoy racing, and when you're training for a marathon, you have to cut way back on the number of races you can run, putting all your eggs in that one basket. I call it the "lottery aspect" of marathoning. If you're unlucky in your one big race, you've lost the whole lottery.

We went back to Denver and a few days later Steve went on to New Zealand. I was staying in the United States to meet up with my mother to do a sightseeing tour, our first time to travel together!

At that time Creigh Kelley and I talked things over and we agreed that with his far better connections in corporate America, Drew Mearns of IMG would be able to do more for me as an agent. It was typical of that he didn't hesitate to put my interests ahead of his own.

IMG represented such luminaries as Arnold Palmer, Greg Norman and Chris Evert, and Drew was the preeminent runner's agent at the time, representing Alberto Salazar, Mary Decker, and other top stars.

Mum arrived and we flew to Cleveland, where I signed a five-year contract with IMG. We were only there two nights, but Mum's early impression of big city America was formed quickly. We were on the 12th floor in downtown Cleveland, and the first night I went to bed with my earplugs in, a habit I had long ago picked up on my travels. At two in the morning, Mum was shaking me awake, frightened out of her wits from a loud banging at our window. Remember, this is 12 stories up! She had been too scared to look out, and had sat up in a chair for two hours letting her imagination run wild. Of course, I hadn't heard a thing. It turned out to be a window cleaner's scaffold that the wind had set to swinging. At three in the morning, we changed rooms. My mother's first impression of America was that of a place where things go bump in the night.

Other than that, we had a great time. I asked her where she would most like to go in the United States, thinking she would say New York, Washington, D.C., or Chicago. But she said Nashville! So off we went to Tennessee, and had a wonderful time visiting all the country music places, buying T-shirts and being typical tourists.

We were even able to squeeze one more race in, Creigh's Zoo Run 10K in Denver. I wanted to run it as a thank you to Creigh, and there was the additional incentive of a new automobile for first place. So my 33:26 first place won a little Ford Lynx, which I would keep for 14 years! And my time was another course record, so I was able to keep my "perfect year" intact.

Mum and I stopped in Los Angeles on our way back to New Zealand and went to Disneyland, then down to San Diego to Sea World. After all my years of traveling around the world, it was great fun to share a trip like this with my mother. I remember looking forward to a time when I could do the same thing with Dad, but sadly it was never to be.

When we got back to New Zealand, the Otahuhu Athletic Club had a parade for me through the city. With Otahuhu's size, it was one of the world's shortest parades. As we drove from the Auckland airport, we switched over to vintage cars, which took us down Main Street, with athletes of all ages from the town running alongside the cars. In that crowd were so many people who had known and supported me for so long, the memories came flooding back and the emotion of the moment was almost overwhelming. Though it must have been difficult for her after all her struggles, my old and dear friend, teammate and neighbor Barbara Moore was there as well, up on the stage with me, my parents and the mayor, gracious as ever. In this moment of glad grace, my heart went out to her and I prayed that she would one day have her moment in the sun.

I was just beginning to realize the effect my Commonwealth Games victory was having on our tiny nation. The population was only about three million souls and apparently every single one of them were tuned to the television the night of the race. Everywhere I went people recognized me and were effusive in their congratulations. They kept replaying the race on television and do so to this day on the anniversary of the event, as well as on my birthday. To this day I am New Zealand's only female Commonwealth Games or Olympic track gold medalist.

Of course, after the race, all the post hoc pretenders came out of the woodwork, laying claim, however tenuous, to some portion of credit. Not the least of these was the New Zealand Sports Foundation, which tried to lay the groundwork for future fundraising efforts by claiming they had financially supported my training! They even presented me with a plaque to commemorate this phantom subsidy!

This was a completely false assertion, and one that would cause me anguish in the years to come. I tried to be diplomatic about it, saying that if it had not been for the chance to compete professionally in America, I would never have been in Brisbane. But this ended up being a long saga, with the result that once it all came out, the head of the New Zealand Sports Foundation ended up in prison for fraud and other offenses. It turned out that for years he had been siphoning off funds that were supposed to have gone to help support amateur athletes in training.

Meanwhile, back in the States Drew Mearns had negotiated a two-year deal with Nike for $40,000 per year plus bonuses. This was overwhelming to me, but it had the right effect: I wanted to run better than ever to prove I was worth it. The contract gave me the feeling of security I needed to really feel like a professional athlete. It allowed me to plan my training and competition with some long-term goals in mind, and not have to hop in every little race that came along just for the money.

A little later, Drew called to let me know he had secured a two-year endorsement deal with Pepsi for the same amount. I was speechless.

For the next several years, during the height of the "running boom" in the United States, I earned what was to me a sizable amount of money. To those who might call it excessive, I can only point out what I had earned for the previous 11 years of extremely hard work: zero.

After weeks of decompressing and enjoying myself, toward the end of November, 1982, I went back to serious training. I had put on about six pounds through this time, but John never minded a little extra weight when I was starting a mileage phase, which for me meant 75-85 miles a week.

One helpful routine started that year. Jon Sinclair had come down to New Zealand from snowy Colorado. He wanted John Davies to coach him, so Jon, his then-wife, Wendy, and three running friends came down to train during our warm months. I was very pleased to have such a compatible training partner. Jon is my height, has the

same stride and rhythm, and we'd always been a good match in training. I took them to our little island and they all fell in love with it.
Winter training "down under" became a yearly routine with Jon
throughout the '80s, something we both believe lengthened our
careers.

Training went well, but I was finding that a lot of my mental
energy was being diverted by outside demands on my time. I spent
five hours one day with a television crew preparing a documentary on
the upcoming Olympic year. And there were thousands of little dis-
tractions as well. People thought nothing of interrupting a training
run to get an autograph for their children, or stopping me in the
grocery store for a lengthy conversation. And heaven help you if you
aren't consistently gracious and accommodating, or you'll hear via
the grapevine that your success has all gone to your head. New
Zealanders demand good sportsmanship from their athletes, which is
one of the many things I love about my country. The problem is that
it's such a small place, once people know you, you can never just
"blend in" again.

Even John was having a hard time dealing with the attention and
requests for coaching and appearances. He already had a full-time
job heading the computer department of a large company, so it was-
n't easy to find the time to even deal with the inquiries. I now paid
him to be my coach—as did Jon Sinclair—because we both considered ourselves to be professionals and it was only fair that our mentor
share in our success. I paid him a percentage of my earnings and
Nike contributed with gear and travel expenses.

On January 16, 1983, I set a New Zealand mile record of 4:33.9,
which was not a particularly fast time. In fact, I was surprised no one
had run it any faster (my 1500-meter time would have converted to a
4:28 or so), but a record is a record, and strangely enough, that one
stood until very recently.

The world record for 10,000 meters on the track stood at only
31:53 at the time, so in mid-February we decided to make a try for it.
Unfortunately, the weather didn't cooperate and at race time it was
pouring rain. A good-sized crowd had turned up at Mt. Smart
Stadium to watch, so we went ahead with it. I was running in ankle
deep water, my shoes getting loose and my feet slipping around, so at
5000 meters I yelled to John that I wanted to quit. He told me to
keep going for the people who had come out to support me, so I did.
I ran a solo 32:21, which I was proud of under the circumstances.

Though it wasn't a world mark, it was another New Zealand record.

We had a wonderful time sharing in the celebration of the gold medal and getting ready for the upcoming season, but by the time March rolled around, I was really ready for my life of relative anonymity in the United States.

36 ~ The Marathon

Steve and I went back to the States on March 10th, straight to New Orleans and the Crescent City Classic, where I was promptly handed my first road loss since July of 1981. I was running well, but the competition was definitely improving. I finished third to Wendy Smith and Joan Benoit in 32:28. We went on to Little Rock for a 10K, and there met Bill and Hillary Clinton when they were still in the Governor's mansion. Then it was back to Denver, where we moved back in with Jenny and Dave Kyle, who had now moved out to Littleton, a suburb that was more convenient to our training haunts.

So how did I suddenly become interested in the marathon, an event I always swore I would never run?

The seed was planted at a 20-mile race I ran in April at the Cherry Creek Reservoir. I did it just to get in a long training run at altitude, but I ended up winning in 1:58:25. Had I been able to keep up the same pace for another 6.2 miles, it would have been close to a 2:35 marathon.

John wanted me to start doing weight training a bit more seriously, so I started going to Steve's Nautilus club in Denver, where I began doing strength workouts for my legs. These workouts would make my legs so tired that I sometimes couldn't run, which was frustrating until I gradually adapted to it.

I won a five-mile race in Dallas, where I met the great American miler Jim Ryun, and also got a chance to talk with my fellow Kiwi, three-time gold medalist Peter Snell, now a highly respected exercise physiologist at the University of Texas.

I was still covering between 70 and 80 miles a week at altitude, in addition to the weight workouts. I soon ran my best time up Lookout Mountain, covering the five-mile ascent in 34:20, which gave me tremendous confidence.

On May 1st, I was back in Spokane for my third Bloomsday, which I won in a course record 39:29. My diary reports: "Felt strong. Eased [up] last mile." A week later, as a training run, I ran the first 18 miles of the Denver Marathon in 1:46:30, again running well under six minutes per mile pace for the distance, and again adding to my growing interest in the marathon. (Perhaps I should have spent some time wondering what Frank Shorter meant when he said "The marathon begins at 20 miles.")

It seemed like a good time to settle some old accounts, so I decided to do the L'eggs 10K in New York. After my humiliating dropout two years earlier, I promised myself I would return and win it someday. Obviously, all the hype was again around Grete Waitz, which was understandable. After all her marathon and other victories there, the whole town loved her, including race director Fred Lebow. As the race day approached, I had a bit of a head cold but my policy was that if I chose to start a race, I would never mention such problems. I was tired of newspaper stories before big races that listed everyone's excuses ahead of time. My philosophy was that if you were on the starting line, you were there to race, period.

After the first mile I took the lead from Grete. This caused great discomfiture on the press truck, where Fred Lebow and Grete's husband, Jack, had formed a two-man cheering section for her.

Now, as I pulled out in front, instead of encouragement, what they were yelling at me was that I had to stay on the right hand side of the road instead of running the tangents. That was curious, because in 1981 when I had run the race we had been allowed to follow the tangents through the park, which is the way courses are officially measured. Road racers know that if you don't adhere to the tangents, over the course of several miles they can add up to substantial extra distance. All I could do was hope that everyone behind me was doing the same, otherwise they were running a shorter race than

I was. Meanwhile, Jack was calling out to Grete in Norwegian and Fred looked like he might have a heart attack as he hopped around the truck, yelling and trying to will Grete back into the lead.

As I've mentioned, situations like this just add fuel to my fire. I never relinquished the lead and won in 32:23 to her 32:42.

After all the years of racing behind her, no one has more respect for Grete as an athlete than I do, and she was gracious in defeat. But her fans and entourage were beside themselves. All I heard at the press conference after the race was how if she hadn't had a cold she would have won. I never mentioned that I wasn't at 100 percent either. But one thing was certain: I had received official notice from all quarters that running in New York City was a closed club and I wasn't in it.

Joan Benoit was supposed to have run L'eggs as well but pulled out late. I was disappointed because I really wanted to race against the best and find out where I stood.

I went on to the Middletown, New York 10K the next weekend and on arrival there found that Joan had entered that race instead of L'eggs. She beat me by seven seconds and said at the awards ceremony she was happy to beat the person who had beaten Grete in New York. So why, I wondered, wasn't she in New York, where she would have had a chance to beat us *both*? It would have been great for the sport. Anyway, I was happy that I had stepped up to the starting line both times.

After several more weeks of training in Denver, I returned to New York for the Pepsi national 10K final on July 3rd. It was an extremely hot day and we stood on the George Washington Bridge for 30 extra minutes in the broiling sun while they fixed some kind of technical glitch.. It was 90 degrees, extremely humid and everyone got sunburned! I ran 32:28 to win and was ecstatic with the time under those conditions.

John Davies and I had been running up our usual huge telephone bills, talking back and forth, and we finally decided that I would attempt the marathon in the 1984 Olympics. In hindsight, I would say that decision was possibly the only wrong one we made throughout my career.

It was an odd situation. Prior to 1972, the longest women's race in the Olympic Games was the 800 meters. It was assumed in all quarters than the female of the species simply wasn't built for anything more strenuous. All poppycock, of course. Olympic authorities succumbed ever so grudgingly to pressure in 1972, adding the 1500 as the longest event (a distance still short of a mile!) With women running marathons and longer nearly every weekend all through the 1980's, the authorities once again responded to the clamor for parity, again in typically illogical fashion, adding both the 3000 meters and the marathon in 1984. But there was still nothing in between. For a runner such as myself, whose best event is somewhere in the 5000 to 10,000-meter range, it was a Hobson's choice. The 3000, at 200 meters short of two miles, is still a relatively short middle-distance race that in good competition will almost always be won by a runner with very good leg speed. And the marathon is the quintessential *long* distance race.

With runners like Mary Decker Slaney and the Eastern Bloc milers in the 3000, we figured that it would be a real toss-up for medals, whereas the marathon might yet turn out to be my strong suit.

Very few who saw that race would ever forget what happened in the 1984 Olympic 3000 meters, when Mary Decker Slaney tripped on Zola Budd's heels just past the halfway point. My Commonwealth Games nemesis, Wendy Sly (formerly Smith) ended up with the silver medal in 8:39.47, three and a half seconds behind Maricica Puica of Romania, so who knows? On the other hand, maybe I would have gotten tangled up, too.

At any rate, we settled on the marathon. It would mean that I would have to run the New Zealand qualifying time, 2:35, before the March 1984 selection deadline. We chose Chicago, a flat course with a fast reputation.

There seemed to be a lot of interest in my running a marathon. I didn't think of it as pressure, really, because I always felt I had control over my own career. But plenty of people were interested in what I could do at that distance.

I had become interested in the distance by now, but I was still cautious. I was concerned about my feet and how they would react to the punishment of racing 26 miles. Since my childhood, I had retained in the back of my mind a simple gratitude that I could run at all, so I always had this little voice telling me not to push my luck. Secondly, as I've mentioned, I liked racing, and marathoners abstain from racing while training for their event.

Still, I trusted John to coach me well for the event. Once we decided that the marathon was it, we put any doubts behind us and got down to work. At that time Alison Roe, Lorraine Moller, Glenis

Quick and Mary O'Connor were all capable of doing the qualifying time, so I was certainly the novice of the group. I started to train for the event and continued to make contract appearances for Nike at selected occasions, but pulled back from other racing.

Alison and Lorraine were the favorites for the team, so to my way of thinking, the challenge was to slip in front of the other two. I lengthened my long runs to over two hours and absolutely hated them. I was bored silly running that far and stupidly thought that if I ran faster they would be over quicker. That used to work when John told me to run, say, 15 miles. Now he was telling me to run, for instance, "two hours and ten minutes." Different concept! Finally I found a runner in Denver named Clyde Sax who agreed to keep me company on these long runs, and that helped immensely. Clyde is over six feet tall, but his stride matched mine, so we ran in sync.

I was going through a lot of training shoes. At the time, Nike hadn't started making air-cushioned shoes. I always liked to run in the nearest thing possible to bare feet, so I did a lot of my training in racing flats with no socks. Nike's lightest racing flats at the time were American Eagles, and they even had some made up for me in New Zealand's black and white racing colors. They were great, but they didn't have a durable enough sole for training, so I'd get a friend at Creigh's store to glue soles from the Nike Waffle Trainer on the bottoms. I ended up with these completely customized Nike black and white American Eagle Waffle Trainers. Even after they started making all their shoes with air, Nike continued to custom-make my training shoes all the way to the end of my career. I never wore anything else.

On September 17, 1983, I raced my first half marathon in Vermont against Portugal's Rosa Mota. I won in 71:20 on a hilly course and was happy with it. It was time to start focusing on Chicago and the full 26.2 mile distance.

Bob Bright, Chicago's race director, seemed to me a good guy and a good businessman. Before I had even made up my mind which marathon to run, he invited me to visit Chicago to see the course, all expenses paid. At the time there was a huge rivalry between the New York and Chicago marathons, and Bob was always getting the brunt of some criticism or another for the way he directed his race. But in my dealings with him he was first rate; he treated athletes like professionals, which was still a rare thing in the sport.

Nike was paying for John and his wife, Patsy, to come up from

New Zealand for the marathon, so I met them in Los Angeles, where I was to run the Los Angeles Coliseum 10K. They brought Bob Johnson, our masseuse, who was on his way to England. It was the only year they held this race, but it was well funded, with a $10,000 prize for first place. The race started downtown and finished on the Olympic track, and it had budget enough to bring in Rosa Mota, Lorraine Moller, Julie Brown, Julie Isphording, Jan Merrill, and others. I won by 20 seconds in 32:20 and felt very strong. It was the first time John had seen me run a road race, so it was wonderful to finally be able to share that experience with him and Patsy.

From there we went directly to Chicago. I was getting a hefty appearance fee, $15,000, to do my marathon debut there. That was a lot of money just to show up, but I always tried to give good value in those arrangements, working hard to help the director promote the event, even to the extent of arriving early in the week to do interviews.

I was apprehensive about the thought of racing 26 miles, not because I wasn't fit enough, but because in the marathon there's always the "X factor." I could usually predict more or less how fast I would run in a shorter race, but in a race as long as this, I knew loots of things can go wrong. But just because I didn't want to predict what I would do didn't keep everyone else from doing it for me! I heard from lots of people what I could expect to run. Me, I was just telling myself I needed to be patient. My natural instincts in any race were to be aggressive, but that's not smart in a marathon.

There was good competition: the gifted American, Lisa Weidenbach; '82 European champion Rosa Mota; England's Joyce Smith; Boston champ Jackie Gareau of Canada; and Dorothe Rasmussen of Denmark.

I stayed up front with the leaders through halfway and felt very comfortable. In fact, I was fighting myself to keep from going faster. At halfway I couldn't hold back any more and started to push the pace. Soon I had two minutes on Jackie and four on Rosa! I got to 20 miles and felt great, with no real appreciation for the pace I was running, which was for a 2:24 marathon. John got around the course to see me at different places and was encouraged by how I looked at each stop. At 24 miles he ran along beside me for a ways and told me I looked great.

"I *feel* great," I said.

A guy I was running with said, "You're running so comfortably, why don't you push harder?"

John said, "Go for it. I'll see you at the finish line!"

I said, "See you!"

Within a minute of that conversation, everything changed drastically. I suddenly felt terrible, like I was going to faint. Here's how Bob Wischnia described it in *Runner's World*:

> ...Audain maintained a healthy lead through 20 miles, but as she turned onto Lake Shore Drive (24 miles), a head wind began to stand her up and the fatigue became evident as her arms drooped and her shoulders began to sway. Although she was clearly in trouble with 1½ miles to go, her lead was still more than a minute on Mota, who was now in second, and only a disaster could prevent Audain from winning.
>
> One disaster coming right up. By the 25th mile, Audain's leg muscles had the consistency of jelly. Not Julie Moss-like jelly (remember her nightmare at the Ironman Triathlon?), but as Audain's legs weakened, she began to weave from the shoulder of the road to the middle and back to the shoulder. A crack in the road almost sent her spilling, but she recovered her balance only to have her right ankle buckle and she tumbled inelegantly—headfirst—to the pavement. Later, she would say that she fell in a hole and was on the street for a minute—indeed, it must have seemed at least that long to her—but a citywide television audience (as well as many spectators at the finish who watched on monitors) saw her scramble painfully to her feet after only a few seconds on the road. She was, however, obviously dazed and disoriented from the fall.
>
> The 25th mile had taken the Kiwi almost 6½ minutes, but the final 1.2 miles would take nearly nine. Mota, urged on by her coach, Jose Pedrosa, who was accompanying her on a bicycle, cruised by the floundering Audain just after she regained her equilibrium. Dead on her feet, Audain couldn't respond to the Portuguese but merely glanced in horror at the smoothly striding Mota.

I do not remember running the last mile, although John and others assured me that I looked terrible. In addition to Rosa, Jackie Gareau and Dorothe Rasmussen went by me before I finally struggled to the finish line in 2:32:14.

It was the fastest debut marathon for a woman ever, and I was well within the New Zealand qualifying standard, but it was a humbling experience, to say the least. I was taken to the medical tent where the diagnosis was that I was just plain hungry—I ate anything they gave me! One of the rookie mistakes I had made was not carbo-loading as much as I could in the days before the race. My legs were fine and after I got some food in me I felt wonderful. I had two badly scraped knees and severely wounded pride, and at the time I thought that was all.

Disappointed but not despondent, I headed back to the hotel where Steve had watched the race on television. Everyone in the room seemed uncomfortable, like they didn't really know what to say. I was the same as I always was after a bad race, sort of, "Okay, *that's* over. What's next?" I showered and went downstairs to the awards ceremony, where everyone commiserated with me as if my favorite pet had died.

The longer I stood there the more my left ankle started to ache, but I thought it was just fatigue. We started walking up the street to a nearby restaurant, and by the time we got there the pain in my foot was so bad I couldn't stay at the table. It got so unbearable I was cry-ing. I told the others that I needed to go to a hospital, that I had a broken foot. They said, let's go back to the hotel. I said, "No! I need to go to a hospital now!"

John and our masseuse, Bob Johnson, carried me back to the hotel and Bob kept insisting that it was just an after-effect of the fall, a spasm. He said that massage would help. I was beside myself with pain. I didn't want to trust him, but John said to hold on and see if massage would work. It actually made sense, as I had been walking on it and it was unlikely I could have done that on a broken bone.

So I took some painkillers from Patsy but it seemed that they took forever to work. Bob was trying to work on my foot and I was crying, swearing at him, yelling at him to stop! I'm glad he didn't lis-ten to me. In the end it worked, but it took a while.

Things were better the next morning, but Steve and I decided not to accompany John and Patsy to New York, where they were going to watch that city's famous marathon. My knees were so lacer-ated I couldn't even wear long pants.

But at least I had finally run a marathon. Now I needed to go home and heal up.

37 ~ *Los Angeles Olympics, 1984*

Now it was back to New Zealand and undertaking the very unfamiliar task of training for an Olympic marathon. I wasn't definitely on the team, but John had been given an indication that the selectors thought my Chicago performance had been sufficient. At this point Glenis Quick and Mary O'Connor had also broken 2:35, but I was the fastest of the three. Alison and Lorraine were not running at all at that stage, so I was fairly secure in the thought that even if Alison and Lorraine did qualify by the March deadline I would still be number three on the team.

Jon Sinclair was down training and I started to put in even more mileage, hitting 97 two weeks in a row, then 100 miles the week ending on Christmas day, 1983! We spent most of our time on Waiheke, running the hills. Every 10 days or so we'd have to go somewhere flatter, just for a break.

In my mind I was training for a marathon that would take place in August of 1984, so I was relaxed and happy, thinking I had a good long time to get fit and ready. I was still questioning whether I should do the 3000, but everyone was telling me I could be a good marathon runner, including Arthur Lydiard. This was the one time in my career that I did not feel totally convinced that I was doing the right thing, and it took a great deal of mental energy to keep reassuring myself that my goal was the right one. This high-mileage training was new to me and kept me so tired that it was hard to feel confident about what I was doing. I was accustomed to using my workouts to bolster my confidence, but these 100-mile weeks felt destructive. I stayed with it, though, and after a while was undeniably getting stronger and feeling better. I was learning something a marathoner *must* learn: patience.

Then along came the news that the New Zealand selectors had given Alison and Lorraine extra time to run the Boston Marathon in April in order to qualify for the team. So now it appeared there might be five under the qualifying standard. Then the selectors said that since I was the novice in the group, I should do a backup performance.

So all of a sudden we had to drastically alter the program so that I could run the Los Angeles Marathon in February, on the Olympic course. John was confident that I could run another qualifying time even though I would not try to be absolutely peaked for it. At the end of January I ran a solo 20-mile time trial along the Auckland waterfront with John following in a car. I ran 1:52:39, despite some strong winds. That's 5:36 per mile, or 2:27 marathon pace. The last five miles I averaged 5:31, so I was strong right to the end.

I tried to run on the road as much as possible because the sidewalk has a crown on it to facilitate drainage. But traffic eventually forced me onto the sidewalk and the crown caused my left leg to get really tight over the last five miles. I felt comfortable with the effort, but my left leg totally seized up on me. A couple of days before I had slipped and jarred my back and this run no doubt just set it off.

Afterwards, I had some severe sciatic pain, but after getting a lot of therapy on it, John and I left for Los Angeles. Of course sitting in an airplane seat for so long doesn't help an injury like that, but we had a week before the race and hoped that would be enough. It was frustrating, knowing how fit I was, but also feeling so much pain from this serious injury. We stayed out in Santa Monica by the ocean, and I would go running along the boulevard and just stop in despair because I knew my leg was not working right. I had always been so careful about my health, immediately taking time off to allow for healing when I got an injury like this, and now here I was trying to run a marathon hurt. It was stupid and I knew it.

But I now felt things were out of my control, that if I wanted to get to the Olympics I had to run this. In hindsight, I should have called the selectors' bluff. I had not only qualified, I had the fastest qualifying time of any woman in New Zealand, yet I was being asked to jump through their hoops once again! I had always taken pride in not running hurt, in respecting my body and being smart about such things. I couldn't believe I had been placed in this situation.

At the exposition the day before the race a chiropractor was offering treatments, so John asked him if he would look at me. He manipulated my lower back and that night I went out for a run and felt a good deal better. At last, a ray of hope! John had asked the chiropractor if he could be at the start the next morning to help me, which he did.

Throughout the marathon my leg gave me no trouble at all. I felt strong and immensely relieved. Jackie Gareau and I ran side by side towards the finish in the Coliseum. With a mile to go she broke from me a little, but knowing that I was by far the faster finisher, I wasn't worried. I assumed we would have one lap around the stadium track when we got inside, so I just concentrated on not letting the gap get any bigger. As we entered the tunnel into the stadium I was gaining on her. Coming out of the tunnel, I started to gather myself up to catch her and suddenly I saw the finish line tape only 70 meters away! There wasn't enough distance to run her down and I finished seven seconds behind.

My time was 10 seconds faster than Chicago, so now I had the two fastest times in New Zealand. I couldn't imagine that they could ask any more of me. I got on the plane back to New Zealand more relieved than anything else.

After a rest, I went back to my mileage program, along with regular visits to my old friend and therapist, Jill Ferguson. She knew me so well and was so skilled that she instilled great confidence just knowing she was watching over me. Just before leaving New Zealand I ran in an Avon 15K, winning in 50:55 with no one else really close. First prize was a trip to the Paris marathon and some of the other runners immediately protested my being in the race because I was a "professional" and could get to international events on my own. What they didn't know was that I had already decided not to accept the prize if I won, and had discussed it with the organizers. When the upset women were told that, not a single one made any effort to apologize for the outburst.

The general public was very supportive of my professionalism, but among the competitive running community there was a lot of petty jealousy. The promoters of the event were thrilled to have me because it drew media attention and gave their race some recognition and competitive quality it wouldn't have had otherwise. But to those few protesting women, I was just an unfair impediment to their winning a prize.

There is to this day in the sport an undercurrent of resentment towards athletes good enough to earn money from it. I've even discerned some understandable bitterness from some earlier generation athletes who missed the movement altogether. The sport never made the full transition from amateur to professional, as indicated by the name of our global governing body, the International Amateur Athletic Federation. The word "amateur" is still there, now honored mostly by the breach. And there are still those resentful of athletes "lucky" enough to be very fast runners.

At any rate, even at this late day I was still not definitely on the New Zealand team until we saw what Lorraine and Alison did at Boston. What happened was that Lorraine won the race in 2:29:28 and Alison dropped out. So I was on the Olympic marathon team with Lorraine and Mary O'Connor. I was still angry about the process, but not in the least surprised. I had been around New Zealand athletic politics for too long. The only thing consistent about it is that it's never consistent and it's a surer bet to know someone than to accomplish something.

We stayed and trained much longer in New Zealand than usual, leaving finally on April 15th, 1984 for the States. As my travel was paid by Nike, Steve and I sometimes traveled on different airlines to get better prices. He didn't particularly like taking those long trips with me anyway because I curled up with my earplugs in place and slept soundly, which he said wasn't much fun.

This time he was on United Airlines and I was on Air New Zealand. He was due to leave the day before me and we would meet up in Los Angeles and continue on together. He was flying via Honolulu and I assumed I was too. That night John Davies got a phone call very late from Steve, who had been unable to wake anyone up at his parents'. He had been stopped by immigration in Hawaii, because of a visa restriction that he couldn't be in the country without me. I had the visa.

This was the first time he had traveled ahead of me, so this caught us by complete surprise. They put him under house arrest at a hotel until I could get there on my way through Honolulu the next day. When John and Patsy took me to the airport the next morning, we looked up my flight and were mortified to see that it was going through Tahiti instead of Hawaii. We notified U.S. immigration about the snag, and they held Steve until my plane had landed on United States soil, at which point they put Steve on a flight to Los Angeles.

Immigration was an ongoing hassle. I had to renew our visas yearly and had to leave the country to do it. There was never any guarantee as to when they would come through and there were times we were held up in New Zealand waiting and pleading with the U.S. embassy to hurry up so we could meet a commitment. American citizens have no idea how expensive and tiring it is to deal with immigration if you're not a political or economic refugee. On top of it all, the treatment you get from the authorities is anything but pleasant.

Anyway, I finally collected Steve and flew down to Little Rock for another Pepsi 10K to fulfill my contract. I was miserable from the travel, but I won in 34:12. Then it was back to Denver. For some time Steve had been arguing that there was too much commotion in Denver for me to train well and that we needed to move somewhere quieter. I wasn't totally convinced but had to admit that Ft. Collins, where Jon Sinclair lived, was enticing, as well as Boise, Idaho, which we had come to like a lot.

Jon lobbied hard for Ft. Collins, and I would have gone but for two things. First, Colorado State at that time didn't have a decent track; second, it was an hour drive to the Denver airport. I still got motion sickness and avoided car trips whenever possible.

So Boise it was! We packed up what little we had and drove to Idaho to stay for a while and try it out. Then I got really ill. As I look back it seems that everything that went seriously wrong in my running career happened when I was training for the marathon. My heart and mind were not in it. I got a very serious kidney infection and I had to really pay attention and get well. I reluctantly passed on Bloomsday in order to recover and stay on track for the marathon. After winning it three years in a row, it was a great disappointment not to go.

As the defending champion, I was paid to go to New York to do promotional work for the upcoming the L'eggs 10K. It was on this trip that I discovered European promoters weren't the only sexual harassers in the sport. Suffice it to say that I got to know more about

Fred Lebow than I wanted to and swore I would never take money again for running in New York when he was involved. I didn't want to be beholden to him in any way.

Another reason I didn't trust him had to do with the L'eggs course record. After I won in 1983 an older official at the finish line rushed up to me after the race and gave me a piece of the finishing tape for a souvenir.

"Congratulations on running such a fast time!" he said.

I said, "How far off was I from Grete's world record on this course?" She had run 31:00 there.

He said, "Oh, that time was done when the course was only six miles!"

I was dumbfounded. A 10K is 6.2 miles, and the usual conversion for that two-tenths of a mile is a full minute. It sounded to me very much like the 1981 New York Marathon "world record" that later turned out to be short, too. Could it be that in addition to his other charms, Fred Lebow owned one of the world's shortest yardsticks?

At any rate, if that official was correct and Grete's 31:00 was run on a six-mile course, it means that I was actually the first woman to run under 32 minutes for 10K on the roads, in the United States.

Interestingly enough, I never did get asked back to the race, even when they had the 20th anniversary event. All the previous winners were invited back except me. Almost out of curiosity, I called and offered to come for airfare and a hotel room and they said no. I did compete in L'eggs again, but at my own expense.

Anyway, I went on to Revco in Cleveland and won there again and a few weeks later was back in New York for the L'eggs race, this year finishing second to Grete, which of course set the universe back in order as far as New York was concerned. This year they allowed us to run the tangents again even though the race started and finished in the same place. The rule seemed to change depending on whether Grete was leading or not. I was quite happy to run 33:29 and felt I was gaining fitness after everything I'd been through in previous few months.

On June 28th, I was back in New York for the Pepsi Final again and this time it was pouring rain, quite a contrast to the sun-baked race of 1983. This time I won in 32:10, a course record and a fast enough performance to let me know I was back on track. Then it was back to Boise and learning to deal with the incredible heat in the summer there. It's not humid, but the temperature is consistently 90-

100 degrees, something I'd never experienced day after day.

One day while I was running out on the Boise Greenbelt I joined up with two guys out training. One was Bob Walker, a Boise high school teacher who had run on scholarship at Boise State. We chatted during the run and he seemed like a nice guy. Since his pace seemed compatible with mine, I asked him if he'd like to train with me sometime. That was the beginning of a great training partnership that lasted for many years until I retired from active competition. In fact, when I'm back in Boise even now we still run together.

In July I joined the New Zealand team at the Olympic Village on the UCLA campus. Every country was there except the United States, which was housed at Southern Cal, next to the stadium. The rooms were cramped and as a late arrival, I was out in the lounge area of one of the suites. Olympic housing is certainly never glamorous. We had two per bedroom and four in the lounge, all sharing one bathroom. My bed was right by the entrance so everyone going in or out walked over me. There was no air conditioning.

It wasn't a good area for distance runners to train, either. We were right in the middle of Beverly Hills, with concrete in all directions.

Of course there were the usual shenanigans, and the fire alarms went off a few times in the middle of the night. The village experience is wonderful in many ways, particularly when you're younger, but I certainly sympathize with the athletes who choose to stay elsewhere if they can afford it. You have to be worried about how the havoc may affect your performance. I was frustrated with the conditions, but tried to put them out of my mind.

I was still having trouble off and on with my leg, so that combined with other factors out of my control—the accommodations, the heat and humidity, the training circumstances—had my confidence at a low level. I knew I was in trouble and it's terrible going into such a big event knowing you are not ready. I considered withdrawing, and if I had really followed my instincts I would have. But then I started thinking of everyone I would let down, and I tried to talk myself up. Everything at that Olympics was a big hassle. I didn't even march in the opening ceremony, because it was the day before the marathon and I thought I should rest.

I went to the starting line feeling that I was fit, but also fragile. It was a terrifically hot and humid day. At three miles Joan Benoit broke away. I was in the main pack with Ingrid Kristiansen, Grete,

Rosa, and Lorraine.

When Joan took off I turned to Grete and Ingrid and said, "You had better go with her or she won't come back."

I knew Joan loved to run alone without the pressure of others. If I had been more confident, I would have gone with her, just to give it a shot, no matter the outcome. To this day when I hear Grete speak of her career, you can tell she is upset about that race. She always talks about how she was catching Joan at the end. It was so frustrating to watch it happen. Had I been ready to run, I would never have let Joan go. But she took the chance and she deserved the gold. Early on that day Grete settled for silver.

I ran along with the pack feeling quite good despite the heat and humidity. It was a miserable course, all concrete and very boring, with hardly any spectators along the way. Then at around 16 miles the pack broke up and I found myself running alone in about seventh place. At around 20 miles I could tell something was wrong aside from fatigue. I was dizzy and had tingling in my fingers, a sign of dehydration and heat exhaustion. I started looking for the medical teams and kept getting told they were just ahead. I kept running but found no one.

Finally I spotted an ambulance on the side of the road by a group of spectators. So I struggled towards them and then just fell down right in front of the paramedics. I didn't realize they weren't part of the race medical staff, they were off duty, just watching the race. They picked me up and took me to their own hospital, which happened to be on the other side of town.

They didn't even know whom to contact to let them know they had me. I was put on an IV. I tried to help them as to where to call, but was still a little addled. My coach, John Davies, was doing television commentating for New Zealand, and after the runners had begun coming into the stadium he became increasingly alarmed. I went missing for six or seven hours, and friends, family, and a good portion of New Zealand were a little panicky.

Finally we established contact and, apart from disappointment, fatigue and general wooziness, I was quite all right. Of course, that was the race where the television audience saw the spectacle of Gabriele Andersen staggering pathetically around the track, and I am sure glad I got out before doing that to myself. Contrary to a lot of sentiment at the time, I did not see anything dramatic or thrilling about her struggle. An athlete in that situation is helpless and risks doing irreparable damage to herself. As Kenny Moore, himself an Olympian, wrote in *Sports Illustrated*, heat is the one thing that can kill even well conditioned endurance athletes. And because we program ourselves not to give up, the outside world must intervene in such situations, or risk losing us. So when I saw the tape later, I didn't think it was heroic, I thought it was sad.

Back at the village I was in the manager's room when Lorraine walked in. I congratulated her on her wonderful fifth place finish.

"Well," she said, "I told you the marathon was tough and now you have been humbled by it."

I was too surprised to reply that I had already been humbled by it twice before. Sure, I was inexperienced at the distance, but I was still proud to have run in the first Olympic marathon for women, considering it was less than a year since my first one, and that I had certainly had to jump through all the official flaming hoops just to be there. I was happy that I had survived relatively intact.

My Dad was devastated by the way I looked on TV. After a marathon you are not a pretty sight under the best of circumstance, and this was an extreme case. He made me promise I would never run another one. That was the only time my Dad ever tried to influence anything about my running. But he was too late, because I had already made that decision myself.

I gave it a good try, I thought, but I'm going back to what I do best. I do not believe I was meant to be a marathoner.

38 ~ *Down and Almost Out*

I bounced back faster than I thought I would from the marathon, though the training and the race itself had taken a toll on me physically. A neurologist's tests revealed I had pressure on a nerve in my back so I began taking strong anti-inflammatories. But after training for a few weeks with Jon Sinclair in Colorado I began to come around again. I was surprised to get second at the Maggie Valley five-mile in North Carolina, and a little later was first at a 5K in 15:45 at 6,000 feet, followed by a 32:52 10K in Denver at 5,000 feet. I was gaining ground.

Back at the Virginia 10-miler at the end of September I won in a course record of 53:47, followed by a third in the Bonne Bell 10K in Boston 32:32. In that race, I turned the corner 150 meters from the finish and planted my foot to try to kick by Judi St. Hilaire. It was a wet surface and when my foot slipped I felt something give in my hip. A scan done later showed inflammation around the piriformis muscle in my hip. I rested, got massage, prayed, and then went to Phoenix where I limped a 32:42 10K. Luckily, I had only one race to go, the Pro-Comfort 10K final in Hawaii on the way back to New Zealand. The race course went by our hotel at the four-mile mark and it took all the discipline I could muster to keep from running right into the lobby and up to my room. As it was, I finished 12th in 34:00. Then they took all the runners to a wonderful luau on the beach. We had a wonderful time, our motley crew of Kenyans, Russians, Americans, Canadians and one grateful Kiwi, soon to drag her stressed-out body back to New Zealand.

Back home during my first run, John Davies noticed that I was favoring one leg. He has always had a great eye for form, but I thought he was imagining things. He took me out on a dirt trail and we measured the difference in stride length between my left leg and my right leg. It was dramatic. Then he got Steve's brother, Ted, to videotape me running. It also showed that one leg was "lazy," dragging slightly. John took me to an orthopedic surgeon friend, Roger Weeks, who diagnosed a torn piriformis muscle. He said I could either take enough time off to let it heal completely or he could operate.

I needed a mental break anyway, and Roger said it would be stronger if I let it heal on its own, so I opted for three months of down time. I don't like swimming or cycling, so I didn't try to cross-train. I went to the island, walked a lot, worked on the cottage, read, vegetated, and tried to forget about my adventures in marathon land.

In early February, 1986, I asked John if it was time to start running again and he gave me the go—ahead. It was Sunday morning, and I set off from our apartment in downtown Auckland, which had a small park across the street. I ran in the park for about 10 minutes. I wasn't in any pain, but I felt so uncoordinated and weak that I just sat and cried. Then I got in the car and drove to John's house where he and Patsy were having a quiet breakfast. I burst through the door crying, "I'm no better after three months!"

John calmed me down and drove me up to the Domain.

"There is nothing wrong with your leg," he said, "It just has bad memories." He meant that I had learned to favor it because of the injury, and now that the injury was gone, my muscles retained the "memory" of the altered stride.

So he taught me to do drills like the sprinters do, saying that I wasn't going to run any further than 600 meters until I ran with a balanced stride again. So we began a six-week program of basically learning how to run all over again. I was hopeless, with no coordination at all, and looked ridiculous doing those drills. John would run beside me, making sure I did them correctly. If I didn't, he would stop me and make me start over. It took a long time for me to get up to even 600 meters.

It took a lot of patience from both of us, but he wanted to make sure that I came back strong and completely healed. It was that kind of long-term thinking that allowed me to have a career as long as I had. Without that kind of attention to a seemingly minor problem, I would no doubt have been on my way out of the sport right then.

I finally got strong enough to go to the island to train and was so mentally revived I couldn't wait to get back to it. On April 8th, 1985, I ran a 10K road race in Auckland in 32:15 and felt great. It had only been two months since I had started back so it was amazing progress.

I had survived the marathon. I had survived the ordeals of 1984.

&

I look at 1985 as the year of my return to sanity. I happily went back to the roads and tried to forget I had ever heard of the marathon. In May I won my fourth Bloomsday in a course record 39:20, followed by another Cleveland Revco 10K in 31:59, a course record on their new route.

At the Cascade Runoff 15K at the end of June I finished second to Grete in 49:45. After the race I phoned New Zealand as I always did, and found out that Nana had died of a heart attack. She would have been 90 the next January, so she had lived a long life. I thought back to that previous April and remembered that when we said our good-byes, she behaved differently than before. She managed to walk outside to wave goodbye, which she usually didn't do. Then, just before I left for the airport, she called on the telephone to say good-bye once more. Looking back, I could see she was saying goodbye for the last time.

It was impractical to try to get to the funeral, so I had to mourn her on my own. She had been such a force in my life and I had so many memories to sort through of our times together on the island, I thought about her a lot over the next weeks and months. I still do.

&

I continued to race well through the summer of 1985, including another win at the Virginia 10-Miler, though my 54:03 was 16 seconds slower than my course record. That fall I ran very poorly at a race in Ukiah, California and couldn't figure out what was wrong. I finished sixth in a slow time, and felt awful. Several days later I came down with a bad sinus infection and had to go on antibiotics again. Hard running will often alert you to impending illness days before you get other signs.

The season was almost over anyway. We had by this time purchased a condominium in Boise and were firmly established in this strange, follow-the-sun yearly pattern of training in New Zealand over the northern hemisphere winter, then racing across America all summer and fall. It's not a bad life, but it's not one many people would identify with.

39 ~ *Commonwealth Games;*
Scotland, 1986

The upcoming Commonwealth Games were going to include a 10,000 meters for women for the first time, and John Davies and I decided to point for it. He set up a comprehensive schedule that took me right from base phase in New Zealand through to the race in Edinburgh at the end of July, working in a limited road racing schedule in between.

As always, as a part of my sharpening process, he included a number of track races in New Zealand. These races were never meant to bring out superlative performances because we always followed the Lydiard principle of "training through" them, meaning I didn't take any real rest beforehand. It was frustrating that some of the press never seemed to understand that I was running "tired" and that these races were part of a long-term building process. I'd read in the paper the next day that I had "failed" in some event that was just part of my training. We explained it over and over again, but they either didn't understand what we were saying or thought we were making excuses.

But John had proven his program to me over and over again and I had absolute confidence in him. I almost never varied from the programs he set up.

On February 22, 1986 I ran a 32:17 10,000 meters on the track at Mt. Smart Stadium. It should have been a New Zealand and Commonwealth record. But after reassuring John ahead of time, they informed us afterward that because there were only two runners in the race, it wouldn't count as a record. This was particularly disturbing because John had a third runner standing by if the officials had said she was needed to make it official.

Ironically enough, the other woman in the race was Debbie Elsmore, who was then living with Gordon and would remain with him for many years. In the race I was essentially running on my own, and after a period of time I had lapped her. Gordon was right on the edge of the track and heaped abuse on me every time I went past.

John's program clearly had me right on track again, and now everyone was predicting a 10,000 gold medal at the Commonwealth Games. I returned to the States for a limited road schedule, including a new course record at Bloomsday, this time by 35 seconds.

By the time I got to Scotland, I knew I was really ready to run well. But even in July the weather in damp and chilly there, and I woke up on the morning of the race with a sore throat. I put it out of my mind and just ran as I had planned and everything seemed to be going fine.

It was a big field and no one wanted to lead, so just as I had done in Brisbane, I took over the lead and started running hard. The only runner who came with me was Liz McColgan of Scotland, and the home crowd suddenly came to life.

Later, watching a tape of the race, I seemed to break her at around four miles, pulling about 20 meters ahead. But the crowd was so loud and there was no sun to cast shadows or stadium screen to watch the rest of the field on, so I couldn't really tell what was going on behind me. I might have been able to put more effort on the pace so as keep her out of the race, but as it was she inched her way back up to me and with 600 meters to go she went in front. When I tried to respond, to my surprise I had nothing left! My legs were dead.

She won in 31:45 and I ran a PR of 31:52, but I knew something wasn't right. As an athlete I'm honest with myself and I know when I've been truly beaten and when some other factor is involved. At the press conference New Zealand reporters were asking "Why silver?" and "What went wrong?" Just like they do in the States, where second place always means failure. The photos in the New Zealand newspapers the next day showed me looking down after the race, and used words like "dejected."

Any mystery was resolved the next day when I woke up really sick with a high fever. It hit me so hard that despite a course of antibiotics it still took a month to recover. To this day I have never had a bout of the flu like it. I must have been coming down with it going into the race, and the intense effort just drove it into my system. I did make myself attend the closing ceremonies on another cold, wet and windy day. I truly love Scotland, but what miserable weather they endure there!

In all our time together, Steve was only interested in accompanying me to major competitions if he happened to have friends or relatives in the area. His mother was born on the Hebrides Islands in Scotland, and because he had relatives there he went on the trip with me. We were invited to stay with some of his family in Edinburgh and they picked us up at the athletes' village in a tiny car and Steve and I squeezed into the back. Both his relatives smoked, and between that and the winding roads I was in rough shape by the time we got there. I barely said hello to anyone and went straight to bed. They were wonderful people, so hospitable, generous and caring that I felt doubly bad being so sick on our visit. They gave up their bed for us and slept on couches. After two days of rest I was able to venture out into the village, where everyone thanked me for "allowing their lass to win." A warm and humble people, the Scots.

I arrived back in Boise to one of the hottest summers on record. There were terrible forest fires all around and smoke blanketed the city. Our house was covered with black ash. It was 110 degrees and the air was unbreatheable. I was still trying to get over the flu, so I had to stay indoors.

I finally got well enough to run a few races. I won the Virginia 10-miler again in 55:02 before heading back to New Zealand. Then I went with the New Zealand team to the Ekiden World Relay in Japan. In that event, six team members each run different distances on the roads against teams from all over the world. Lorraine was on the team, along with Mary O'Connor, Hazel Stewart, Ann Hare, and Sue Bruce. Most of the others hadn't run against this level of competition that much, so I got the impression they weren't giving us much of a chance. I told them Lorraine and I were in great shape and all they had to do was run their best and we would end up in the top three. We started talking it up amongst ourselves and soon they were convinced we could do it. Everyone ran well and on the next to the last leg I gave Ann Hare a ten-second lead over her Russian counterpart. After handing off to Ann I said, "If you don't win now, you'll have to answer to all the rest of us!"

I got in the bus and got to the hotel in time to join the others in watching her win on TV. She was a mess afterwards, laughing, crying, overcome with relief. She told everyone what I'd said, and apparently must have believed it! Although it's a little-known event, that year's Ekiden relay was such a tough, competitive team effort that it stands out as one of the high points of my competitive career.

40 ～ *Finding my Birth Parents*

I was back in New Zealand that fall, training near the seaside at Tauranga, when I woke up one morning and announced to John, Patty and Jon Sinclair that I was going to try to find my birth parents. The idea may have been bubbling around in my subconscious for a while, but the decision to actually do it just seemed to come out of the blue.

Steve had remained in Auckland, and when I told him about it later, he asked, "You've hardly ever spoken of it. What made you decide to do it now?" I told him I didn't know, and that was the truth.

The laws relating to adoption secrecy had been liberalized some years earlier, and my father had brought home a brochure about it, which I read. Neither he nor Mum opposed my looking into it, which was a great comfort to me, but at the time I wasn't ready to do anything about it, so I tucked the brochure away and did nothing.

Now I was ready.

I sent off for my birth certificate, the first step in the process, having no idea what, if anything, I would find out about my origins. My birth mother had been 17 when she gave me up and I expected that she would have gone on to marry—probably someone other than my biological father—and have had a family of her own. Would I represent just a painful time from her past that she would rather not be reminded of? Would my existence be a shameful secret she had kept from her husband and children all these years, only to be thrust into their faces suddenly by my meddling at this late date?

I was dealing with some deeply buried and swiftly running emotional currents here—some of them my own—and I was going to have to proceed with great caution.

The birth certificate arrived from the Bureau of Social Welfare. It had my mother's name, and her age at 17 when she had gone to the Home of Compassion to give birth. Her grandparents had been born in Switzerland and, as expected because of the religious affiliation of the home, she was Roman Catholic. My birth father's name was not given, but the name they had given me was: Eileen Maria. My adoptive name was also on the document: Anne Frances Garrett.

The next step was to search the marriage records, to see who my mother may have later married. We wrote for that information and learned that a year after giving birth to me, my mother had indeed married a farm laborer ten years her senior. His nationality was listed as Dutch.

I was beginning to get excited, nervous, and a bit fearful. It had been remarkably easy up to this point and I was beginning to wonder how I would actually go about approaching these intimate strangers with whom I shared blood and ancestry but no life whatsoever.

Now that we had her married name, we went to the registrar in Auckland to search each province's voting roll books. There were hundreds of them. Steve and I were beginning to relish our detective roles and went through the dusty records with growing anticipation. But as we went through journal after journal with no results, we began to realize that we might be searching for something that wasn't there. She may have left New Zealand entirely years earlier. Or possibly have passed away.

At this point a remarkable coincidence occurred. Jon Sinclair had been reading the biography of Jack Lovelock, the famed Kiwi miler who won the Olympic 1500 meters in 1936. The book mentioned Lovelock's sister, Olive Anne Butler, the same name as my birth grandmother. It was a tantalizing thought, that I might be related to one of the great icons of New Zealand sports history.

It turned out not to be true, but it started us on a new direction.

The birth certificate listed my maternal grandparents' address as being in Te Puke, not far from Tauranga, where I had been training when I began my search. As best we could tell, there was no longer anyone by the name of Butler living in the area, but a search of telephone directories for nearby towns turned up a woman named Olive Butler.

I had Steve telephone the woman, saying he was trying to track down relatives of Jack Lovelock, and might she be his sister? She said she wasn't. Then Steve asked if she had a daughter named Margaret Anne Butler. She said no. Steve thanked her for her time and rang off. We were puzzled but not discouraged. If we were indeed on the right track, there might be two possible explanations. One, the lady might be quite elderly and simply not have responded to her daughter's maiden name, which she wouldn't have used for many years. The other possibility was that she knew exactly what the phone call was about and was denying it.

We waited a day and then Steve called again.

"Sorry to bother you again," he said, "But I'm confused. Do you have a daughter named Margaret Anne, who lives near Te Puke?"

"No," she said. "I have a daughter named Margaret Anne, but she's married to a Dutchman and lives in Cambridge." She said *Dutchman* quite emphatically.

Cambridge is about 80 miles southeast of Auckland. We called directory assistance and within a matter of minutes had the telephone number of the person I believed to be my birth mother.

Then we had a lengthy discussion about how to make contact.

We wanted to approach her in such a way as to give her an out, a way she could deny everything and keep her secret safe, if that's what she wanted. I tried to put myself in her place. How would I feel about hearing from a lost daughter after all these years? I certainly empathized with her plight as a 17-year-old in trouble, having gone through my own young adulthood in mortal fear of an unwanted pregnancy.

But I wanted to tell her something. I wanted to tell her that however painful it was, she had made a good decision. I wanted to say that I didn't blame her for anything, that my life had been wonderful and that I was happy. I wanted to let her know that I understood.

We decided that Steve would make the first call. I sat in the room, a bundle of nerves, listening to our half of the conversation, fighting back the tears. Jon Sinclair was there, trying to comfort me, but it wasn't long before he was blurry-eyed too.

A woman answered the phone.

"Hello, this is Steve Audain calling. I think we both may be related to the same person. Did you give birth at the age of 17 to a baby girl?"

"Do you mean Anne Frances?" she said.

"Yes," Steve's voice was hushed.

"Is she still alive?" she asked.

"Very much so," said Steve.

"I've prayed for her every night since the day I gave her up," she almost whispered.

"She's my wife," Steve said.

In the conversation that followed, we learned that my birth mother had married my birth father a year after I was born. That came as a complete surprise. An even greater surprise was the fact that I had six full brothers and sisters I had never met, nor did they even suspect that I existed!

She told Steve that she did indeed want to meet me, and that she had tried to find me shortly after the law on adoption information had changed, but all she was able to find out was my given name, Anne Frances. She decided to wait until her family had grown and then try again. She wanted to meet my adoptive parents, to tell them thank you.

"Have you ever heard of Anne Audain?" Steve asked. "She's a runner."

"No, but my husband might have. He follows sports," she said.

Steve told her that a book about successful New Zealand women had just been published, and there was a chapter about me in it, if she wanted a convenient way to find out what I'd been doing with myself.

I had not told my adopted parents about my search, so Steve asked her to wait to tell anyone about it. It was a well-kept secret among her family; even her brothers and sisters never knew she had become pregnant at 17. They were told she had been sent away to school for a year in the city.

Just before leaving for the states in March, Steve and I drove to a hotel halfway between Auckland and Cambridge to meet my birth parents for lunch.

It would be hard to imagine a more awkward situation. My birth mother was very nervous, smoking the entire time. My birth father seemed quite shy and reserved. Sitting across the table from them, Margaret and Johanes Oosthoek, it was difficult for me to feel anything remotely like the emotional ties I felt for my adopted parents. Yet, the more I spoke with them, the more I studied their features, watched the way they moved and gestured, the more I realized that everything I had started life with I had inherited from these people. The woman across the table had given birth to me and I looked like her. The genetic ability to become a world class athlete had come directly from them. But it was another couple, the people I called Mum and Dad, who had taken the gifts I was born with and nurtured them.

I shed few tears at that first meeting. The search and the hard training had left me emotionally exhausted, running on empty. I wondered how different my life might have been living in a farm community, the first of seven children. Would my deformed feet have been fixed? Would I have been as successful academically? Would I have become a runner? Would I have been allowed to leave home at age 17 to run in a world championship race in Europe? Such a big family, working so hard to keep a farm going, would have had little time for or understanding of academic pursuits, much less a career in athletics.

My destiny was changed drastically the moment I was adopted. That's the way I look at it now. The life I have now would almost certainly have not come about had I not been given up.

My birth parents promised to tell their family about me and I did likewise, though I would wait for the right time to do it. We were due to leave soon and I didn't want to drop this bombshell on Mum and Dad and then just leave. My biggest fear was that someone in the press might learn about it, perhaps from a tip by a clerk in one of the government offices, and write a story about the whole thing. In such a small country, it would have certainly received a great deal of attention. None of us wanted our families finding out about it from the newspapers, so we all agreed to keep our story among our families.

Family. I hadn't really thought much about it before, but it was really dawning on me now that I had a whole separate family that had grown up in almost a parallel universe a few hundred kilometers away geographically, but light years away emotionally.

And the one who bore the brunt of that knowledge most directly was my birth mother, who had told Steve in their first conversation, "Whenever I sat down at the dinner table, I'd look out at my six children sitting there, and I always knew that one was missing."

41 ~ Injured!

Despite the distraction of the search, my training had gone well. In early March I won the New Zealand Championship 5000 in a gale in Wellington with a time I was proud of given the conditions: 15:32. On March 17th, 1987, I ran a 10,000 meters on the track in 31:57 to qualify for the world championships later in the year. It would have been a New Zealand record but the paperwork wasn't filed.

In that last race my left leg began bothering me again, so I came back to the States with not only family matters on my mind, but the pall of a nagging injury as well. It was my own fault. With all the emotion and distraction of the search for my birth parents, I had become lax with my therapy routines for the leg.

In my first race of the season, the Cherry Blossom 10-mile in Washington, D.C., I finished second in 52:30 to Lisa Martin, with both of us under the world best time. But after the race I knew my leg was worse. A few days later I reluctantly withdrew from the Bloomsday race.

Because of our long-standing working relationship, I did go to the Cleveland Revco race. I told the director, Jack Staph, that I had an injury problem but he wanted me to come anyway. Adding misery to misery, I arrived with a terrible head cold but resolved to do the best I could. I finished second in 34:14, beaten by a local runner.

I went back to Boise determined to start faithfully doing my drills and therapy again. In retrospect, it was obvious that the emotion of the past few months had caught up with me. I was a wreck.

At the end of June I tried to run the Cascade 15K, and was only able to manage a 15th place. I knew that I had to make some decisions about the rest of the year. John and Patsy Davies came to Boise on their way to London and the World Championships where John would be a team coach. After talking it over with him, we agreed that I should withdraw from the team to take some pressure off. But John persuaded me to come to London with them anyway so that he could coach me back to health. Anytime I could get together with him was helpful, because it got lonely at times, trying to stay motivated to do all the workouts alone. The whole New Zealand team was staying close to Crystal Palace so we could train there.

In August, Steve returned to New Zealand. His father, Frankie, had become very ill with emphysema, and it was clear the end was near. One day Frankie called me in London and though his old spirit was there, I could tell he was very weak. It was obvious to both of us that this was our last conversation. He had always been one of my biggest fans and supporters and now here he was using his last ounce of strength, telling me to keep going and keep accomplishing great things. He was always the loudest person in the stands when I ran, criticizing the more reserved spectators around him for not showing more enthusiasm. I could always hear his voice over everyone else!

He was a wonderfully colorful man, full of life. He loved horse racing and betting on his favorites, and I'm quite sure that if he could have, he would have bet on me. I was sad for days after that call.

After his death, I received a note from Kitty. "He was always so proud of you… Countless people have remarked to me this past week what a great joy you were to him. The last ten years were a wonderful bonus for just these reasons."

It's ironic that as my relationship with his parents only grew stronger my bonds with Steve were beginning to crumble. While he was home during his father's last days, Steve took it upon himself to get my father aside and tell him the whole story about finding my birth family. I was stunned when I found out. I couldn't believe he had deprived me of the opportunity to tell them in my own way and in my own time. Although we never discussed it, I'm sure my father was extremely disappointed to have found out about it that way. My mother was due to visit in October, and my dad told Steve that he wouldn't tell her before that because she might not come on the trip.

When she did arrive that fall, the three of us took a car trip up to Sun Valley in our little car, with my mother in the back seat. Steve was driving. Out of the blue, he turned to me and said, "Oh, Annie, have you told your mother the story of last summer?"

I was speechless. I stuttered and stammered for a few minutes and he pulled into a gas station. "I'll give you two some time alone," he said, and hopped out of the car.

It took me a long time to understand why Steve had gone out of his way to put me in such a painful and awkward situation with my parents, and when I did it was the beginning of the end of us.

I finally understood that what he had done was manipulate the situation for his own entertainment and gratification, putting himself at the center of something he should have been peripheral to. It was the act of an adolescent, and my emotions, the sensitive feelings involved, were entirely secondary to him, if they mattered at all. He had helped play the detective game, he had learned "the secret," and he was determined to play a role in the final scene. The whole thing hurt me terribly and left me with an insight into the man I married that changed everything between us.

Nonetheless, when I told Mum the whole story, she took it very well, particularly considering the circumstances. When we got back to Boise, I telephoned my dad to tell him that she knew and that everything was fine. I knew he'd be worried.

At the end of September I won my fifth Virginia 10-miler by a scant three seconds, but then could do no better than sixth in a 12K in Dallas. Though I was physically fine, I knew I was running out of emotional energy. It had been quite a year.

☙

On returning to New Zealand that fall, I agreed to meet my entire birth family.

I was nervous but I think it was worse for them. My siblings were not just meeting a 32-year-old sister they never knew existed, but a sports figure that they had all grown up reading about in their newspapers. In fact, my birth father and brothers occasionally visited a pub in their town that for several years had a poster of me winning the Commonwealth gold medal. They turned out to be a close-knit, humble, and extremely kind group of people who received me with great warmth and love. They could not have been more understanding or sympathetic.

In a wonderful moment much later, my birth mother finally met my adopted mother. As these two most important women in my life embraced, my birth mother said, "I just wanted to say thank you."

Nowadays on most of my trips home my birth mother gathers everyone together for a visit. It's quite an undertaking. In addition to brothers and sisters, there are in-laws, nephews, nieces, and cousins in all directions. And through it all, I think my relationship with my adoptive mother has only grown stronger. I think she truly knows now that she is and always will be my mum and that she could never lose me.

42 ~ *The Seoul Olympics, 1988*

My birth family now wanted to be in contact with me, which was certainly understandable, but I hadn't felt ready for the two families to meet yet, and it was becoming harder to juggle the situation and keep everyone happy. Added to that was the pressure of an Olympic year, and I was in for another ordeal to qualify for the team in the 10,000 meters, which was being run for the first time. The qualifying time was 32:20 and I would probably have to run another solo effort to achieve it.

I had decided to run a 5000 meters in Hamilton, an hour south of Auckland. I had always had good support from the people there and thought it would be a good change of scenery. In hindsight it was probably not that good an idea. My entire birth family lived in the area, so naturally my birth parents, siblings, nephews and nieces all turned out for the race.

Normally Mum, Dad and Kate didn't venture far from Auckland to watch me run, but this time they decided to come. I couldn't say no, but I had no idea how I was going to manage what was beginning to look like a situation comedy. I know I could have done introductions right there, but I myself was still coming to terms with the whole process and I wasn't ready.

The weather on race day was terrible but John and I decided I should run anyway so as not to let the people down. Mum called that morning to ask if I was going and I tried to persuade them that it would be cold and miserable. They went anyway. Dad had a cousin there he wanted to visit.

So now I had both families sitting in the stands without knowing each other were there. All the kids from my birth family were shouting, "Go, Auntie Anne!" I looked up at the stands before the race started and thought, "Oh, how am I going to deal with this?"

John and Patsy understood perfectly and took it upon themselves to save me. They kept the families apart by going to the other side of the stands and introducing themselves to my birth family while Steve and I chattered away with Mum, Dad and Katie. Once the race was over and they had left to visit relatives, we could join the other group and no one was the wiser. But it was nerve-racking, to say the least.

On March 1st, 1988, I ran a solo 10,000 meters in 32:05, another New Zealand record, and this time it was ratified. It had been a good winter. Training had gone well, I had qualified for another Olympic team. And despite Steve's ham-handed interference, the most intensely emotional part of my birth family drama was behind me.

I left for the States on March 10th and finished second to Liz McColgan in a 10K in Los Angeles. Then I went on to Boise and within a week or so I started to feel really good about my running again, very healthy and strong. Finally I had a lot of turmoil behind me and could get back on track again.

I won Cherry Blossom in 53:25. It was a very wet and windy day and I won by a healthy margin over Kim Jones.

Nike asked me to participate in promoting Junior Bloomsday, a race for kids, something I was delighted to do. I went to Spokane area schools and spent a lot of time with the kids, talking to them about the race, about running, and about overall health and fitness. It was a wonderful program to get kids interested in being more active, and I wish there were more like it everywhere.

I won my sixth Bloomsday on a cold and windy May Day, running 39:35, a great thrill. In a sport known for "shooting stars," I was really proud of my consistency and longevity. Spokane had become a special place for me, and Bloomsday one of my favorite events. And not just because I had been athletically successful, but because I had "grown up" with the race and had always contributed as much time and energy as I could to help build the event.

It was a special challenge as an athlete to keep winning, though, because people really got to know me in that town. And while it's wonderful to be stopped and asked for autographs or a handshake, when you're trying to juggle other promotional activities and the competition itself, you find this little troubling thought tucked away in the back of your mind: My opponents are all back at the hotel resting right now. That's why I'm doubly proud of my Bloomsday successes.

I went on to Revco and got my fifth win there. Then the L'eggs Mini in New York invited the Who's Who of the sport, so it was a great opportunity to race everyone who was running well at the same time.

There is a classic photo in *Runner's World* of all of us spread across the road in the first mile: Ingrid Kristiansen, Lisa Ondieki, Mary Decker Slaney, Joan Benoit Samuelson, Margaret Groos, Francie Larrieu-Smith, and others. It was a great photo, capturing in an instant just how competitive the sport of women's running had become. In fact, I was only able to manage a fifth place behind Kristiansen, Ondieki, Larrieu and Decker.

I went to the Cascade Runoff and won my third title after quite a hiatus—I had won back in 1981 and 1982. It was a gratifying victory, given the race's history and the fact I ran a PR 48:55 for 15K. What was not so reassuring was that Nike had obviously decided to de-emphasize the race that had launched the professionalism of the sport, as well as my own career. First prize had actually been lowered from $10,000 in 1981 to $7,000 this year. It's hard to imagine any other sport allowing such a thing to happen. But it was clear to me that year in Portland that the bloom was off the rose, and it was a sad thing to witness. Nike had discovered basketball, soccer and other sports, and started to forget its roots. Sadly, the Cascade Runoff no longer even exists.

After Cascade I took a little break and then started to train for the upcoming Olympics in Seoul, Korea. John and Patsy were going to come to Boise again and then he and I would go on to Japan and Seoul. He was a team coach again.

We flew to Japan via Los Angeles and Honolulu, a long and miserable trip made worse by all the extra security surrounding these Olympics. We went to Fukuoka where we would stay for 10 days of training. Upon arriving, I made the mistake of allowing John to convince me to go for a run immediately. That was something I had never done because my feet always swelled up badly on long flights and I always waited until they were back to normal before training.

But we went running and I was just miserable. I could barely get my shoes on and we ran on a gravel trail, which made for bad footing. I was completely dehydrated, my feet and legs were sore, and the outcome was that I must have traumatized my calves and lower legs so much that I didn't really recover fully until after the games were over. No matter what I tried, I could not retrieve the situation.

Once we were situated in the Olympic village I decided to go it alone in terms of getting myself to the starting line in the best physical and mental state I could. I told John I just wanted to be left alone for the last few days before the heats of the 10,000 so that I could gather myself together. My calves were still sore so I made the decision to do no workouts at all, just to rest, jog a little and do a few strides.

It was a good decision. The first eight from each heat and the four fastest losers would make up the final 20. It was hot and humid and the heats were at 10 in the morning. I drew the first heat, which was stacked with all the top-ranked runners with the exception of Liz McColgan. Ingrid Kristiansen took off fast and split the field wide open, spreading everyone around the track in single file. We were running a good pace and with one lap to go I looked up and saw Ingrid finishing and started to count where I was in the field. I was thinking, the next heat is not going to run this fast so I have a chance to be in the final if I get my act together.

So I really worked hard and caught an Australian runner right on the line. It made me the 4th fastest loser, in 32:10. She was devastated as she had not heard me coming. I went to the press room and the New Zealand media was all over me about not making the final. I just told them, "Wait until the next heat is over. I bet I make it." Sure enough, the next heat was much slower and I made the final!

It may seem like a small consolation, but at this stage I was happy I had salvaged something from the trip. All I did before the final was rest my legs again. I ended up 11th place in exactly the same time as the heat, and I was honestly very satisfied with my effort and the outcome, given the circumstances. I hadn't given up, and I had assessed my situation realistically and made the best of it. It's funny, but when athletes look back on their careers, they often cite such instances as among their proudest accomplishments. These lesser triumphs are certainly not ones the fans notice, but we athletes truly understand what we had to overcome and how much it took to accomplish these seemingly minor achievements.

Toward the end of the year, after a long expensive haul with U.S. immigration, I finally received a letter giving me employment status, the final step before getting a green card. They requested that I stay in the country until they notified me to come in for fingerprinting, medical tests and final interviews, all of which would take place in Boise. They only give you four days to appear after you receive the letter, so you tend to stay on pins and needles until you get through the process.

Because of that, we decided not to make our usual winter trip to New Zealand. I would have to miss my parents' 40th wedding anniversary; it would be my first Christmas ever away from them. They were disappointed, of course, but understanding. And since there was no way I could train in the snow in Boise, we decided to migrate south to Tucson when winter set in.

Steve's sister and her family were in Florida for Christmas, so we met them along with our Australian friends, the Thomsons, in Orlando, which was fun and *warm*.

We went back to Boise for New Years and I tried running in heavy snow for a few days. It was definitely time to head south. We packed our little car up to the roof liner with everything we would need for two months and started driving. We barely made it out of northern Nevada with a huge snowstorm nipping at our heels. It was scary and dangerous to be on the highway in that kind of weather in our little car.

In Tucson we found a one-bedroom unfurnished apartment near a National Park that had trails and some hills. We only had a mattress on the floor and small TV, so it was like camping out. I can't say I thought the town was very attractive; I'm too partial to the green of vegetation. But it was a good place to winter and I was soon training well.

Through all the years I had been in the States, my Dad was never truly at ease with me being so far away. He wasn't a telephone person, and though we spoke regularly, the conversations were never very long. On New Year's Day I called home and when he got on the phone, he talked for a long time. At one point he changed the subject and said out of the blue, "You know everything is in order here and you don't have to worry if anything happens. Your mother and sister are well taken care of." I thought it was a bit strange but didn't think too much about it at the time. We planned for him to make his first trip to the States that year and we were going to travel together. Mum had come twice and I had finally persuaded him it was his turn.

We didn't have a phone in the apartment in Tucson, but had given Kyle Cundiff, our neighbor in Boise, the manager's number in case the notification letter came from the INS.

On January 13th, 1989 there was a knock on the apartment door. It was the manager, saying we had a phone call. We assumed Kyle was calling about the INS notice. Steve went down to the manager's office and came back looking pale. He said my dad had died suddenly.

In a daze, I called Mum. They had been away on vacation and on the way back he was driving really fast to get home. When they arrived she said she was going to the post office to get the mail and he said he would mow the lawn. When she got back, she found him lying in bed, saying he felt bad. She took him to the doctor, which he had always had a tremendous fear of. He went in alone and, knowing Dad, probably downplayed everything. He came out saying the doctor thought he was fine, got behind the wheel and had a massive heart attack and died there right in front of Mum and Katie. He was 63.

The autopsy showed he had suffered several minor heart attacks, so he probably had some intimation that something was wrong, and that was the reason he had tried to reassure me on the phone on New Year's Day. Both his mother and brother had died the same way.

Mum told me not to try to get home. She knew about the situation with the immigration notice, and that I would be such a hopeless mess at a funeral. She was right about that, but I still felt guilty. Since I hadn't been at Nana's funeral, I had no experience handling grief like that in public. Mum said that Katie did really well and rose to the occasion.

Unknown to any of us at the time, my birth mother slipped into the back of the church and sat in the last pew with one of my brothers. As the services drew to a close, she stood and with tears in her eyes, whispered two words: "Thank you."

I was comforted by the knowledge that I had a great relationship with my Dad, and there was nothing left unfinished except that trip we were going to make together. It still saddens me to think of it and I still miss him. I find myself wishing he could have lived long enough to have seen me finish my career and to see that everything turned out fine and that I'm happy.

After getting word of Dad's death, I went into a kind of numb trance. Steve had for several years been involved in all kinds of New Age spiritualism and though I had tried to be open-minded about it, none of it was any comfort to me. I felt very alone dealing with the death of my father.

I went through the motions of running. There was nothing wrong with me physically, but emotionally I had nothing.

We finally got the notice from Immigration and flew back to Boise, right into 20-below temperatures and lots of snow. It was stressful, dealing with all the regulations and requirements, while living in a winterized house we couldn't get warmed up in such a short time. I was also waiting for a new New Zealand passport that I needed to take into Immigration, and it had still not arrived.

We had medical tests and went to our interview where I was told that I couldn't proceed without the passport. I said that I thought it would come in that morning's Fedex delivery so they sent me home to get it.

Thank goodness it did arrive and I was able to go back and complete the process. They took me into a room by myself where they had a file a foot high on me. Then they asked a lot of questions that I had answered many times before, as if they were trying to trip me up.

But we finally dotted all the i's and crossed all the t's and were cleared to get our green cards. At that time I asked if I could leave to go back to New Zealand and they said I had to stay until the card came.

So I flew to Tampa, because I had originally planned to run the Gasparilla 15K anyway. I started the race thinking everything was fine, when suddenly after the first mile it was as if my engine just shut down. I had no energy whatsoever and was just going through the motions. I barely remember finishing the race, in 19th place.

I was confused and worried that something was really wrong with me, but friends said it was too soon after Dad's passing and I would be all right. I went back to Tucson and back to training, feeling like a robot. I then flew to Jacksonville, Florida, for the River Run 15K while Steve hauled our belongings back to Boise. I ran only 54 minutes, so I was getting worse.

Steve got his temporary card to go to New Zealand to visit our mothers I kept training for Bloomsday, where I finished third in the second slowest time I had ever done there. I had none of my usual fire and could tell the difference physically. It was amazing, as if without that all-consuming passion to excel, I was a different person.

I flew straight to Washington, D.C. for an all-woman's race, but by the time I got there, I had such a case of flu I was barely able to stand up.

I pulled out of the race but did other commitments, getting out of bed to smile through interviews. The next race was Revco and I arrived feeling somewhat better, only to have Lorraine fly in the night before. I did my best to win but faltered in the last stretch. I was happy to just have survived it and to be feeling better.

I raced fairly well the rest of the summer, including a 52:30 10-mile PR at the Bobby Crim race in Flint, Michigan, just barely catching Lisa Weidenbach at the line.

My last race of the season was the Philadelphia half-marathon in mid-September, where I was pleased to finish second, losing by only six seconds in 1:12:31. I hadn't run that distance in quite a while, and a good performance over such a distance after all the recent emotional stress was gratifying.

I went back to New Zealand early because the Commonwealth Games were going to be in Auckland in January of 1990 and I had chosen this event to be my swan song for New Zealand athletics. In hindsight, by announcing this in advance, I probably brought a lot of extra attention to myself, but it was what I wanted and I thought I could handle it. The trials for the team were in December.

This was my first time to see my Mum and Katie since Dad died. All in all, there would be a lot going on, so naturally on arriving home I got the flu again.

There was a huge media buildup to the trials, because the triathlete Erin Baker, new star Anne Hannam, and my old friend Barbara Moore were all running well and were all considered serious contenders in the 10,000 meters.

Anne Hannam had raced really well on the U.S. circuit in 1988, winning a number of races and setting course records. However it was obvious that she was now suffering from an eating disorder. I said something about it to John Davies, but he didn't believe she had a problem and said in jest that maybe I should consider losing some weight, too. I had seen far too many of these girls through the years to not know the symptoms. It was sad to see pictures of her in the press, so pitifully thin, and yet no one would openly acknowledge the problem. Eventually she began the familiar downward spiral that ended the careers of so many promising women runners: injuries, stress fractures, and bouts of illness. She tried to keep ignoring the problems and training through all of it until finally she had nothing left and was out of the sport.

There is no question that women who become anorexic, bulimic or both get a short-term surge in their performances due to their lighter weight. But the price they pay in the long term, not just in sports but in their overall health, is terrible. I have always questioned the integrity of coaches who continue to train athletes in this situation instead of getting them help. It especially makes me angry when the media glorifies the "look" of these painfully thin creatures, but then never print the follow-up stories on what happens to their careers and lives when they start getting sick and hurt. Or when some of them die.

But at the time Anne Hannam was being built up as a favorite, along with Erin Baker, who had beaten me in the Bix 7-mile road race in July. Everyone now thought she might switch from the triathlon to track. And Barbara Moore was the one with the real credentials to make the team if she got herself focused. She had always had a lot of talent but had never accomplished what she should have. She had good moments but no consistency when it counted.

There were some comments in the press that I was too old to be on the team. I was accustomed to being everyone's favorite "target" to knock off, so it was only fueling my fire. Sometimes though, I have to admit, I would go out for a run and have an argument with myself about whether they might finally be right after all. On November 1st, 1989, I turned 34, so the years were undeniably adding up. When I began competing I would never have thought I would still be running at this age. Becoming a professional had allowed me to have a much longer career than I would have otherwise. As an amateur, I couldn't have afforded to take good enough care of myself to last so long at such a competitive level.

The 3000 trial came first, and I ran that as a tune-up race, finishing fifth. Of course, everyone was ready to write me off immediately. Some of my competitors even got cocky enough to begin talking about beating me. All I said was, "The 10,000 is still two weeks away."

It surprised me that after all these years that no one understood the way John structured my training to get me ready on precisely the right day for one supreme performance, and that everything leading up to that was prelude.

We all went to Wellington for the race, John and Patsy, Steve, Mum and Katie. The 10,000 was to be run at night, thank goodness, as Wellington could have such bad afternoon weather. I was very nervous, having gotten myself all worked up over the media buildup and the challenge of proving whether I still "had it."

It was a calm night and when the gun went off I waited as usual to see if anyone was going to set a pace. I don't know why I thought this race would be any different. They always tucked in behind me, knowing I would do the work. To this day there are a lot of New Zealand runners who got their best times by following me through races.

So there I was again, leading everyone on a nice even pace. But I was running fast, so it was a risky pace for most of the others who had to protect their chances for the other two spots on the team. After a few laps I was running alone out in front of everyone.

I went through the halfway mark in 16 minutes flat and then ran exactly the same time for the second half, finishing in 32:00, a New Zealand record. (They hadn't yet ratified my earlier 31:57, which, in a delicious irony, meant they would be paying me a newly instituted $5,000 bonus.)

It was a particularly sweet victory in the face of all the hoopla and I still think of it as one of my best performances. It meant a lot to me that I could still deal with all the pressure and rise to the occasion.

However it used up a lot of my emotional energy, and though I didn't know it at the time, it would hurt me in the next few weeks going into the Games themselves.

43 ~ New Zealand Swan Song

Oh, hindsight is a lovely thing!

In retrospect it's quite clear that I should have done something to try to insulate myself from all the distracting activity surrounding the 1990 Commonwealth Games in Auckland.

But I decided to stay at Steve's family home, in a familiar environment, rather than the athletes' village. In most situations, that would have been a perfectly logical thing to do. In this case, however, I was directly associated with a huge international athletic event taking place right in my hometown.

For more than a decade, New Zealand had been my refuge, my special place of physical and spiritual rejuvenation. I had gone there to get ready for a world record, for the Olympics, for big road races and marathons, and it had always worked.

But this time I wasn't hiding myself away, building up my reserves, getting ready to go do battle somewhere else in the world. The world was coming to me, right into my front yard! Not only that, I was favored to win another gold medal in my farewell appearance on a New Zealand track. I confess that I allowed myself to get worked up over the whole thing. Added to everything else, it was the anniversary of Dad's death and I was distraught that after all these years he would not be there to see me run in a big event.

My birth family was also now very much in the picture and needed a certain amount of time and attention. And then Mum, Katie, Steve and his family, everyone seemed to have gotten caught up in the building anticipation and excitement. People would turn up to visit who we hadn't seen in years. I'd be out training on the streets and people would stop and want to have their photographs taken with me.

All of it was understandable. I look back and have to conclude there was nothing I could have done. Everyone was keying off me emotionally. They looked to me for strength, for leadership, for emotional control. And when the pressure got to be too much, in the current parlance, everyone around me seemed to just *lose it*. I was able to stay focused for a while, to keep everyone reasonably happy and keep my training on track, but then it all got to be incredibly draining. I was unable to stay focused, unable to gather and marshal my mental energy the way I usually did. There was nothing wrong with me physically; my training was fine, but I was getting emotionally and mentally fatigued.

I could have gone into the athletes' village. I was assigned a room there and I had always enjoyed village life before, even though the accommodations had sometimes been Spartan. But I was still in my hometown and would have known the officials, the press, and many of the athletes. There was really no place to hide. I had even considered flying to Australia to stay until just before the races. But then I thought, well, that doesn't make sense. If I can't cope with everything in my own home environment, leaving won't help. It got so bad that sometimes I would just get in the car alone and drive around, sometimes in tears. I had nowhere to go.

I was a little disappointed that after all those years nobody really had an understanding of what it took to go out on the track and win an important long distance foot race. Everyone saw the final results, but not what was behind it. I don't know why I expected them to; I normally didn't expect anyone but fellow runners to empathize. But at the time I think I had become a little emotionally needy myself, I wanted someone to understand my world, what I was going through. But I was alone.

I became bothered by things that normally I would have shrugged off. I was disappointed, for instance, that I wasn't chosen to carry the flag into the stadium. There were rumors that it would be me, and I thought that after all these years representing my country I had earned the honor. But it went to a male swimmer instead.

Additionally, in the back of my mind the whole time was a fear that the story of my birth family would break out. A few of my friends in the media knew, but out of respect for me hadn't done anything about it. But one member of the birth family, an elderly gentleman, got on a radio talk show at one stage and started saying he knew some secrets about Anne Audain's family and he wanted to tell them. Fortunately the host was a good friend of mine and he knew exactly what the man was talking about and managed to cut him off before he could blurt it out. There were still a great many things that had to fall into place before I could bring everyone together, so I just prayed that nothing broke loose in the final days before the event.

The race day was a blur. We lined up, the gun went off, and we took off with everybody running dead slow; no one would take the lead. So I got out in front as usual. But this time I just didn't have the emotion. It was just like when I tried to run after my dad died. There was nothing there. Physically I was fine; emotionally, the fire was out.

For the first time ever in a track race my feet blistered badly, probably because I was running so flat-footed that by the end of the race my heels were just bludgeoned. It was miserable, going round and round out there in front of my home town crowd so far behind the leaders, but I was determined to finish. I ended up in 11th place in 33:40, more than a minute and a half slower than the race I'd run to make the team.

There was one silver lining. Barbara Moore, my childhood friend and neighbor, my training partner for all those hundreds of miles, ran wonderfully and won a bronze medal! After all those years and all the set-backs and slights she had endured, I was thrilled that she was finally able to get some of the recognition she deserved, and the fact that she did it on Auckland soil made it all the more gratifying.

I was disappointed after the race, but not dejected. It was not the way I had intended to end my long track career in New Zealand, but in athletics we are not allowed to write our own final scenes. We just do the best we can and the endings write themselves. The crowd was very supportive and empathetic, giving me a big ovation as I finished.

I ran one last slow, nostalgic lap around the stadium, thanking them for all their support over the years.

44 ~ End of the Roads

It was a tremendous relief to have it over. I was disappointed but when I went out running the next day to see how I felt, even with my badly blistered feet, I *flew*. For the first time in weeks I ran with abandon. It was a wonderful feeling. I thought, *that's it!* There is nothing wrong with me, I was just mentally gone. But now I felt great.

Unfortunately, it wasn't quite that simple. The blisters became infected and I needed very strong antibiotics. In fact, they almost put me in the hospital. But when they began to improve, I escaped to my healing place, the island. There I walked in the salt water, read, wandered around the island and generally got my head back on straight. It was a much-needed time off. My feet needed a long time to heal and a lot of antibiotics. It was good for me.

I came back to the States in March of 1990 and on April Fool's Day finished second in the Cherry Blossom 10-miler in 53:18, a respectable time, indicating that I was actually in fairly good shape. I ran several more races in April and then returned to Spokane on May 6th to try for my seventh Bloomsday title.

The field was great, and American Olympic marathoner Janis Klecker had just come off a very fast 10K, so the pressure was on. I took off early and led, and from what I was hearing from the crowd I was way out in front of second place. But no one was seeing Janis, with her short hair and diminutive stature, tucked in 20 to 50 meters behind. At about the five-mile mark as I started up Bloomsday (or as we called it, "Doomsday") Hill, she came up beside me.

That was quite a shock! I thought I had the race won and now I had to quickly change my thinking. I let her get in front as we ascended, and then when we got on the flat I pushed ahead. Then she just pushed back! This was going to be a race!

We went all along Broadway, which is a straight mile until you take a turn to run into the finish line. All I could think was to hold on, hold on. We swapped the lead maybe 10 times down that stretch, and the whole time I was thinking about how Jon Sinclair had won the race one year by getting to the corner, taking it as hard as he could and then just sprinting all the way to the finish.

That's what I did, and fortunately it worked. It was the closest finish I'd had since the first time I'd won in 1981 and I really had to fight for it, winning by only seven seconds in 39:40.

&

I was beginning to sense that I wouldn't be able to keep it up forever. I still loved to run, but other components of the lifestyle were getting to me. The travel, for instance, was now tiring instead of exciting. And I noticed that it was getting to be a chore to train twice a day, which I had been doing for years. I was growing weary of the routine, the schedule, of going back to the same places year after year. I found myself searching for the motivation to keep going.

Money wasn't it; it never had been. My heart and soul went into running and my whole life was built around simply training hard and racing well. If I could do that and be happy doing it, I knew everything else would fall into place. But I could sense the emotional fire was beginning to drain away.

I remember reading a magazine article in which tennis stars Martina Navratilova and Chris Evert said that the big difference at the end of their competitive careers was that it took longer to "get up" for an important event, and longer to recover physically and mentally than when they were younger. All I could say was, amen.

But I always made a special effort in races with which I had a long history. So on May 20th I was thrilled to win my sixth Revco 10K in 32:50. But then a month later at the Cascade race in Portland I felt as if someone had let the air out of my tires. I managed only eighth place, and was struggling again. I knew I needed a new challenge and had several long phone conversations with John Davies about it.

We decided that I would try another marathon. It was funny that with the passage of time I always seemed to forget how bad my last marathon ordeal had been. We didn't want to jump into the pressure cooker of one of the really big events like New York or Boston, so we picked Twin Cities, a popular but moderate-sized race with a lovely meandering course through Minneapolis and St. Paul.

So I trained through the Boise summer, once again logging a lot of miles with my ever faithful training partner, Bob Walker. I convinced him to go on those hot, boring two-and-a-half hour runs by bribing him with an air ticket to Minneapolis to run the race with me. He had run Boston once but no other marathons, so we both felt like novices as we began getting back into marathon training.

It was really tough training in heat that was often over 100 degrees. But we were proud of our perseverance, and I doubt I could have done it without him. At the same time I couldn't help thinking back to 1983-1984 and how much I had *hated* training for a marathon. I was frankly miserable, bored, and didn't even think it was healthy. But I had a new goal and I was determined.

Several slow races in August and September didn't help my confidence. To me, the marathon was an event where I felt no sense of control. So much depended on your luck on a given day, where something very small could go wrong early and affect you for 26 miles. In the shorter distances you had a chance to overcome the problem or at least gut your way through it.

Also, the training didn't build my confidence the way it did for shorter races. I felt like all I was doing was beating myself up, just piling the miles on. I wasn't suited for it mentally, I knew that. At least I admitted it to myself, whereas a lot of athletes don't.

The Twin Cities race was of a piece with my past marathon experiences. Everything went wonderfully until I hit 20 miles and, sure enough, my feet just shut down. I finished the race feeling just fine except for my devastated feet. I ran second to Sylvie Bornet with a 2:31:41, my best time, but it was frustrating to think I had a much faster marathon locked inside me that I couldn't get out. I can apparently run 20 miles up on my toes and feel absolutely fine, but then my feet get tired and I turn into a flat-footed six-minute-per-mile plodder.

We returned to New Zealand for the winter and while we were down there Steve managed to negotiate a lucrative agreement for me to run the Los Angeles Marathon in March of 1991. I hadn't changed my mind about the marathon as an event, but I thought, why not? I'm not really interested in much else. I don't want to run track any more. My interest in road racing is waning. Why not give it another shot?

❧

By the time John, Steve and I headed to Los Angeles in February of 1991, I was up to two-and-a-half-hour runs and feeling strong. I had done a 15-mile tempo run along the Auckland waterfront in 1:25, which is 5:40 per mile, or 2:28 marathon pace. But the day before we left, I was out running and my calf went into a spasm. I didn't think it would be too serious, but it caused me to literally limp onto the plane for Los Angeles, certainly not a great confidence-builder.

The race turned out to be the same old story, with my feet falling apart at 20 miles. I thought about dropping out, I was so miserable. But I had an extra incentive to stick with it. My fellow Kiwi, John Campbell, and I were teamed up in competition for what they called the "Friendship Cup," a $25,000 prize to the winning male-female team from the same country. The American team of Cathy O'Brien and Ivan Huff were in contention, with him in 10th place and Cathy in first. We had been told it would be scored like a cross-country race, with low score winning.

That was keeping me going, but just barely. I was stopping at every water station and each time had a hard time getting my feet to move again. John and Steve were meeting me at various points along the course, and at miles 22 and 23 they encouraged me to keep going because John Campbell had in fact finished in fourth place. They said if I stayed where I was, we would win the team contest because the American team was already in. Ivan was 10th and Cathy had won. They had 11 points, and if I could keep from getting passed, we would have 9 points and the victory.

I ended up finishing fifth in 2:34:30, and was never so glad to cross a finish line.

We were sitting around afterwards when John Davies and Steve came up and said that they'd already given the prize to Cathy and Ivan. They'd had a ceremony and given them the check already.

When we approached the race director, Bill Burke, he said they had given the prize based on which complete team was across the line first. If you thought about it, that didn't make any sense. Because all elite men are going to finish ahead of all the elite women, what it really meant was that the prize would be awarded to the team that had the highest finishing woman. The American man could have finished in 30th place and still been ahead of all the women, so it was a nonsensical way of doing things. Additionally, it wasn't the way the competition had been explained to us, and it was certainly unfair to change the rules after the fact.

We thought about it for a while and talked it over with some other friends in the sport, nearly all of whom agreed we had been done in. John Campbell and I asked for another conference with Burke and a representative from AT&T, the sponsor of the Friendship Cup. They finally agreed to award us an equivalent prize in exchange for our not talking to the press about the matter. Though we would get no recognition in New Zealand for the victory, we agreed that it was a fair resolution to the problem.

But the race itself had been another horrendous marathon experience and I swore I would never run another. To tell the truth, I was disgusted with myself for running almost solely for money. It went against everything I believed to jeopardize my health for the sake of financial gain. I had always assumed that even after I retired from competition that I would want to continue running for health for the rest of my life and I wasn't willing risk that for a few extra dollars.

Back in Boise it took a long time to recover. Coming off the Twin Cities race in October and then continuing marathon training all winter had done a number on my feet, as well as my head.

By May I was healthy enough to return to Bloomsday, where I finished third in what turned out to be the last time I ever raced there. I was pleased that I could still be competitive. In fact, I was in fourth place with about a mile to go and managed to move up a place, so I went down fighting. My record over all those years at Bloomsday ended up being seven wins and two third places.

By now I really started to sense that I wasn't into it anymore. It had become such a chore to train twice a day that I started to develop tightness in my chest that felt like indigestion. I would often get an attack of diarrhea after a tough race or workout. I was bored. I had to face the truth: I didn't want to do it anymore. But I was committed to a schedule of races for the rest of the summer, and I had never summarily pulled out of a race I had committed to.

I went to Revco in Cleveland and dug really deep to run 32:56, winning by two seconds. That was my seventh title at Revco, making my overall record there seven wins and two second places.

In June I made a trip up to the Alaska Women's Run 10K. Nike was a sponsor and asked me to help race directors Vicki and Larry Ross promote the all-woman's event. It was such a wonderful event that I think a seed was planted. I began to think, What a wonderful thing it would be to put on an event like this back in Boise. I liked the whole celebratory atmosphere of the event, the way they kept everyone entertained, the way they turned the awards ceremony into a big party. I ran 33:34 for a course record, so it was pleasing to see that despite my mental fatigue I still had some running left in me.

Later in June I finished fourth in the Cascade Run-Off in 50:28, making an even decade of running that event. After a short rest, I placed fourth at the Bix 7-mile race in a very tough field. At Falmouth it was 85 degrees with 95 percent humidity and a hurricane approaching! I ran a minute slower than I had in 1989, but finished sixth in another tough field. A week later at the Bobby Crim 10-miler, Kim Jones edged by me in the last 100 meters, leaving me in third place.

My mother-in-law, Kitty, was visiting at the time, and because she wanted to look up some genealogical information there I took her with me to the Philly Half-marathon. Through all the ups and downs with Steve, Kitty and I had always been close, and still are.

Though it was mid-September, the conditions in Philadelphia were really tough for a longer race, with temperatures in the high 70s and humidity at 95 percent. I was leading until about a mile to go, and then just shut down. I was well aware of how bad the conditions were, but they were no worse than Bix or Falmouth had been, so I was surprised to fall apart so badly. I had a bad blood blister on one foot and was totally done in by the effort.

As we were walking back to the hotel, Kitty put her hand on my shoulder and said, "Annie, this is starting to kill you. It's doing you no good whatsoever. You really should think about finishing it up. "

Well, that thought had been bouncing around in my mind, too. But it had been the way Steve and I had earned our living and my thinking had been, well, I'm going to be 36 and maybe I can go a few more years and then get out of it. But her saying it like that brought me face to face with reality. I had to come to grips with my struggle. If I hadn't been facing what was going on within myself, Kitty saw things clearly.

Two weeks later, I flew to Lynchburg for the Virginia 10-miler and won it for the sixth time. I didn't know it at the time, but that would be the last race of my competitive career. The fact that I won my last road race and that it was in Lynchburg is still a source of great pride to me.

I was scheduled to run the Tufts race in Boston on the second Monday in October, so I came back to Boise and already had my air ticket for the event. That race doesn't provide airfare, but if you finish high enough, they reimburse you. It was the first time in all those years I had actually purchased an air ticket to a race.

I was due to fly out Saturday, October 12, 1991, and race the following Monday. On Wednesday, I met with Bob Walker for a typical pre-race workout, which consisted of a warm-up followed by an all-out mile time-trial. As we warmed up, we chatted as we usually did and I felt very fragile emotionally. A lot of things I had been repressing for a long time were finally boiling to the surface.

We got to the starting point and I began to run this all-out mile time trial, which on a good day I would run in around 4:50. When we got to the half-mile mark, Bob turned to me and said, "Annie, when are you going to start the mile?"

"What do you mean?" I said, "We're already halfway through!"

"Annie," he said gently, "We're only running six-minute mile pace."

And I just stopped right there on the trail and started to cry. I said, "Okay, that's it. I quit."

Bob thought I was talking about ditching the workout. He was saying, "Look, it's okay, you've only got one race to go in the season, this workout doesn't matter that much..."

And I said, "No, no. I mean I *really* quit."

And he said, "Yeah, I know what you're saying, but you've only got one race, you don't have to do this time trial, just rest up."

I said, "No, Bob, what I mean is, it's *all* over."

The emotions had been building for longer than I realized. Steve was running elsewhere in the park, so we went and found him, and all kind of sat down in a circle to talk about it. I just cried and cried.

I came back to the condo, where Kitty was still staying with us, and I walked in and said, "Kitty, I've quit." She jumped out of the chair and gave me a hug and said, "Oh, Annie, that's great! I'm so pleased!"

I felt an immense sense of relief. It was October 10th, 1991. I had been running competitively for more than 20 years.

I had run races of every description: track, cross country, road, marathon, relay and orienteering. I had won Commonwealth gold and silver medals, had run in three Olympics and had set a world record. I had logged thousands of miles in training, in all kinds of climates and geography. I had run up volcanoes and through snow-dappled mountain meadows. I had run by raging seas and bubbling streams. I had circled the world many times, had made cherished friends all over the globe and had homes in two different hemispheres. For 10 years I had been a professional athlete and had made a good living from my sport and my passion.

Running had taken me light years from scrawny stick figure of a girl in a billowing school uniform hobbling around on bulky corrective shoes, tormented by her classmates.

And now it was over.

45 ~ *Aftermath*

That was the only time I ever committed to a race and then pulled out. I was always proud that in a sport infamous for no-shows, I had never missed an event that I said I was coming to.

But it was over.

I didn't tell John Davies about it right away. I thought I would wait until I got back to New Zealand to tell him in person. We had been through so much together, I thought I owed him that. Unfortunately, Steve went back earlier than I did, and being Steve, he went ahead and told John. I went back later and formally announced my retirement on November 21st, 1991.

There were varying reactions to my decision. John Davies and Jon Sinclair, along with some others in the sport, didn't think I was really quitting. They thought that after a rest my competitive drive would come back and that I wouldn't be able to stay away. I think Kitty was the only one who understood why I was doing it and how serious I was about it.

Even the six masters races I ran when I turned 40 in 1996 didn't rekindle the competitive fires, although two of them were U.S. masters championships at 5K and 12K, and as a new U.S. citizen, I was proud to win them. I ran them to prove to myself that I could still compete if I wanted to, but I knew I had made the right decision in 1991. It was over and I've never regretted the decision.

It was a tough transition, going back to being a non-athlete. After all, I'd thought of myself as a runner for more than 20 years, my self-image was completely tied to that. For all those years my first thought when I awoke in the morning was when, where and how I was going to run that day. I rarely did anything, went anywhere, or ate anything without considering what impact it would have on my running. Now all of that was gone, and it left me in a strange kind of limbo. When I got up in the morning, I wasn't really sure what I was supposed to do.

For the first time in years I had the time and energy to take a good hard look at my life. Once I had made a comment to a writer that when I retired from running all I wanted to do for a while was sit under a palm tree. But then I added something telling: "That is, if Steve will let me."

It was a comment that came back to haunt me. I can't bring myself to look at that article anymore because it so painfully pin-points something missing in my life at the time. I was beginning to see more clearly problems in my marriage that I had either not seen or glossed over.

I really did want to take a year off. I had worked long and hard since I was 16 without ever really stopping. Even though it looked to others as if my life was one long vacation because I didn't have a "real" job, anyone who understood the stress and pressure of such a life would know how draining it can be.

So I felt I needed and deserved a good rest. We didn't need a great deal of money, and it seemed to me that if Steve could get some kind of job—even something part-time—that we could manage easily until I gathered myself. But he said, "Oh no, everyone's going to forget you quickly if you don't continue working in some capacity." He wanted me to continue my relationship with Nike, maybe look into the possibility of a corporate position. I resisted that idea. Earlier I had spoken with one of my contacts with Nike, Steve Miller, about possible opportunities with the company after my retirement.

"Yes, Annie," he said, "There would be such opportunities, but my recommendation is that you never come to work at this place. It would just destroy your enthusiasm for the sport."

That was very good advice that has been ratified by others over the years and to this day I'm grateful that he offered it.

But I still had to figure out something to do. What I really enjoyed was going into the schools, working with the kids. So I put together a proposal for Nike wherein for a nominal sum I would continue do that kind of work around the country in 1992 and I would take responsibility for my own schedule. I would still be under contract, but it wouldn't be too stressful. Hopefully it would give me a chance to relax a little bit. I had never been with any other shoe company and I wanted to remain loyal to them after all these years. It never entered my mind to go elsewhere.

There was quite a lot of media interest in my retirement and for the first time Steve allowed himself to be interviewed and photographed. He was well into his New Age projects, giving seminars on his "alternative healing system," and now wanted to let people know what he was doing. Not only that, he wanted to give the impression that I was endorsing these ideas.

From England came word that Gordon Pirie was very ill. I hadn't had any real conversation with him since I left him in Holland all those years before, but those who had seen him on his last trip to New Zealand noted a marked deterioration. Dick Booth, in *Impossible Hero*, wrote:

> Robyn Hames, an experienced veteran runner in New Zealand with an eye for the running scene, saw something of Gordon in his last days in Auckland. 'A marvelous man, who gave so much to athletics. And there he was at the end, living in his car on the Domain."

He had returned to England and his health got progressively worse. When he finally went to the doctor in early 1991, they discovered an inoperable tumor in his bile duct. He was given six months to live, but Gordon being Gordon, naturally took that as a challenge to prove the experts wrong. He remained relatively active through the summer, but then began to go downhill rapidly. He died in a hospice on December 7th, 1991. He was 60.

For all our problems, I was saddened to hear of Gordon's death. I never begrudged him credit for all that he did for me as an athlete. But his dogmatic, manipulative and mercurial personality, his insistence on being in complete control of everything and everyone around him neutralized much of the good that he did in the sport. It had driven me very close to a mental breakdown.

But he was a tireless motivator, a unique and fascinating character, and for good or ill the sporting world probably won't see his likes again.

ᘒ

When we arrived back in the United States in the spring, Steve announced we should sell our condo on the golf course because with my smaller income we couldn't afford the mortgage. I was so disappointed because I loved that place and was finally feeling at home there. I went along with it, but couldn't help feeling that if Steve had contributed a very small amount to the family income, we could have kept the place. Instead, we sold it and moved into one of the two apartments we owned in downtown Boise. We had to sell or give away a lot of nice furniture, going from three big bedrooms to one was a big change.

Steve was becoming more involved in his own projects, and participated in fairs and workshops around the country and in Boise. He started doing "readings" and talks at various events. It wasn't my cup of tea, but I tried to be supportive because I believe people should follow their own philosophies and walk their own path. But I had been supporting Steve both emotionally and financially for a long time, and I was beginning to feel that he should be willing to reciprocate. I was beginning to think anew about something he'd always said about our relationship. He said that I was lucky to have a husband that let his wife be an athlete, because not many men could handle it.

That began to grate on me, because from my perspective he'd had it pretty good. As I've said before, he rarely traveled with me to events unless he had his own reasons for going. In truth, I usually would have preferred to go alone anyway. Like Gordon, Steve tended to be argumentative with people and I didn't need that kind of distraction while competing. Meanwhile, he traveled whenever and wherever he wished. At various times he went alone to England, Scotland, Peru and Australia while I continued to race and train.

Through 1992 I did some promotional work with several races around the country. With that and the money from the sale of our condo and other savings we got along.

We returned to New Zealand again for the summer, where I gave a proposal to the ASB Bank to work with a program they had started that involved 20,000 children in races. That was the kind of work I really enjoyed doing.

I began talking with Nike about the upcoming year, and it soon became obvious that our long-standing relationship meant little to the new people in the hierarchy. Alberto Salazar was now the director of running programs; I'd long been under the impression that ex-runners who got into corporate positions at athletic shoe companies were fairly stingy when it came to dealing with outside athletes, and Alberto was no exception. Fortunately, my long time colleague, Steve Miller, found some money in the marketing budget to keep me stumping for Nike for another year, but things were clearly changing in the running world.

When I offered to appear as a Nike representative at various races on the 1993 schedule, no one turned me down, so almost immediately I had a full travel schedule. With another Boise woman, I began putting together a women's event, which we called the "Idaho Women's Fitness Celebration."

I worked hard for Nike. Once I was to speak at a "Women's Mornings" at a large mall in Seattle. I did many such events. I was to fly from Boise Friday evening to speak at 7:30 the next morning. However my flight got diverted to Spokane because of fog and I was stuck there until the next day. I got three complete strangers from my flight to share the driving and we rented a car to drive five hours through the night. I arrived in Seattle at five the next morning, got an hour of sleep, then went to give the speech at the mall.

The year went well; I continued to run for health and didn't miss racing at all. As time passed, I was more convinced than ever that I had made the right decision. We held the first Idaho Women's Fitness Celebration in September of 1993 and it was a wonderful event, built around a 5K race, but really more of a participation event to encourage women to think about health and fitness. We de-emphasized the "race" aspect and made it a women-only event so that those who had never participated in a road race wouldn't be intimidated by either the "jock" atmosphere or the "thin" culture. Women of all ages and abilities came out by the thousands, many walking, some pushing baby carriages, some holding hands with daughters and friends. Husbands, fathers, brothers and boyfriends took part as race volunteers, entertainers, officials and spectators. At the finish area we held a big party with food, bands, and other entertainment.

That first year we had 2,400 participants, including three guys in drag who did such a good job with their makeup they were hard to pick out! In 1994 we nearly doubled to 5,600. Over the years the Celebration has grown to be one of the largest women's events in the country, with more than 16,000 women taking part in the 1999 event.

But it was tough going early on. There was a lot of work involved beating the bushes for corporate sponsors and handling the organizational details of an event of that size. We knew it would be successful eventually, but the early days of any venture are almost always a struggle.

Steve and I had a lot of arguments about the growing intensity of his New Age ideas and his intolerance of the views of others. I grew concerned as I heard him making promises to people that he couldn't possibly keep. Sometimes these were people with serious illnesses, desperate people, and Steve was telling them he could help them with his alternative medicine "system."

He had begun talking with a resort owner in West Virginia about setting up his programs there, and was making plans for us to move there. I was trying my best to be supportive, but couldn't help be concerned about where all this was leading. It only added to the other strains in our relationship.

Then one day he made one of those pronouncements that started me thinking. He said, "You know, you're lucky I let you spend all that time on the Celebration. You'll have to tell your co-workers all this will end when we move east."

I was stunned by his attitude. It started a period of serious soul searching for me during which I began to recall hundreds of incidents from the past that I had suppressed so I could train and race. I also realized I had been using my training as a way to literally run away from the problems in our marriage. I was willing to own up to my share of the responsibility, but I also knew that I had given everything I had for 17 years. I was now faced with a difficult decision that I had been avoiding for years. I would find myself walking around doing errands in downtown Boise with tears in my eyes, realizing there was nothing left. It was over.

I came back from a trip and told Steve I had had enough. I encouraged him to go east so I could have some time to myself to think. He left for West Virginia and I felt only a tremendous sense of relief. We had filed for U.S. citizenship and he came back for interviews and the ceremony, but every moment he was back was a strain. When I took Steve to the airport the last time I promised I would take the next three months to think things over, but for me the decision was all but made. The 1995 Celebration was an even bigger success than the first two years, but it all went by in a blur for me.

Once I'd made up my mind, I felt a tremendous weight off my shoulders, a great relief. As time went by I realized I was my old self from years ago, laughing, fun, happy, relaxed. It was such an obvious change that people commented on it.

I felt like I was practically starting my life over again. Becoming a U.S. citizen—one of the happiest days of my life—was a milestone in that regard. The ceremony was so moving to me that I often accept invitations from the federal court to go back and take part in them, something that never fails to fill me with joy. No one appreciates the privilege of citizenship like a naturalized citizen, and I encourage those about to take the oath to vote and to participate fully in this great democracy.

I reorganized my life and my apartment. We had been living such an itinerant existence for so long that we had slept on bunk beds in our apartment for two years! I bought some furniture and began enjoying living on my own with my adopted stray cat, Puss II, who seemed to realize that I needed nurturing and began following me around and sleeping on my pillow beside me, something she'd never done before.

I filed for divorce at the end of 1995 and agreed to split everything down the middle. I wanted to get on with my life and was not going to waste money going to court to fight about money. We had been sensible and had invested mainly in real estate, and we would both come out of it fine. When it was finalized, I felt only relief, no sadness. I had done my crying a long time ago. My real regret was about Kitty, Steve's mom, but she understood and supported me. My mum cried, but knew how long I had struggled.

It's amazing how once something is gone from your life you realize how much energy you were using up dealing with it. I was a new person. I wished Steve well, but it was more obvious than ever just how much we had been living in different worlds.

In 1996 I began dating—long distance—Chuck Whobrey, whom I'd met several years earlier at a Nike-sponsored summer running camp. A runner and divorced father of one daughter, he was a Teamsters representative in Evansville, Indiana, with a wonderfully upbeat and irreverent take on life. We'd hit it off immediately. He couldn't believe I'd been in America for as long as I had had remained so unassimilated that I hadn't heard of Jimmy Buffet! Chuck took it upon himself to become my cultural mentor and was constantly sending me tapes with cuts from Buffet, John Prine, and

Hoyt Axton.

Several years earlier he had invited me to Evansville to help promote a race he was involved with, the Arts Fest River Run, where I met his daughter, Lizzie, and friends Pat and Lisa Shoulders. Pat is a lawyer and frustrated entertainer, and he did such a wonderful job as announcer for their race that I recruited him for the same job at our Celebration, something he has done ever since.

My friendship with Chuck already had a running start, so once I was single again it didn't take long before we were seeing each other as often as we could. Chuck is kind, honest, generous, funny, smart and compassionate, in addition to being a wonderful father. He's comfortable in his own skin and I came to realize very quickly that I had a truly wonderful man in my life, even though he required something of a commute to get to!

Our visits became more frequent and in June 1997, we were married in Evansville, with Pat Shoulders, Esq., presiding.

46 ~ *After all these Years*

The big change occasioned by our nuptials was that I began commuting the other way. I now spend most of my time in Evansville, and travel to Boise for Celebration business, to races and other events to speak. I'm the executive director of the Celebration's non-profit association, a wonderful job that fulfills my passion for educating and motivating women and kids about health, fitness and self-esteem.

I don't want to leave the impression that I'm phobic about running races. In fact, I occasionally hop into local races, particularly ones that Chuck wants to run, and it's not unusual for me to win the women's division. I can still run a 36 or 37-minute 10K without a great deal of strain, such are the dividends of all those years of serious athletic investment. But there's no pressure, my livelihood's not on the line, my self-image is not all tied up in crossing the finish line first.

I'm a very happy former athlete.

I usually get to New Zealand once a year to visit with Mum and Katie, who still live together in the next suburb over from where I grew up in Otahuhu. I usually get by to see my birth family on those trips, and we've all grown to know each other now, so that it really does feel like a family get-together, and a large one at that. Even

Mum and Katie have gone with me.

And nearly every day, no matter where on the planet I find myself or what else is going on in my life, I still head out the door and put myself in the wind. My feet pick up and move to the beat of an ancient melody, my arms swing in time-worn arcs, and as I begin to move, slowly at first, then faster, I become a little girl again, flying across the sandy beaches of Waiheke Island in the South Seas while my grandmother watches from a windy hill.

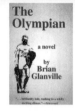